Communicating for Development
Experience in the Urban Environment

Edited by

Catalina Gandelsonas

ITDG
PUBLISHING

Published by ITDG Publishing
103–105 Southampton Row, London WC1B 4HL, UK
www.itdgpublishing.org.uk

First published in 2002

ISBN 1 85339 542 0

A catalogue record for this book is available from the British Library.

ITDG Publishing is the publishing arm of the Intermediate
Technology Development Group.
Our mission is to build the skills and capacity of people in developing
countries through the dissemination of information in all forms,
enabling them to improve the quality of their lives and
that of future generations.

Index by Indexing Specialists (UK) Ltd, Hove, East Sussex
Typeset by J&L Composition, Filey, North Yorkshire
Printed in Great Britain

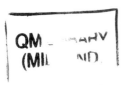

Contents

Foreword – DIFD's Point of View in Relation to Knowledge Transfer

The idea of improving the links between development research initiated in high-income countries and effective urban development practice in developing countries gives rise to several key arguments that have been explored in recent research funded by the UK government's Department for International Development (DFID).

The first is that the amount of effort researchers devote to doing research itself is disproportionate to the effort devoted to publishing and promoting the results. There is a need for researchers to plan consciously for knowledge-transfer strategies designed to produce outputs that effectively target potential users – as an integral part of the research process.

The second is that too much research in urban development is 'supply-led'. It is generated by the interests of donors and researchers in developed countries, rather than by the needs and interests of the intended beneficiaries of the research – households living in poverty, and poor communities in towns and cities in developing countries. This second argument suggests that, in developing their research, researchers in developed countries need to look beyond a limited, one-way process of disseminating research results. Instead, they need to consider a many-way exchange of information with the urban poor themselves and the variety of intermediaries involved in applying research knowledge in development practice. Knowledge transfer should form part of a more general research communication and networking strategy based on the ideas of partnership and knowledge exchange.

In response to these concerns, researchers are seeking a better understanding of need; more effective communication of research findings; and a broader take-up of good or improved practice. Increasingly, they are aware of the need to form a more inclusive relationship with partners in developing countries, and are developing a wide range of communication techniques to make their work more effective. This shift is aided by other developments, such as improved communications technology and increased capacity in developing countries to undertake or partner research. However, communication is often seen as incidental to the core focus of the research and, as such, is not subject to the same rigour. While much good practice exists in the field of communication for urban development cooperation, it has not been extensively or systematically studied and applied. Certainly, more can be done to collect, share and enhance such practice among researchers.

The pivotal aim of poverty reduction underpins much of the research undertaken in urbanization and urban development in developing countries. This reflects the increasing attention paid to explicitly poverty-focused development targets by donor governments, multilateral organizations and international finance institutions – the foremost target being halving the proportion of the world's population living in abject poverty by the year 2015 (OECD, 1996; UN, 2001).

Rapid urbanization has transformed the spatial distribution of the world's population in the twentieth century, and will continue to do so into the twenty-first century. Already, half the world's population live in towns and cities, and the numbers living in urban areas will double in the next 30 years. All of this increase (equivalent to half the current world population) will take place in developing countries that already contain the majority of the world's urban population. Although urbanization, if properly managed, can contribute to poverty reduction, and the proportion of those living in poverty can be reduced, poverty itself will inevitably become more urban in character and the absolute numbers of those vulnerable to urban poverty will increase.

In recognition of this trend, DFID, the World Bank and other bodies concerned with development cooperation have been developing specific strategies to address urban poverty (DFID, 2001a). Effective local development in towns and cities, properly managed by municipal authorities, is the key to eliminating urban poverty. Local government itself needs to be properly resourced, trained and equipped, as well as being democratic, responsive and accountable in its procedures.

Moreover, for urban management to be informed, effective and sustainable, all citizens and communities must participate fully in the decision-making process. This applies particularly to communities of the urban poor. Such communities are frequently excluded from the decision-making process and lack political leverage. Improved urban governance also implies a greater willingness on the part of local authorities to facilitate rather than to direct, and to form and encourage the formation of partnerships among the variety of stakeholders with an interest in urban development and the provision of urban services.

This urban governance agenda can be seen as a means to achieving the reduction and elimination of urban poverty – in the sense of 'income poverty' – but also contributes to reducing the sense of powerlessness that is an aspect of poverty in its broader definition. The UN Human Settlements Programme (UN-HABITAT), in recognition of its central importance in achieving sustainable urban development, has made urban governance the focus of one of its two global campaigns (the two Habitat Global Campaigns, initiated in 2000, are Security of Tenure and Good Urban Governance).

An effective say in decisions about development interventions at the local level that will affect the lives, lifestyles and livelihoods of individuals, households and communities should be seen as a basic human right. This is of critical importance to the urban poor who may be disenfranchised through a lack of legally recognized tenure, excluded on the basis of status, caste or social stigma, and disempowered through lack of education and access to information and knowledge resources.

The empowerment of the urban poor is a practical as well as a human rights issue. A full understanding of the nature and causes of urban poverty and how it varies with time and place can only be achieved with the participation of poor people themselves. Similarly, development strategies intended to overcome poverty and improve the quality of life for urban communities can be sustainable in the long term only if those affected are involved in the decision-making and have a commitment to their outcomes.

Michael Mutter

The Urban
Management Series

The Urban Management Series focuses on demographic and economic change in the towns and cities of developing countries. The series offers a platform for practical, in-depth analysis of the complex institutional, economic and social issues that have to be addressed in an increasingly urban and globalized world.

By 2025 it is estimated that two-thirds of the poor in Latin America and a third to almost half the poor in Africa and Asia will live in cities or towns. An estimated 600 million people currently live in life and health threatening homes and neighbourhoods. One of the UN's Millennium Development Targets calls for significant improvement in the lives of at least 100 million of these slum dwellers by 2020. This is a very modest target, but challenging nonetheless. Clearly, the livelihoods and rights of the poor must be at the centre of any strategy to manage urban growth.

Cities and towns, and the industrial and commercial activities located in them, are a positive force for national economic growth. This is why cities are popular: where you find the mass of bees is where to look for honey. Urban areas provide consumer markets and services for agricultural producers. They are also gateways to larger national, regional and international markets. But the opportunities from urban development are not equitably distributed. The rights of the poor are curtailed and they are often excluded from accessing secure land, shelter, services, employment and social welfare due to the discriminatory practices of government, the private sector and civil society.

This series of books addresses the many challenges facing urban management professionals. First and foremost, they aim to improve understanding of the impact of urbanization on the livelihoods and living conditions of poor people. With better understanding, the institutional and political conditions for poor people to participate and benefit from the urban development process may be improved. New knowledge from research and dialogue should show how best to shape the relationship between the public and the private sector and with civil society, and to mobilize our resource for more equitable and sustainable development. It is essential to mitigate the impact that poor environments and natural hazards have on the poor, to enhance the economic synergy between rural and urban economies, and to strengthen efforts by the international community to coordinate support for a positive urbanization process in the poorest countries.

Communicating for Development tackles all these issues by focusing attention on the most fundamental of questions about development: how can the lessons of good practice and innovation and results of research benefit the poor? This is a book about managing information and it begins by exploring the difference between information and knowledge. How is new knowledge created, managed and exchanged? Thematic analysis and case study chapters show that a great deal can be done to ensure that innovative research shapes new policies and leads to more sustainable urban management.

This book explores the impact and the value of new information technologies. And it unpicks current development jargon – networking, sustainability, stakeholder participation, gender equality, enablement policy, poverty reduction, public/private partnership, social capital, civil society and so on. In questioning how researchers and academics can share their knowledge more effectively, this book presents a challenge for the whole development community.

The key challenge for this millennium that shines through in this book is that new ways must be found to encourage and to ensure public engagement in the way that we run our communities and cities.

Nick Hall
Series Editor

Acknowledgements

I am indebted to my husband Geoff Denison for his total support. Without it this book would have not been finished.

I also wish to thank Michael Mutter, who made the ITDG Publishing book series possible, Tony Lloyd-Jones and Pat Wakely for giving me the opportunity to edit the book, and Nick Hall, with whom working to put this book together was real fun and a lovely experience.

Finally, a special thanks to the Max Lock Centre Director, Mike Teis, and researchers Bill Erickson, Ripin Kalra and Luisa Vallejo, who contributed to the Inter-School Conference, the Charney Manor Seminar and the research project 'Knowledge Transfer' financed by the Department for International Development (DFID).

The editor and the publishers are grateful to DFID for making the publication of this book possible. They would also like to make it clear that the views expressed in the book are those of the individual contributors and are not necessarily the views of DFID nor of the editor.

The publishers would like to thank Chris Stowers/Panos Pictures for permission to use the cover photograph.

Figures

Tables

Acronyms and abbreviations

BASIN	Building Advisory Service and Information Network
CBO	community-based organization
CDP	Community Development Programme, UN-Habitat
CEHS	Centre for Environment and Human Settlements, UK
CERCA	Resource Facility for the Sustainable Development of Human Settlements in Central America
CIVIC	Citizens' Voluntary Initiative for the City of Bangalore, India
COICA	Coodinadora de las Organizaciones Indienas de la Cuenca Amazonica
DFID	Department for International Development, UK
EPDP	Environmental Protection Department Punjab
ETF	Employees' Trust Fund
ETPI	Environmental Technology Programme for Industry, Pakistan
EXNORA	Excellent, Novel and Radical Initiative, Chennai, India
FIRE	Financial Institution Reform and Expansion Project, India
FPCCI	Federation of Pakistan Chambers of Commerce and Industries
FUNAI	Foundation of Indigenous Peoples, Brazil
GARNET	Global Applied Research Network
GEF	Global Environment Facility
GTZ	Gesellschaft für Technische Zusammenarbeit (German Development Agency)
H&H	Housing and Hazards Group, University of Exeter
HIC	Habitat International Coalition
IBRD	International Bank for Reconstruction and Development (part of the World Bank Group)
ICBL	Institute for Computer-Based Learning, Heriot-Watt University, UK
ICT	information and communications technology
IRFD	International Research Foundation for Development
ITDG	Intermediate Technology Development Group, UK
KIS	knowledge and information systems
MKSS	*Mazdur Kisan Shakti Sanghatan* (struggle for empowering workers and farmers), India

N-AERUS	Network for Research on Urbanization in the South
NGO	non-governmental organization
SC/UK	Save the Children Fund, UK
SDI	Shack/Slum Dwellers International
SEWA	Self-Employed Women's Association, Ahmedabad, India
SPARC	Society for the Promotion of Area Resource Centres, Mumbai, India
TVE	Television Trust for the Environment
UN-HABITAT	United Nations Human Settlements Programme (formerly UNCHS)
UNAIDS	Joint United Nations Programme on HIV/AIDS
UNCHS	United Nations Centre for Human Settlements (now UN-Habitat)
UNDP	United Nations Development Program
UNEP	United Nations Environment Programme
USAID	US Agency for International Development
WHO	World Health Organization
WWF	Worldwide Fund for Nature
ZOTO	Zone One Tondo Organization Network, The Philippines

Introduction

Catalina Gandelsonas

This book reflects current thinking about communicating knowledge and good practice for development. It represents the work of 22 authors. The subject of 'communicating knowledge' for the benefit of the urban poor was selected because urban poverty is a research priority for many development agencies, given the scale of the problem.

Poverty is 'an attribute of urbanization' (Chr. Michelsen Institute, 2001). UN-HABITAT (formerly the UN Centre for Human Settlements) places particular stress on poverty in urban areas (as opposed to rural poverty), because of its ultimate social, economic, political and cultural consequences. According to this organization, urban areas are places where social issues such as homelessness, illness, unemployment and crime will become more complex and consequently more difficult to tackle than ever before (Habitat, 1994).

In recognition of the depth of urban problems, many agencies, including the World Bank (IBRD) and the UK Department for International Development (DFID), have supported research on good practice in communication aimed at improving knowledge transfer, with the hope of reducing urban poverty levels.

The book examines communication from a variety of perspectives. It offers a critical analysis of communication methods that have been employed over the past 50 years, and suggests ways of overcoming gaps and barriers. It stresses the importance of networks and intermediaries and the value of many different types of media, and shows how specific communication tools can best be used to transfer knowledge to different urban contexts and cultures.

DEFINITIONS

The title of this book, *Communicating for Development: Experience in the Urban Environment*, contains terms that need clarifying.

To communicate means to convey, exchange or share information with people; to impart knowledge, information and ideas; or to exchange thoughts. *Communication* is any method by which human beings pass information to one another, and is generally recognized as the process of successful transfer of meaningful information. This description may equally be applied to the problems of communicating knowledge or development skills, particularly in situations when the meaning of the message may be alien to the receiver's cultural values, beliefs, language or frames of reference. Communication, evidently, may be a one-way, two-way or circular process.

Dictionary definitions of *development* are generally unhelpful. A developing country, according to one respected dictionary (*Concise Oxford Dictionary*), is a 'poor or primitive country that is developing better economic and social conditions'. Clearly, 'development' is a value-laden term whose meaning will change according to one's definition of 'better' economic and social conditions. In the post-colonial years following World War II, development was widely thought to mean economic growth and industrialization, and the European or Western example was presented as the model for the rest of the world. But over the years, social and political considerations have come to the fore. Now development is considered to depend as much on improved governance, democratization and respect for human rights as it does on economic growth, although it is by no means clear which of these characteristics comes first. More useful for a book about communication for development is a generally acceptable definition of what is meant by 'develop'. To develop means 'to come or bring to a later or more advanced or expanded stage' (*Times Dictionary*, 2000). Change through dialogue is implicit in this definition.

The concept of *knowledge* dates back to the Greek philosophers Plato and Aristotle, and is commonly defined as the facts, feelings or experiences known to a person or group of people, or the awareness or familiarity gained through experience or learning. Only recently have Polanyi (1966) and Nonaka and Takeuchi (1995) explored why differences between tacit and explicit knowledge are important in the communication process. Whereas explicit knowledge is information that can be verbally shared and may well be written down, and is thus easily exchanged, tacit knowledge is said to represent the inherent, embedded experience of individuals. Together, these two forms of knowledge combine dynamically to create new knowledge.

Communicating for Development: Experience in the Urban Environment refers to the need to place the communication of knowledge for achieving development in the *urban* environment. It is estimated that by the year 2050, most of the world's population will have become urban and a very high percentage will be poor (DFID, 2000b).

COMMUNICATION FOR DEVELOPMENT: A HISTORICAL OVERVIEW

One-way communication models

A number of theories about effective ways to communicate development ideas were created after World War II, and gained recognition during the 1950s and 1960s. Typically, these communication theories promoted one-way, non-participatory communication models with the objective of encouraging the industrialization and economic growth synonymous with the model of development that prevailed in the 1950s. Such theories were clearly designed, according to many writers (e.g. Lerner, 1958), to limit countries in the developing world to a subsidiary role in an emerging hierarchy of the international world structure. The communication models used to promote this idea were one-way, non-participatory processes, with most messages being 'intentional' and 'persuasive' (White et al., 1994: 154). These models were reinforced by economic theories developed during the 1960s in which underdevelopment was considered to be a consequence of industrial and technical backwardness. This could only be resolved by borrowing modernization strategies and importing know-how and capital from the industrialized countries of the North (Kumar, 1994: 77).

Two-way participatory communication models

Increasing poverty in many countries has triggered criticism of one-way communication approaches, and has led to the development of alternative communication models. Two-way communication methods were developed in parallel to one-way, top-down models from the 1950s onwards. Buber (1958) was an early advocate of more open and respectful dialogues between human beings, which led to two-way dialogue as opposed to the one-way monologues that he believed to be the root cause of underdevelopment, poverty and alienation.

Buber was echoed by Freire, a Brazilian researcher on development issues, whose views were drawn from his own experience of work with poor communities in north-east Brazil. Freire's books became the foundation for theories of participatory development that came to dominate development debates during the 1980s. He advocated communication strategies that would raise poor communities' awareness of the cause of their problems and conditions. Freire asserts that knowledge 'given' to people only vaguely relates to what they really need to learn, and that 'the authoritarian transfer of knowledge to a passive audience did little to promote human development' (Freire, 1967).

Following Freire's ideas, during the 1980s and 1990s a great variety of two-way participatory communication techniques and theories developed, all with the aim of encouraging self-confidence and self-determination. The intention was to ensure the active involvement of poor communities in decisions that would affect their lives (White et al., 1994; Chambers 1995; Guijt and Shah, 1998; Holland and Blackburn, 1998).

THE FAILINGS OF TWO-WAY COMMUNICATION MODELS

The application of participatory approaches to communication has not guaranteed that (neighbourhood-based) communities[1] have access to information about ideas and practices that may be useful and applicable to their particular socio-economic and political contexts. One important reason for this is that many development initiatives that are said to be participatory have failed to take adequate account of the very real differences that exist within a given community.

A community, in the current rather loose definition of the term, tends to be viewed as an amicable and equitable collective of people. But this simplistic definition fails to recognize that communities are affected by internal differences, sometimes in conflict, and always made up of individuals with different needs, interests, skills and educational levels. In these circumstances, optimum forms of communication have to involve all sectors of the community. While the interests of particular needs-based groups ('communities of interest' in the original sense of the term), such as women, the elderly and young people, may have some representation within a given neighbourhood, it is frequently the case that community 'representatives' fail to represent or even recognize such interests. An in-depth understanding of cultural differences, religion, ethnicities, class, education and income is essential if effective communications between different interest groups are to be achieved (Evans, 1992; Guijt and Shah, 1998).

In recent years, although a great deal of research and writing about development practices has stressed the importance of participatory methods, most of it has been inaccessible to the poor. Often this research is effectively unavailable in developing countries, partly because studies about development have typically been packaged in formal reports and densely written documents.

Evidently, both communication and the sharing of knowledge are fraught with difficulty. Despite the best of intentions, cultural differences between researchers and poor people in urban communities are sometimes an insurmountable barrier.

ORGANIZATION OF THE BOOK

This book offers an in-depth discussion about how the communication process works, or doesn't. It questions and challenges. Who are the stakeholders, what are the best media or vehicles for transferring knowledge, and why are networks and intermediary agencies important vehicles for communication? In effect, it shows why gaps and barriers in the communication process occur. Although many of these issues have been discussed elsewhere, it is hoped that bringing together in one book a diverse range of expertise and opinion will extend debates about development and communication theory.

The book is organized in two parts. Part I covers theoretical issues relating to communication and development, with chapters on communication models, media, intermediaries and networks. It also includes a discussion of development theories. Part II includes a number of case studies focusing on various communication issues. Topics covered include the worldwide use of print and television media; networks as a vehicle for communicating knowledge to the South; overcoming barriers in communication by tailoring specific strategies to communicating knowledge and good practices; and an explanation of communication problems in a large and diverse developing country such as India, with growing numbers in urban poverty.

Part I Theoretical issues

The first two chapters in Part I consider communication models.

In Chapter 1, Tony Lloyd-Jones affirms that researchers have yet to take on board the full implications of recent changes in networking and media practice in their own research practices. He suggests ways in which researchers can make better use of media and networks in developing their knowledge-transfer strategies to impact on urban poverty. He then goes on to explore the concept of good or best practice as a form of knowledge generation and sharing, which addresses a new paradigm in knowledge transfer.

Lucky Lowe, in Chapter 2, combines a theoretical discussion of communication models – describing the development of a new model which explores communication flows – with practical examples drawn from case studies carried out in Peru and Zimbabwe. New theoretical models of knowledge and information systems provide an insight into the understanding of the communication processes and constraints in effective information exchange in those communities.

Social and academic networks are the theme for Chapters 3–5.

In Chapter 3, Richard Barbrook discusses academic networks and media as vehicles that produce a 'gift economy' resulting from the free exchange of knowledge and information. He argues that academic networks supported by presently developed electronic media have generated and encouraged this gift economy of intellectual production, and affirms that the system has a global scope supported by the self-interest of Internet users.

Norma V. Madrid analyses the differences between communities and social networks in Chapter 4. She describes communication problems that may arise when people have insufficient time to meet, or when meeting places proved unsatisfactory. Such problems, coupled with psychosocial environments of increasing violence and crime, are the main factors that deter people from communicating with each other.

Chapter 5, by Otto Ruskulis, gives an overview of types of social network, their characteristics and functions, and their differences with coalitions and alliances, and summarizes a number of case studies on networks researched in different developing countries. Types mentioned are nested and social networks, the latter being especially important because of their value as social capital. How social networks develop social links based on kinship, employment, trade, associations and neighbourliness is also discussed.

The following three chapters examine barriers and gaps in the communication process.

Chapter 6 outlines barriers in communication relating to cultural differences, values, beliefs and reference systems, and proposes a number of ideas for developing better communication through a more legible and culturally compatible type of media. Nabeel Hamdi describes the difficulties of communicating between various cultures with different languages, beliefs, values and reference systems, all of which produce communication gaps. Graphically illustrated communication ideas are suggested as ways of overcoming communication gaps and improving the legibility of the messages.

In Chapter 7, Robert Brown discusses communication gaps that exist within the same context and culture, and result from different backgrounds and reference systems of those attempting to communicate. Given the disparity between the value systems of architects and communities in general, a shared examination of each others' meanings and values is suggested. The techniques proposed aim at developing a common language between the parties involved to create a common ground for discussion.

Catalina Gandelsonas, in Chapter 8, examines the mechanics of the communication process and ways by which knowledge is generated, codified and transferred, in order to determine the possible roots of communication barriers and gaps that exist between researchers and communities. She outlines various ways by which the transfer of knowledge and best practice to urban poor communities might be improved through the application of knowledge-management tools.

The final two chapters of Part I reflect on development issues from different perspectives.

Kathleen Richardson addresses issues of development and communication by examining bad communication practices between development organizations and various Amazonian groups. A description of how Amazonian indigenous groups use an environmental/developmental language to gain land rights and support is included in Chapter 9. The author concludes that better communication practices should be implemented to ensure that indigenous groups express their development objectives, free from the influence of the latest fashionable development agendas.

In Chapter 10, Carl O'Coill controversially argues that development is not a tangible process or goal, but a theoretical discourse that is more concerned with power and control than with achieving real development. He states that this approach does not provide the scenario for a democratic dialogue between Western and non-Western people, as it prevents both parties from understanding the common problems and interests that span the developed world/developing world divide. He also challenges the development theorists' idea that the developed and developing worlds are different places.

Part II Case studies

The second part of the book contains seven case studies, the first three of which look at communicating knowledge through electronic and multi-media communication.

In Chapter 11, Janet Boston discusses new methods of communicating with the poor around the world, describing *Hands On*, a multimedia global dissemination initiative. Programmes are broadcast on BBC World, linking appropriate technology approaches in the North and South. *Hands On* has, to date, broadcast 150 five-minute television programmes that reached 700 million homes in virtually every country in the world, sharing information on local solutions with a global audience. The programmes are also made available to a range of television, radio stations and networks, and concentrate on those with access to Southern audiences.

The authors of Chapter 12 discuss theoretical and practical issues relating to the establishment of Internet-based research networks, and describe potentials and problems encountered in practice by two of these networks: UK-based North–South Research Network (national, in the 'North'); and the Central American initiative INVESTIGA (regional, in the 'South'). Harry Smith and Paul Jenkins draw lessons for the creation of similar networks elsewhere. Internet-based technology to support such networks is available and increasingly affordable; however, the appropriate choice of financial support for network management is crucial to achieve sustainable research networks.

In Chapter 13, Mansoor Ali and Darren Saywell describe their experience of putting together electronic conferences, explaining the practicalities of using electronic conferencing for academic discussions related to development. Based on experience gained through organizing three electronic conferences, a number of ideas, lessons and specific organizational steps are discussed. This chapter offers innovative ways that professionals from anywhere in the world can discuss development-related issues in detail. It also discusses technological constraints which still restrict a number of developing countries from accessing knowledge and information.

Chapters 14 to 17 highlight barriers and gaps in relation to communication. To begin, three interesting case studies describe practical ways of overcoming communication barriers and gaps in relation to development issues, including pollution abatement, building technology and AIDS prevention.

Jeremy Raemakers and Rizwan Hameed discuss the importance of using communication tools to achieve pollution abatement in Pakistan, by offering a programme that promotes a culture of abatement. The authors of Chapter 14 argue that, although there were some signs of awareness that pollution is a problem among industrialists, attempts to resolve the problem without state intervention failed, either because of technical ignorance or as a result of unwillingness to find solutions without state financial assistance.

In Chapter 15, Iftekar Ahmed and Matthew Carter debate how the Housing & Hazards Group, a non-governmental organization (NGO) based at the University of Exeter, developed a methodology in partnership with a grassroots Bangladeshi NGO aimed at communicating building ideas that villagers could implement and pay for themselves to reduce the vulnerability of the traditional housing (*kutcha*) in relation to flooding. Communication was through participatory workshops that brought villagers and builders together to discuss techniques and try out practical ideas. The project was supported by a traditional song team which keeps alive the concepts learnt through this experience.

Chapter 16 examines the importance of communication for HIV/AIDS prevention by emphasizing the importance of communicating to people alternative approaches to HIV/AIDS prevention in Vietnam. The success of this approach depends tremendously on communication tools, such as the language, styles and approaches to the messages used. Toyoko Kodama and Le Thi Minh Chau suggest the application of communication media to achieve a mobilization of communication resources, building capacity in relation to these issues and empowering people, as efforts on these lines could promote awareness for avoiding the disease as well as changing attitudes towards HIV/AIDS.

Pachampet Sundaram, in Chapter 17, elaborates on the communication difficulties of a large democracy such as India, a country with substantial numbers of poor people. He examines the problems related to the transfer of research findings at the level of research institutes and scholars and bureaucrats. He describes various recent approaches of the Indian government and civil society for sharing experiences among stakeholders, and for dissemination of information and knowledge to citizen groups. He advocates the need to achieve transparency, accountability, equity and the participation of people within government and donor agencies.

The book concludes by reflecting on all the arguments presented and making recommendations that should be useful for researchers, policymakers and development practitioners. This book shows how global communications technologies can be effectively used to promote pro-poor development. Equally, they can be irrelevant or even a hindrance to sustainable development. Communicating ideas about development depends on dialogue, humility and respect for the differences between people, whether they be academics, politicians or urban residents in Southern cities.

PART I

THEORETICAL ISSUES

CHAPTER ONE

Communicating urban research knowledge in international development cooperation

Tony Lloyd-Jones

The argument of this chapter is that researchers have yet to take on board the full implications of recent changes in networking and media practice for their own research practices.[1] It suggests ways in which researchers can make better use of media and networks in developing their knowledge-transfer strategies to help reduce urban poverty. It goes on to explore the concept of good or best practice as a form of knowledge generation and sharing that addresses a new paradigm in knowledge transfer.

How can research knowledge be produced in a form that can quickly and effectively reach the key actors in urban development processes that improve the conditions of the urban poor? To address this question we need a better understanding of the range and use of media available for receiving, delivering and storing information. There is also a need for more conscious identification of the potential targets of research outputs, knowledge of the best 'media routes' for reaching them and clarification of the role of intermediaries in the communication process, as well as their role in the development process itself.

The transfer of research knowledge is part of a larger exchange of knowledge and information, with flows in many directions. It is primarily a question of communication, with researchers as part of a larger network of stakeholders in urban development. The issue of improving communication between researchers and key actors in the development process forms part of a larger issue of how to improve the channels of communication and knowledge transfer between all interest groups – public, private and civic society – including poor communities themselves.

'Communication in development' is a field that is currently scattered across a number of disciplines, from the broad theoretical and policy-focused concerns of media studies to a more practical focus on health and education, with a rich mix of theory to draw upon in cultural and social anthropology, psychology, political, management and other social sciences.

Recent developments in information and communications technology (ICT) have led to a sharper focus on the need for better understanding of this field. Technological innovation in communication is giving knowledge producers and communicators an increasing array of media to get their message across to a variety of audiences within a shorter time scale. At the same time, greater ease of communication on a global scale, particularly through the electronic media, is making networking an increasingly large component of research and development practice.

One effect of the growth of technological innovations in knowledge and communications infrastructure is the vast increase in the quantity of information and formalized knowledge that can be more easily shared through both traditional dissemination routes and new global, regional and local networks. 'Knowledge management' is another field that researchers will need to address in response to the practical demands of those working in urban development practice and the pressing needs of the training and research institutions.

Improving the communication process means identifying and overcoming any gaps that may impede it (see Chapter 8). Addressing the broader communications and networking issues also requires a focus on the knowledge, information and communication needs of the urban poor. The more informed poor people are, the more they are able to initiate and negotiate development changes in their settlements that reflect their real needs and concerns – and in the research needed to inform these changes. How can poor urban communities gain better access to media, networking, information and knowledge resources in a way that empowers them in decision-making about urban development and getting their needs understood? As Michael Mutter points out in his Foreword, empowerment, along with poverty reduction, is a principal goal of international development policy.

Much of the effort needed to address the broader issues of communication, knowledge exchange and urban governance falls beyond the remit of researchers, and much more is involved than simple improvements to research practice. Nevertheless, research does have a central role to play, and researchers need to address these larger issues as a part of their research process.[2] Given the huge variety of cultural, social, economic and political contexts, the crucial area of empowering the urban poor through better access to knowledge and information is indeed large in scope, and is being explored in ongoing DFID-funded research.[3]

THE NEED FOR NEW MODELS OF RESEARCH PRACTICE

For research to be more demand-led and responsive to the needs of the poor requires a departure from the traditional scheme of research production and dissemination. Different models of research are called for, involving two-way and many-way communication and information exchange. Rather than being the passive recipients of knowledge or, more commonly, of the consequences of its application, urban poor communities should have a role in initiating and directing research. This might be through direct involvement in participatory and action research; alternatively (and indirectly), the urban poor can ensure that the knowledge produced and communicated better reflects their needs through the involvement of intermediaries representing their interests.

It is not possible simply to substitute a traditional top-down model with a crude bottom-up version. The complexities of interactions between the various stakeholders involved in the urban development process, and the realities of power and inequality of access to resources, rule this out. Greater participation by communities in local decision-making is clearly possible and research should address this as an objective. On the other hand, donors and governments in developing countries, at both national and local levels, will continue to make decisions about expenditure and interventions affecting urban development and urban poverty on the basis of broad policy and political aims rather than the needs of particular urban communities.

Thus researchers will continue to be required to generalize from the experience of particular households and communities, gained through participatory forms of research, alongside the use of more traditional, 'scientific' and quantitative research methods. In this way, they may influence new policies and assess the impacts of previous policies as well as devising knowledge 'products' to facilitate education, training and development practice. The effectiveness with which they are able to do this will remain the main yardstick by which research in developed countries is assessed.

A PARTICIPATORY, NORTH–SOUTH PARTNERSHIP MODEL

Institutional inertia and research culture in developed countries can inhibit the broad take-up and utilization of research knowledge. The traditional, pedagogical model of research might be characterized along the following lines:

- identify a need
- undertake background study
- conduct field research
- argue conclusions
- disseminate findings.

This model, as applied in urban development, supports the tendency to objectify the urban poor as recipients of development practice informed by research knowledge, most often produced in the North. It presents research communication as a series of one-way flows: data collection (South to North) and dissemination of findings (North to South), the former toward the beginning of the process and the latter at the end. This process can be represented graphically, as in Figure 1.1, representing the actors and information flows involved.

This is a highly simplified representation of what is in practice a complex process involving a variety of time frames and media routes. Much

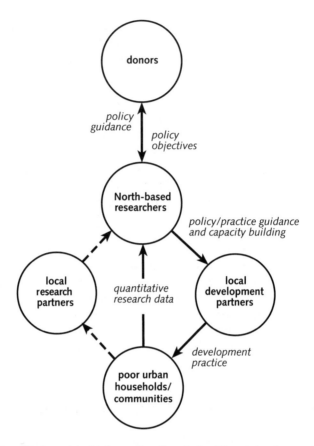

Figure 1.1   Simplified model of information flow in traditional development research practice

knowledge dissemination is typically slow and long term, with new knowledge as the product of research informing theoretical debate and academic practice through conference papers, journals and books. This, in turn, informs the education and training of development practitioners. Over time, this new knowledge is tested in practice and becomes the subject of new research. Alongside the traditional, long-term academic pathway, new knowledge may influence practice through more immediate routes. Examples include commissioned policy research, practical research disseminated in the form of practice manuals or briefing notes, or the use of the mass media to put across the essentials of major research findings to a wide audience.

In all these instances, however, whether short term or long term, the flow of knowledge is one-way, following the classic top-down dissemination pathway. People living in, or vulnerable to, poverty hardly ever access knowledge in this process – they are the objects of actions initiated by others informed by research knowledge. One of the key issues for researchers in developed countries is how best to assist those people to have more say in such actions. Research, and its dissemination, should be designed to influence and enable local decision-makers to be more open to the participation of poor communities in decisions that affect them, and should facilitate their better access to knowledge resources. It should be formulated to achieve better communication and understanding between all local actors to enable more effective and equal partnerships in urban development.

What should be the role of developed country-led research in addressing these needs? The initial findings of the research providing the basis for this chapter suggest the following objectives.

1. There should be a greater emphasis on involving local partners and carrying out participatory and action-based research so that research is demand-led and, from the beginning, feeds directly into projects and programmes that reduce poverty and its impacts.
2. The experience and lessons of research and development practice in achieving urban poverty reduction and empowerment of the urban poor should be generalized and made transferable to wider geographical and policy contexts.
3. Research-based knowledge should be disseminated in a form that is accessible to the urban poor and/or their immediate representatives, as well as targeted at other stakeholders in the urban development process.
4. Methods should be identified for improving access to knowledge resources and improved communication channels for the urban poor.

Most funding for research in urban development is channelled through researchers in developed countries. While this is the case, the main responsibility for realizing objective 1 lies with donors and researchers in developed countries. In the longer term, there seems to be no reason why donors should not ensure that Southern researchers are funded directly or take the leading role in research partnerships.[4]

In terms of addressing objective 2, researchers in developed countries are likely to maintain their traditional comparative advantage, at least in the short term, through networking strengths and technological superiority in ICT. Objective 4, like objective 2, is generally a matter of generalizing and disseminating good practice and lessons learned and, again, Northern researchers are in a position to continue to add value.

Given the diversity of social and cultural contexts in which poor people live, however, it follows that North-based researchers are not necessarily best placed to achieve objective 3 – making knowledge accessible to the poor – even though this is an assumption that has tended to inform much of the research currently being undertaken in this field. If empowerment is our aim, researchers in the North might best direct their efforts to producing knowledge in a form that is useful and communicable to intermediaries on the ground. It is they who are best placed to relate it to the experiences of local poor communities, to put it in context, and to translate it into a form that is accessible to those communities using local media channels, languages, forms of expression and networks.

In summary, our research suggests that we should be looking at a new networking model of research, one that is already practised to a certain extent, but needs to be reinforced, founded on concepts of North–South partnership and participation (Figure 1.2).

INTERMEDIARIES AND NETWORKS IN RESEARCH KNOWLEDGE TRANSFER

This chapter argues that empowering poor communities through improving their access to knowledge and information, and improving their means of communication with other stakeholders in the development process, are fundamental to the urban governance and poverty reduction agendas.

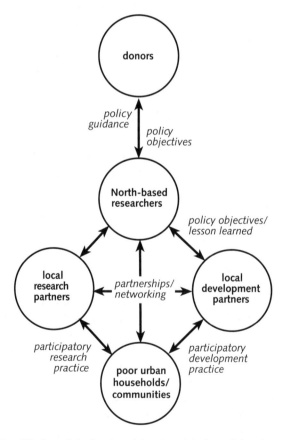

Figure 1.2   Simplified model of network/partnership-based development research practice

However, this does not mean researchers in developed countries should turn exclusively to generating research outputs tailored to the requirements of poor communities. The diversity of such communities and their needs, and the economics of knowledge production, mean that we still have to produce knowledge in a generalized form that can be interpreted for local use by those most able to do so.

These might be particularly informed, respected or educated members of the communities concerned or, more frequently, various forms of intermediary who represent or interpret their needs and interests directly in the service provision and development decision-making processes. An understanding of the different intermediaries in the urban development process and their roles and interests is therefore critical. Typically, interventions in urban development can involve any combination of interest groups, of which only a minority may be interested in improving the conditions of poor people, and any of which might be targeted as users of research knowledge, whether they are initiating the development, are subject to it, wish to be part of it, or to modify or oppose it.[5]

The links between knowledge producers in high-income countries and users in developing countries, even where identified as local intermediaries rather than intended beneficiaries, may be remote. There will be other intermediaries involved at different stages of the knowledge transfer food chain. In the traditional pedagogical model of knowledge transfer, these would typically be educators, trainers and publishers. But contemporary methods of knowledge transfer are equally dependent on other media-based intermediaries whose concerns are not directly with urban development interventions at the local level, but more with the process of knowledge transfer itself.

Figure 1.3 represents this contemporary form of knowledge exchange in diagrammatic form. Knowledge resources and users at the local level and those at the macro level of national government, international development agencies and donors, and global and regional knowledge centres are linked by media specialists (mass media, publishers, broadcasters) on the one hand, and by their own interconnecting networks on the other. In some instances, particular individuals or organizations may be responsible for managing the flow of information through such networks but, more often than not, the networks are ad hoc and the exchange of information, although limited by the common interests, language and jargon of the members of the network, is largely uncontrolled.

These networks are the means by which decisions about the flow of resources are made, and are not merely concerned with knowledge exchange as such. Knowledge flowing through such networks has tended to be tightly focused on the purpose at hand, in the form of correspondence, face-to-face discussion or technical reports. With the advent of the Internet such networks have assumed a greatly augmented role in the broader processes of knowledge dissemination. A wider range of potential knowledge-users can be accessed in a much shorter period. What was a

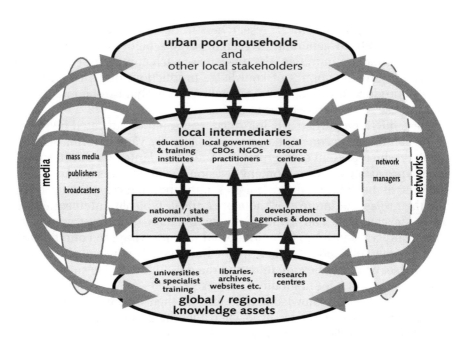

Figure 1.3   Contemporary knowledge exchange and access to knowledge assets

correspondence becomes, through e-mail, a form of targeted broadcasting or leafleting, and knowledge managers can become website publishers and propagandists.

Computer technology has also provided cheap access to types of media that were previously the preserve of professionals and commercial media organizations. Desktop publishing, digital video and multimedia presentation have widened the choice and degree of professionalism in presentation of information. These technologies have also heightened researchers' awareness of how more professional types of media in general can be used to get their message across. We have seen the 'mediatization' of knowledge networks and an increasing crossover with the professional media. In this process, the quantity and quality (in form if not in content) of information and knowledge exchange through networks is greatly enhanced. As a result, we can begin to see the particular shape of a new paradigm of knowledge exchange and transfer arising out of advances in ICT. Since McLuhan (1994) talked of an electronic 'global village' in the 1960s, this has long been predicted, although the media hype that accompanied the commercialization of the Internet has tended to obscure the real social implications of the transformations that have accompanied its growth (see Chapter 3)

In all aspects of the research that informs this chapter, the increasing importance of networks and networking has come to the fore. The new model of network/partnership-based development research practice in Figure 1.2 is clearly based on this idea. For development research and practice, the main consequence is an ever-increasing demand for knowledge to be applied and tested in practice in the shortest possible time, through good practice guidance, evidence-based practice and capacity-building.

Among donors and practitioners there is increasing dissatisfaction with traditional, academic forms of research and the slower, pedagogical forms of knowledge dissemination. There are dangers in this – that knowledge generation itself becomes completely market-led, and the forms of pure, in-depth research without which development knowledge, at the level of its theoretical foundations, cannot advance, are completely sidelined. This is a challenge for researchers, but one that they need to confront directly, recognizing the significance of ICT for the ways in which we generate and communicate knowledge, and making the most positive use of the changes it has brought.

IDENTIFYING THE APPROPRIATE MEDIA FOR COMMUNICATING RESEARCH KNOWLEDGE[6]

The remainder of this chapter explores two aspects of these new developments of communication in development: the use of different types of media in conveying development research knowledge; and the growing importance of the concept of good or best practice in knowledge exchange.

It is evident from the discussion thus far that there are many possible targets for the dissemination of research knowledge. Researchers need to be aware of the different potential audiences for their research outputs. Awareness of how different types of media can be used to reach these targets is critical for designing knowledge-transfer strategies. Researchers should consider the purposes of different media. They should be able to identify different media routes, selecting the right media to ensure that the message is accessible to the intended target audience.

The mass media – newspapers, radio and television – usually serve to raise awareness of issues without necessarily exploring them in any depth. Journals, reports, books, documentaries and other print, tape or electronic reference materials can provide the in-depth information lacking in more immediate forms of communication. A news report is often prepared in a matter of hours, and can reach thousands or millions. Books and reports take weeks or months to prepare and reach a far more targeted audience, and the quality of information they contain will often be superior to more immediate forms of delivery.

Different types of media may be used in combination to get across a distinct message in a tailored way, to reach a particular audience and/or to improve communications between particular groups of people. Certain media routes allow less control of the message that is sent out to the end-user, making it open to distortion and interpretation. Control over the mass media and how it is used by or on behalf of the poor, for example, is almost always impossible to achieve.

The more immediate, awareness-raising media should include route markers to more in-depth, long-term sources of information. Any knowledge transfer and communication strategy should be designed around this 'cascading' of knowledge through different types of media, ensuring the message is accessible.

More often than not, the audience will be more general and researchers should earmark resources for market research and exploring and utilizing the appropriate media to achieve effective knowledge transfer and exchange. Intermediaries and networks may be used to build the capacity to access large groups of people over the required period. Preferences for and availability of media will vary from place to place, and among different social groupings in a particular place. Where knowledge is narrowly targeted at a known user group, they may be consulted on the media of preference.

Local advice should be sought when media are selected, as standards, language, cultures, technical capacity, literacy and logistics can all be constraints. Having an individual at the user end who understands the needs

Table 1.1 Characteristics of selected media

Media	Potential to reach poorest	Participatory potential	Potential number of people reached	Potential for distortion of message	Cost-effectiveness
Leaflets, news sheets	+	−	++	—	+
Interpersonal meetings	+	++	—	—	−
Video	−	+	+	+	—
Television	—	—	++	++	—
Schools	+	++	+	−	+
Audio cassettes	+	−	+	+	−
Radio	++	+	+++	+	++
Slides	−	−	−	—	−
Posters	+	−	+	—	−
Theatre, folk media	++	++	++	++	++
E-mail, Internet	—	++	++	—	++

Quality of delivery and quantity in terms of audience reach is important in the choice of media. There is often a trade-off between these two factors. +++, Most likely to be applicable; —, least likely to be applicable.

(Max Lock Centre, 2001b; adapted from New Economics Foundation, 2000.)

for and application of reliable information is important. Ultimately, all knowledge transfer rests on the assumption that the source can be trusted, and trust can be established only through direct communication or through a trusted intermediary. Word-of-mouth and the lessons of experience are the ultimate guarantors of more formal knowledge sources.

The Internet greatly increases the potential ease of access and range of audience for a relatively low additional outlay of resources. However, apart from the evident lack of access by poor people, it should be recognized that electronic communication and publishing can be unreliable, and are likely to remain so. One way of overcoming the limitations of electronic communication and achieving the reliability (and readability) of printed documentation is to transfer information in digital form for local printing and distribution.

The full potential of research knowledge to affect practice rests on its access and use by all stakeholders. Researchers can do a great deal by giving appropriate attention and devoting sufficient resources to their knowledge-sharing and communication strategies. This should be seen not only in the immediate terms of disseminating the knowledge produced in a particular research project, but also in the longer-term aims of developing local capacity and building effective communication networks between stakeholders in development.

However, much of the effort needed to turn development knowledge into effective practice for the urban poor to improve their living conditions rests with the capacity-building efforts of governments and donors. At a basic level, this can be achieved through improvements in social infrastructure – schools and colleges, libraries, learning centres, information centres and archives. At another level, it means developing the knowledge and communication capacities of a range of local actors in civil society and local government.

THE GOOD OR BEST PRACTICE MODEL OF KNOWLEDGE TRANSFER[7]

The networking-based paradigm of development knowledge transfer demands new forms of easily communicated, practical knowledge that by-pass traditional, long-term routes for knowledge transfer. In this context, the good or best practice model of knowledge transfer is of increasing importance. In this approach, it is essential in the adaptation of the practice to a new context that the knowledge beneficiaries become active in the knowledge-generation process.

The good or best practice approach has been widely adopted in urban development research and practice throughout the 1990s. In particular, it has been used as one of the two key tools promoted by the UN Centre for Human Settlements (UNCHS) to promulgate and encourage the implementation of the Habitat Agenda, the international human settlements policy framework.[8] The aim is to establish models of process, conveying knowledge and skills applicable in any context. The issue of context is critical, and one of the main criticisms of the approach is that insufficient effort has been addressed to the issue of how practices can be transferred to different contexts or transformed into effective government policies. If good or best practices are to be successfully applied, they should be framed in ways that are sensitive to specific political, cultural and behavioural contexts. 'There are two related aspects to this problem. The first is formulating appropriate conceptual frameworks that enable practices to become tools, which are easily adapted to different contexts. The second is developing methodologies for understanding and communicating within the different contexts in which practices can be applied' (Gandelsonas and Lloyd-Jones, 2001).

In devising appropriate conceptual frameworks for cases of good practice in urban development, much work needs to be done. Urban theory has long relied on a deductive approach, adapting a priori, theoretical models, often drawn from other sciences, to the complexities of urban reality. These often quite sophisticated theoretical economic, spatial and sociological models have seldom found much resonance in development policy and practice, and the influence is indirect at best. On the other hand, policy-makers seldom pay enough attention to learning from experience, or the outcomes of detailed monitoring and evaluation exercises, preferring to follow fashions or re-invent policy in their own image. Similarly, practitioners prefer to follow their own ways, sticking to habits good and bad, long learned and not easily unlearned.

As far as the Habitat Agenda is concerned, good or best practices have been firmly associated with the concept of partnership involving the range of stakeholders, including governments and local governments, NGOs, community-based organizations (CBOs), academic institutions and others. Although, in practice, partnership is far from being a simple concept, in the Habitat framework it is seen as aiding closer dialogues between knowledge-formulators and communities, and as better geared towards producing ideas that are more adaptable to specific development conditions (UNCHS, 1998). Whether or not partnerships can be made to work on an equal basis, adapting practices to local circumstances that recognize the need for particular kinds of stakeholder involvement is an important first step in arriving at a more general model of good or best practice that is sensitive to different cultural contexts.[9]

The argument put forward here is that 'the transfer of knowledge of good or best practice is only effective when coupled with the use of appropriate forms of knowledge and when channelled "horizontally" through networks and partnership arrangements' (UNCHS, 1998). Thus communicating good or best practice involves identifying existing social networks, applying knowledge management tools for the communication of explicit and tacit knowledge, and creating partnerships by drawing on networks at various levels, in particular at the local level.

THE ROLE OF NETWORKS AND SOCIAL CAPITAL IN ADAPTING GOOD OR BEST PRACTICE

Local networks, in this context, are defined as interconnected groups of people who are in direct intercommunication with one another and share knowledge of some sort to meet specific community interests – for example, maintaining social contact, mutual aid and sharing common struggles, and establishing and maintaining a common sense of identity (Johnston et al., 1986). From this perspective, local networks are an aspect of social capital (Chapters 4 and 5 herein; Phillips, 2002) and, given the importance of word-of-mouth communication in the knowledge-transfer process, are the natural medium for the transference of knowledge or good/best practice in poor urban communities in developing countries.

Once key or representative members of local networks are identified, it becomes easier to understand how such networks gain access to knowledge, what the local tacit knowledge is, and what the basic needs of a community are. Tacit knowledge is here understood as knowledge possessed by communities which forms an integral part of their everyday practice, and is not formally set out or learned in a formal setting (White et al., 1994).

As an aspect of social capital in urban areas, local networks may be weakly established or carry negative connotations but, where well established and of positive social value, they may certainly carry strategic significance in the transference of good practice. 'Members of such networks can be key in offering support and access to local knowledge, neighbourhood contacts, network relationships, a large membership for consultation, energy, time and, above all, commitment. In building the capacity of communities to share their experiences and local knowledge and to absorb better forms of practice, networks provide a potential point of focus' (Gandelsonas and Lloyd-Jones, 2001).

The importance of networking at the local level is emphasized here, but it is also necessary to draw on wider networks in identifying and sharing different models of practice. In recent years, networks of cities and local authorities have grown in number and significance, and have a potentially important role to play in the transference of good practice.10 International NGOs, through their internal networks, have similar potential for conveying good practice, although there are greater dangers in unitary organizations, even where decentralized, that practice can become ossified and unresponsive to local realities. Of particular interest are international networks of CBOs, as illustrated in the case study of Slum Dwellers International, Chapter 8.

CONCLUSIONS

The experience-based model of knowledge transfer, of which good or best practice is a special case, is most effective where mediated forms of knowledge transfer are backed up with direct experience of good practices, and of face-to-face communication between those involved in the good practice and those who wish to apply it elsewhere, as in the case of Slum Dwellers International. This implies that even where ICT has lowered or eliminated the costs associated with transferring information across great distances, sharing good practice on a local or regional basis would still have advantages over more globalized networks of knowledge sharing.

The argument of this chapter has grown out of the contention that researchers in developed countries need to look beyond a limited, one-way process of dissemination of research results to a many-way exchange of information with the urban poor themselves and the variety of intermediaries applying research knowledge to development practice. Knowledge transfer should form part of a more general research communication and networking strategy based on the idea of partnership and knowledge exchange.

Empowering people in poverty through access to knowledge and information, and improving their means of communication with other stakeholders in the development process, are fundamental to the urban governance and poverty reduction agendas. This does not mean tailoring all research outputs to the requirements of specific poor urban communities. Most knowledge will continue to be produced in a generalized form and interpreted for local use by the intermediaries closest to poor urban communities. Understanding of the different types of intermediary involved in the urban development process and their respective roles and interests is therefore fundamental.

Through ICT, and the increased accessibility of professional forms of media to knowledge workers, there has been a 'mediatization' of knowledge networks and an increasing crossover with the professional media. In this process, in which the quantity and quality (in form if not in content) of information and knowledge exchange through networks is greatly enhanced, a new paradigm of knowledge exchange and transfer is emerging. The impact on knowledge generation and exchange in urban development is demonstrated in the dynamics of a new model of partnership and network-based development research practice (Figure 1.2).

Researchers have yet to take on board the full implications of changes in networking and media practice for their own research practices. The chapter explores ways in which researchers can make better use of media and networks in developing their knowledge-transfer strategies to impact on urban poverty. It suggests that researchers should make far better use of the great variety of types of media available, often in combination, to get their message across and communicate with the variety of interests involved in the urban development process. Finally, it outlines how the concept of good or best practice as a form of knowledge-generation and sharing addresses the emerging new practice-orientated paradigm in knowledge transfer.

CHAPTER TWO

Modelling demand in order to meet it: can the information and knowledge management systems of the urban poor be understood and strengthened?

Lucky Lowe

'Knowledge is of two kinds. We know a subject ourselves, or we know where we can find information upon it.'

Samuel Johnson (1709–1784)

INTRODUCTION

Communication is the oxygen of change; in the dynamic and fast-moving urban environment people have to be aware of opportunities in order to use them to their advantage. Sustainable livelihoods literature emphasizes the multifarious nature of poverty, but also the diverse and dynamic nature of livelihood strategies which the most marginalized members of society adopt in order to survive (DFID, 1999). People need access to resources but, in order to gain access, they first need an awareness of where resources exist and how they can be obtained. They also need the necessary information, knowledge and skills to turn those raw materials into positive livelihood outcomes. Within and between low-income settlements, women and men engage in complex patterns of exchange with family and friends, interact with private sector entrepreneurs, and engage in formal and informal commercial markets and with public sector bodies in order to meet their daily and longer-term needs for survival and growth (World Bank, 1998). It is the nature and substance of these socially, politically, economically, technologically and personally defined interactions, which exist in any society, that are referred to by the term knowledge and information systems (KIS).

Research and the information services supplied to Southern individuals and organizations are often supported by donors such as the UK Department for International Development (DFID), with the overriding goal of reducing poverty. Concern among development agencies that their research findings, knowledge and information assets are not reaching the urban poor is increasingly apparent in current development strategies. A strong desire exists to ensure that the considerable body of information and knowledge being generated by Northern researchers and development agencies enhances the capacity of poor women and men to create and sustain urban livelihood strategies. An increasing realization is emerging among development donors, non-governmental organizations (NGOs) and researchers that they need to be able to adapt current practices and policies to increase effective outreach and demonstrate the impact of knowledge and information initiatives.

This chapter describes the Intermediate Technology Development Group's (ITDG) modelling research applied to specific case studies. As a small international NGO, ITDG has always sought to scale up the impact of its work through information and knowledge creation and dissemination. Action research and development initiatives that support lesson learning through undertaking research, implementing pilot projects, and the development of longer-term programmes and partnerships to meet local needs, all inform development practices and influence policies. The range of communication processes, and the information types and media employed in meeting these aims, are diverse. Products and processes cover from generic to specific topics, providing practical 'how-to' guidance on a range of technological issues, approaches, tools, equipment, production processes, social and institutional development organizations, and policy issues.

COMPLEX COMMUNICATION PROCESSES: THE ROLE OF MEDIA AND INTERMEDIARIES

Information dissemination is an extremely complex process. Factors such as culture, linguistics, educational and economic realities of both senders and recipients, competition for people's attention, individual and organizational motivation and objectives, and access to and appropriation of communications technologies all contribute to determining the effectiveness of information-sharing that results from any development initiative.

The choice of dissemination media has a significant bearing on the effectiveness of interactions between information provider and recipient. The media greatly affect the value of information, and influence whether target audiences receive the message in a format that is accessible, credible and useful (Shadrack, 2001). Certain communication media and presentation formats may be inaccessible if they depend on levels of literacy higher than those that actually exist. Messages are likely to be ignored or more forcefully rejected by target audiences as being irrelevant if the format is unfamiliar, whereas familiar sources may be given credence even if the quality of the information received means it is of little real value. The media and the message are inextricably linked.

Traditionally printed media have been a common vehicle for sharing information. The availability of a range of document types makes print a versatile medium, able to provide anything from individuals' opinions, historical accounts, impartial data, entertaining stories and academic musings to practical guidance. Technical briefs, visual and graphic message boards, posters, exhibitions, leaflets, reports, newsletters and specialist journals might all provide details on how to construct an affordable house using locally available materials; or how to manufacture household goods such as an energy-efficient stove to meet the demand from low-income urban households. The degree to which such materials are able to respond to local literacy, language and other requirements will vary.

The rapid increase in electronic communication and mass media is causing increasing debate about North–South, South–South and South–North information flows (BSHF, 2001). Access to the Internet is improving, but it is difficult to assess its global state or to give any realistic indication of how universal a medium the Internet will be in 10 or 20 years' time. Donor agencies such as the World Bank and the UN Development Program (UNDP) are taking an active interest in the development of electronic communications. The current divide between North and South in access to the global Internet is stark. For example, approximately two-thirds of the 'Internet population' resides in the USA and Canada; the 23 per cent of the world's people living in South-East Asia include 1 per cent of the world's Internet users (World Bank, 2000a; DFID, 2001c). Connectivity varies within regions and between rural and urban populations. At both household and institutional levels, capacity to access information electronically will be limited not only by the lack of communications infrastructure, appropriate hardware and software, but also by the necessary attitudes, confidence and skills. The emphasis on modern information and communications technologies (ICT) by international development agencies is running high, but opinions are divided as to whether or not the potential is as great as optimists suggest, or as divisive and unsustainable as the pessimists believe. Macro-level support and a growing body of micro-level pilot initiatives do not yet constitute a coherent force for change (O'Farrell, 2001).

Supply-led information provided by Northern development agencies often fails to 'go the last mile' – a range of resource constraints and limited human capital, especially in terms of limited literacy and technological capability, have been effective barriers to potential benefits being secured by poor women and men. Yet the potential for new ICTs to reach out and meet the needs of people living in poverty is tantalizing. The current tendency to focus on the technology is perhaps deflecting attention from the need to increase understanding of the information requirements, the existing knowledge base and the preferred communications media of poor urban residents (O'Farrell et al., 2000).

Development intermediaries are, nonetheless, increasingly focused on how modern and traditional ICTs can be better deployed to meet the needs of people in poverty. Provided that there is an adequate literacy level, and access to ITC hardware and communications infrastructure is available, significant amounts of information may be obtained from web-based databases, intranets or e-mail conferencing. Rapid advances in technology mean that literacy-dependent media can be supplemented by interactive and other more accessible formats. Employing local languages, visual and oral/aural techniques allows access to information to be increased and a voice for the urban poor to be created, for example by employing participatory video production to record local realities and raise awareness of priorities defined by poor urban women (Foster, 2001; Development Alternatives). The telephone is shown to have the capacity to link rural communities to urban resources providing information on markets and trading, strengthening kinship relations, accessing health services, etc. (DFID, 2001b). The same research concluded that the potential of radio remains underexploited; radio is often cited as the preferred medium at local level (see also Mhonda, 1997). Researchers in Peru found that radio provides company for people, but will only be considered effective in supporting livelihood strategies when the information is strongly contextualized to the local environment and designed to meet specific local requirements (Saravia, 2001). Mass media, dependent on electricity and communications infrastructure, are more likely to be available to the urban rather than the rural poor. Access to mass media by the poorest remains highly restricted, often only via wealthier friends, relatives or community-based collectives. The nature and quality of the information available will be variable, and is often unrelated to livelihood needs.

Innovation is required at all levels of the communication chain, among information generators, institutional conduits and intermediaries operating locally, nationally and internationally. The combined use of several media, creating a communication continuum, may allow a wider or more targeted audience to be reached. Information can be disseminated in a coordinated and complementary way by using the most appropriate media for different kinds of audiences and messages. For example, the multimedia global dissemination initiative *Hands On* (Chapter 11) uses broadcast media to increase exposure of development issues and development solutions in mainstream broadcasting. Broadcast on BBC World TV, linking appropriate technology approaches in the North and South, the aim is to build synergies and strengthen the case for appropriate technology approaches in meeting development objectives.

MODELLING INFORMATION FLOWS BASED ON LOCAL REALITIES IN PERU, SRI LANKA AND ZIMBABWE

The above overview of communications activities and issues, incomplete as it is, demonstrates that attempting to represent the array of indigenous and exogenous information flows, methods and media in any given context will be a gross simplification of a complex and dynamic reality. A two-dimensional representation of information exchange may provide only an illusion that information dissemination is understandable, while in reality it is fraught with unknowns. Most information providers have developed an intuitive feel for what media to use, how to identify their target audiences and how to structure messages accordingly. Nevertheless, the development of a model based on empirical evidence of local realities aims to identify specific audiences, media, intermediaries and information channels. Representational models of reality aim to assist in synthesizing certain aspects of existing intuition and experience to help non-specialists and specialists to improve the range and impact of their dissemination activities. A function of modelling KIS among the urban poor is to enable development agencies to listen, learn and put in place baseline understanding that will enable indigenous knowledge and information systems to be understood and strengthened.

Figure 2.1 shows a simplified representation of the flows of information between various stakeholders involved in the process of disseminating information aimed at supporting development (Lowe, 1998). Some important aspects of the model are the linkages between various providers and users, showing a two-way flow of information. Numerous other lines could be included and the nature of those lines further defined to demonstrate that, despite the suggestion of a two-way information flow that is equally balanced, reality is rarely like this.

DFID-sponsored development research tends to be supply-driven, of a 'handbook' type, but information flow in the other direction is less substantial and is often limited to feedback by way of post hoc evaluation, rather than early, ongoing dialogue about information needs and options. The model in Figure 2.1 represents the 'push' of information: from exogenous agencies, placed at the top of the diagram, representing their desire to drive information and knowledge assets, which they own, to poor urban households. This model was subsequently developed, putting people in poverty at the top of the diagram and thus raising the question as to what information and knowledge assets they have to supply, but also what they seek and need to draw on in order to support their livelihood strategies (information 'pull'; Max Lock Centre, 2001b).

The model (Figure 2.1) essentially considers information flows which are thought to be typical or widespread: from Northern research institutions, through intermediaries such as Southern universities, NGOs or community-based organizations (CBOs). A variety of media and structured dissemination channels may be employed for disseminating knowledge. Information also flows along informal routes; someone will talk with an acquaintance who has access to information resources: 'a friend of mine worked in the head office of the university, and she told me and I decided to give it a try' (Agreda and Contreras, 2001). The strength, frequency and diversity of such unstructured information-sharing are significant. The horizontal information flows, which are assumed, such as might occur

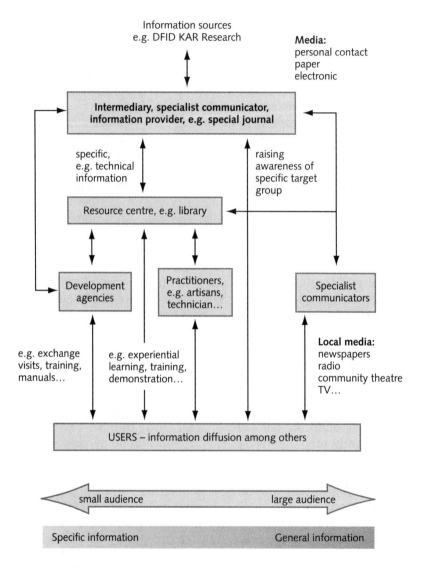

Figure 2.1   Information flows – a simplified model

between community members, among artisans or in academic institutions carrying out related research, are also numerous, yet very little of that information appears to flow across to other levels. The concern of donors and development agencies to enhance flows between all stakeholder groups aiming to reduce poverty is perhaps only superseded by the desire to see information reach the most marginalized and poorest people (DFID, 2001a).

Recent research undertaken by ITDG among low-income urban neighbourhoods in Zimbabwe, Sri Lanka and Peru, aimed to increase understanding of existing knowledge and information systems at the grass-roots level, so that resources can be applied to strengthen them. By creating an explicit understanding of the available resource base among all stakeholders, defining information assets and needs, and identifying preferred media, researchers aimed to learn lessons and provide recommendations as to how the flows of information, both supply (push) and demand (pull), can meet in support of urban poverty reduction.

Figure 2.2 presents a 'windmill' model developed during the research. In workshop discussions ITDG's researchers decided to expand on the areas of focus identified during the pilot phase as pertinent to urban women and men: income, infrastructure, housing and facilities. The expressed desire to reflect current holistic thinking about sustainable livelihoods and move away from sector-specific areas of focus contributed to the model shown in Figure 2.2. Key features of the model include the 'sails', representing various assets and services required to sustain livelihoods. By breaking livelihoods issues into certain areas, researchers were able to begin to make sense of the various information flows. Researchers undertook surveys involving structured and semi-structured interviews and group discussions, observed local realities and reviewed secondary information sources.

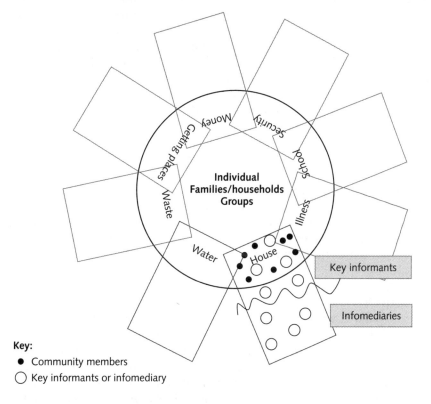

Key:
- ● Community members
- ○ Key informants or infomediary

Figure 2.2   Livelihoods based on the KIS model

Efforts were primarily focused on residents of low-income neighbourhoods in the capital city of each country, and a secondary town.

Information flows were studied at the individual, household, neighbourhood and city levels. In populating the windmill's sails, local researchers adopted different approaches but essentially reflected current practices used in social mapping. Developing each of the sails in depth, researchers in Peru produced eight diagrammatic representations of information flows, one example of which is given in Figure 2.3. In the final report, researchers list the types of information received, its sources and the means by which it reached them (see Table 2.1 for the findings in relation to education).

Table 2.1 clearly shows that the nature of information sought by people ranges across issues of moral, economic and physical wellbeing at both personal and collective levels. The sources of information also span the formal and informal networks that people interact with, from household level (exchanges between parents and children) to municipal-level institutions, which are responsible for providing details about the services they offer.

Intermediaries were identified as critical actors in bridging the divide between local residents and exogenous information suppliers and stakeholders in the urban development process. Variously called key informants and/or 'infomediaries', key individuals and organizations were identified in each of the research locations. In Zimbabwe, key informants were defined as 'respected people, opinion leaders and agenda setters within a community', but the political context meant people were reluctant to identify individuals for fear of repercussions. Nonetheless, informal discussions and surveys carried out with a number of respondents at service centres, shops, organizations and institutions within the community led to the identification of three types of key informants with traits identified as either constraining or beneficial to information flows.

- Key informants from organizations and institutions providing a service may have different attitudes towards enquirers. As their workplace may be frustrating and demoralizing, some employees may vent their anger on clients; however, some are very responsive and try to do their best to provide services, although constrained by their circumstances.
- Key informants may be individuals respected and sought out by respondents, and responsive to the information needs of the beneficiaries.
- Political appointees as key informants are found in almost all ongoing activities, and usually act as the informers or intelligence for the political party they belong to. They may be feared gatekeepers, or occupy decision-making positions in CBOs, NGOs, churches, local schools and local government institutions that work directly with urban communities. They may vary widely in terms of their resources, the means at their disposal to access information, and the acquisition and dissemination capabilities of their staff. They may also be criticized for being information hoarders.

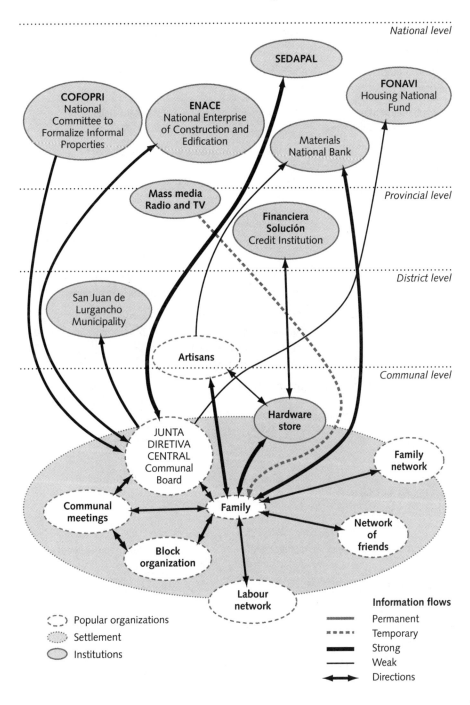

Figure 2.3   Information flows relating to housing in Peru

Table 2.1 Information types, sources and media relating to education in low-income settlements in Tarapoto, Peru

What information do they receive?	Where do they get the information from?	How is information received?
Access to elementary and high school education (free)	Relatives, friends and neighbours	Person-to-person
Cost and quality of higher education	Pre-university academies, technological and pedagogical institutes, university	Visits to provider
Educational centres, technical and/or professional careers	Media, friends and relatives	Radio and TV advertising, person-to-person, visits to provider
Scholarships and easy terms	Institutes of higher education	Provider visits the school, provider visits houses
Sexuality and reproductive health	Regional health direction, educational centres, teachers, relatives, church, national police, media	Talks, educational campaigns and programmes, person-to-person
Religious and moral training	Church, educational centres	Book reading (Bible), magazine reading (*El Atalaya*), teachers' advice
Basic information for students	Internet	At institutes and academies
Technical education (agricultural and livestock training, accountancy, sewing)	High schools	Formal education
Education information and motivation	Relatives	Transfer of experiences
Information about the students' progress	Teachers	Parents visit schools, school for parents
Artistic and sports activities, and others	Educational centres	Workshops, courses of manual work
Information on institutional work/others	Municipalities, other institutions	School work

Institutions identified as information providers: educational centres, pre-university centres, Tarapoto Public Pedagogical Institute, State University of San Martin, Private Pedagogical Institute, technological institutes (*Ciro Alegria, Blaise Pascal, Nor Oriental de la Selva*), *El Huayco* Health Centre – DIRES, media (*Radio Tropical*), Jehovah's Witnesses, Provincial Municipality of San Martin.

In Peru, researchers concluded that it would be more helpful to focus on defining types of information providers, rather than key informants. Table 2.2 summarizes the findings in relation to a small sample of the information- and knowledge-providers researched, their methods of developing content, and dissemination activities (Staeheli, 2001).

Table 2.2 highlights the finding that institutions tend to develop areas of specialism depending on organizational interests and priorities, rather than local demand. Those policies will often be derived from implicit and/or explicit views of development. Institutional policies also determine work methods, for example, staff working on gender issues 'go out into the field' with a series of ideas based on previous experience of gender relations and roles.

The predominant means of providing information and supporting target groups to build their knowledge capital is through training. Trainers and trainees will employ support resources such as 'modules', workbooks and other printed media. Oral means adopted by the sample organizations include radio promotions and school-based competitions to promote experiential learning. Web-based information is seen as increasingly accessible, but not as a replacement for other means.

While some of the organizations studied in Peru employed external evaluation of their efforts, most were found not to focus on gathering opinions of target populations or measuring satisfaction levels, although some specific initiatives adopted more participatory approaches. Face-to-face exchange and experiential learning have been shown to be the most effective means of South-to-South support among poor women and men, enabling people to meet, talk, inform each other, and develop new ideas for coping with and reducing poverty (ACHR, 2000). The complexity and significance of social capital of all types, linking, bonding and bridging (World Bank, 2001), has been shown to have both negative and positive impacts on livelihood strategies and outcomes in low-income urban settlements (Beall, 2000). Research in Suduwelle, Sri Lanka, highlighted the fact that information about employment opportunities was often gained from friends and family, but also from local politicians (Figure 2.4). The majority of the inhabitants make a living from fishing in the Beira Lake, and share information with each other on where to sell the fish, where to catch fish and other related issues. The Beira Lake Restoration Project is being carried out in order to clean the lake and its environs. The value of knowledge held by the fisherfolk, effective in the conservation of the natural asset base, has not been recognized by institutional stakeholders in the public sector. Local people have not been consulted in the lake restoration planning, or considered for employment opportunities which the restoration activities will generate.

The relations of NGOs with governmental organizations are significant in ensuring coordination and collaboration. Methods generally include information exchange networks and joint projects, but these may be limited to ad hoc examples of good practice rather than institutional ways of working.

Table 2.2 Comparison of three NGOs' information strategies in Peru

Subject area	NGO ALTERNATIVA	EDUCA	TAREA
Stakeholders	Grassroots leaders from students, sports and other interest groups Women involved in community-based initiatives Young people Small entrepreneurs	Marginalized urban residents	Teachers, community
Geographic area	North side of Lima Los Olivos and San Martin de Porras, currently expanding to cover *Rimac*	San Juan de Lurigancho (SJL)	North and south side of Lima
Selection criteria	Institutional goal of developing leadership capacity among younger generations Local leaders under age 50	Need to focus limited resources Extreme poverty in SJL and lack of service provision by any other NGOs	Previous networks
Content, type and means of dissemination	Primary stakeholders taught about leadership, social management and participation Health education Participatory assessment of settlement area and development of the *Independencia* Development Plan Dissemination of plan for further consultation and awareness-raising	Education	Education New methodologies Citizenship Empowerment of organized population

Table 2.2 (Continued)

Subject area	NGO ALTERNATIVA	EDUCA	TAREA
Criteria for definition of content	Interests of population in context of NGOs' interests Ongoing interaction with students informs work methods and content	Based on planning informed by institutional policies and current pedagogic practice	While the contents are defined with a participatory methodology, they build on their interests and policies
Media of dissemination	Training Website *Independencia* www.alter.org.pe Dissemination material – ex-students continue to visit the offices and use IT facilities to access e-mail and web-based information		*La Red*: incipient; free software In general, training, teachers, materials, modules, etc.
Feedback on information use	Physical proximity with primary stakeholders is seen as significant in ensuring needs are understood No systematic evaluation of stakeholders' satisfaction but builds on requests from students to develop new content		Participatory methodology in elaboration of materials
Inter-institutional relationships	Particular experience with the Municipalities of Independencia and Comas Mediation between local residents and local government bodies is significant; 'the relationship you know, has to do a lot with politics. . . it depends who the mayor is'.	Operates through smaller NGOs and uses local networks of governmental and popular organizations Recent focus on a penal procedure faced by the mayor has displaced residents' issues and stifled collaboration	Intense coordination with schools, some USE (Educational Services Office) on the south side of Lima, Ministry of Education and other NGOs

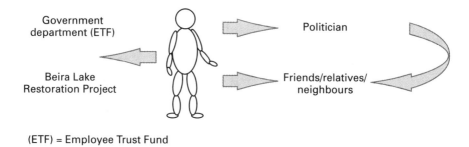

(ETF) = Employee Trust Fund

Figure 2.4   Modelling local information sources about employment in Suduwelle

Perceptions of the relationships between public sector bodies and NGOs vary from being highly competitive to being usefully collaborative. Effective partnerships were seen as dependent on the development of mutual understanding and commitment to long-term joint initiatives; without such collaboration the likelihood of duplication and contradictory information flows is increased, and information-providers may lose credibility. The political nature of many public sector bodies and offices clearly impinges on the capacity of all stakeholders to engage in a long-term process. Issues of transparency and accountability to poor residents would be likely to challenge the status quo in most countries, and is likely to be strongly contested by more powerful stakeholders.

The organizational culture, political will and operational environment found in the public sector evidently have an immense impact on the nature of information flows from local service providers, in particular affecting the performance of civil servants. In Zimbabwe, researchers found numerous documents produced by government departments, such as the legislative instruments and guidelines on accessing a myriad of basic services, but these are rarely shared. 'Requests for documented information sources at the Ministry of Labour ended in a futile encounter with the Labour Relations Officer who jealously guarded his copy of Statutory Instruments.' Researchers felt that lack of information flows and political ill-will were not easy to model. In ministries concerned with provision of social services, officers were found by the same researchers to be more outward-reaching: 'information is taken to the communities by officials of the Ministry through meetings and workshops' (Chitonga, 2001).

Many community-based organizations take a proactive role, encouraging communities to innovate, developing skills and local organizational capacity, facilitating access to resources and overcoming bureaucratic constraints. In order to fulfil such roles effectively, people need access to a wide range of information – both technical and non-technical. Midwives and Public Health Officers are often cited as critical sources of information on health issues, but also on other subject matters. In Epworth, Zimbabwe, the midwife's exposure to several external agencies means she is well informed.

Her extensive knowledge of the people within the neighbourhoods she serves means the information she provides is felt to be relevant and is generally appreciated as being valuable in meeting people's needs.

The interaction between CBOs, NGOs or an extension of public sector workers and communities varies according to the individuals concerned. 'WARD 26 Councillor Mr K. Ramirez deals with the supply of information on virtually all ... key livelihood issues and is the focal point of all information that comes in and goes out of the area' (Chitonga, 2001). Individuals might adopt quite different ways of working with and relating to the members of communities which impact on the availability, cost and value of the information exchanged.

Modelling the complex reality of knowledge-sharing at the level of abstraction of the windmill diagram proved problematic, if not futile, at the local level. Researchers developed their own models to represent local preferences and realities, giving substance to the windmill's sails, exploring in their deliberations which areas of interest concerned people, whether information was *push* or *pull* in nature, and using maps to represent the horizontal and vertical information flows. In Suduwelle, Sri Lanka, for example, the researchers concluded that with regard to issues about housing, water and employment, health and sanitation *pull* information flows mattered most, as decisions were made on a demand basis. It was recognized that many information flows were two-way, but a lack of *push* information from public sector bodies could be turned into *pull* when NGOs supported people to make demands on public sector service providers.

ASSESSING VALUE AND IMPACT: AN ELUSIVE PRACTICE

By populating the models, researchers were able to identify where information resources were held and to identify the predominant flows of information within low-income settlements, gaining quantitative and qualitative knowledge of the impact of available information resources or specific knowledge creation and sharing initiatives. Generally, a lack of empirical evidence, or analysis of actual experiences of information provision and its impact on poor people's economic and social livelihoods, is reported (Michiels and van Crowder, 2001). There is concern that the lack of information about development initiatives and programmes affects livelihoods and has resulted in alienation of the majority from decision-making processes (Norton, 2001).

Impact assessment remains an elusive aspect of information dissemination; many people measure the success of their activities based largely on anecdotal evidence or measures of outputs (Roche and Bush, 1997). Information users will be operating in a diverse set of contexts, using information for many different purposes. The various actors in the communication chain may double as users and providers. At each stage there is potential for information to become distorted, misinterpreted or improved from value added to the content or packaging. An accurate assessment of the validity and usefulness of information could be made only if the assessor has a good understanding of the use to which the information is to be put, and the capabilities and needs of the users of the information (Ruskulis, 1998). Many institutional information providers felt that adopting a participatory approach in designing and producing information resources ensured that it was pertinent to their target audiences (Table 2.2). Commercial information providers, such as the information booth studied in Lima, have a clear measure of the monetary value of the information sold – the commercial viability of their service provision is a good indication of whether or not they are meeting local demand. However, few examples exist of formalized impact assessments.

The complexity of the processes and distance (in space or time) from the sender to the end-user is often a major barrier to effective monitoring and evaluation. Beyond the first recipient of information it is likely to be expensive, if not impossible, to trace what happens to the information provided. Additionally, the recipient will have received information from a number of sources; any subsequent decisions made and action taken will reflect the sum of the information obtained, rather than any causal link to a single component of it. Therefore, assessing the impact of information shared by way of journals, books, enquiry services, Internet or many other communication methods in which the sender and recipients are distant from each other is problematic. Nonetheless, the need for accountability of all development agencies is clear, as is the imperative to put limited resources to best effect. Measuring and evaluating development initiatives must include consideration and assessment of communications elements of the process in order to assess the direct and indirect impacts, intended or fortuitous.

One example of effective impact assessment of information provided to individuals and small-scale entrepreneurs emerged from ITDG's evaluation efforts in Sri Lanka and Peru. The journal *Food Chain* has been published twice a year for over 10 years, initially based on 'widespread perception' of the lack of information available to field workers. It is distributed, free of charge, to development institutions, NGOs and individuals working with poor communities in the South. Circulation has increased steadily with each edition, from an initial print run of 350 to 3000 in 2001. The journal's approach and content have been adapted, informed by experience and feedback gathered from two 'mid-term' evaluations in 1993 and 1996 undertaken by postal surveys of readers. The nature of the journal's readership, and the ways in which information was put to use, were better understood, but the surveys did not provide any in-depth information about impact. More recently, new evidence was generated from face-to-face interviews held while the evaluator followed an information trail (Judge, 2001b). The resultant case studies provide anecdotal evidence of direct positive impact on beneficiaries, including enhanced income generation and improved nutrition. Journal materials were used in training courses translated or used as a source for publishing articles locally. For example, Mr Gamini Ratnayake of Matale is self-employed and runs 'Growers and Processors', which produces organic vanilla, vegetables, fruit, spices and medicinal plants, and processes tomatoes, spices and medicinal plants. Mr Ratnayake uses the information for domestic purposes and to garner new ideas about technological options. He shares information with people in the village, and is willing to explain the processes to those who are unable to read. Mr Ratnayake can read *Food Chain* because it is in simple English. He would prefer it to be written in Sinhala because then all the housewives would be able to read it and use the information directly.

During the KIS research in Zimbabwe, examples of impact monitoring by Epworth Poly Clinic included systematic use of data forms to gather and consolidate information, generating statistics to monitor whether information is reaching the intended beneficiaries. Comparative analysis of the number of cases of malaria from one year to the next gives an indication of outreach achieved. A decrease in the number of malaria cases is taken to show that target beneficiaries have accessed and applied the information supplied. Should there be an increase in the number of cases, new information dissemination strategies are sought (Chitonga, 2001). There may be limitations on the validity of simplistic, quantitative monitoring, but data collection and analysis systems must be pertinent and also affordable.

Qualitative research findings demonstrate that face-to-face discussions can give clear indications of how local information systems could be strengthened. Mr Rambire of Gadzema was often unable to access essential services due to the lack of communications – the distance of this peri-urban informal settlement from the formal city increases residents' isolation. He clearly felt that access to a telephone would increase his capacity to be an effective intermediary for his constituents and the service providers located beyond his neighbourhood. In Sri Lanka, information-sharing initiatives introduced by the Arthacharya Foundation met the (hitherto latent) need for information about waste management. Even though the Galle Municipal Council collected garbage regularly, people were unaware of the alternative means of disposal. Training on recycling resulted in new income generated from composting, the product of which is sold and used to improve food safety in urban agriculture (Hidallage, 2001).

The principles and practices of participatory development are more widely accepted now than ever, yet 'cultural barriers, as well as attitudes of arrogance about knowledge and vertical practices, have not allowed donors, planners and governments to establish a dialogue with communities of beneficiaries. Indigenous knowledge is at best perceived as an acceptable claim from communities, but rarely considered as one of the main components of development' (Dagron, 2001). Michiels and van Crowder (2001) conclude that external agencies rarely undertake participatory needs assessments and priorities for the adoption of ICT, which is often driven by outside agendas. The number of community-driven ICT initiatives remains limited and content creation more often than not lacks local ownership.

There is increasing recognition of the need to involve poor women and men in the assessment of current issues in formulating and monitoring poverty reduction policies (Estrella, 2000). DFID places new emphasis on popular participation in urban governance and recognizes the need to enable the poor to participate in the decision-making processes driving urban development (DFID, 2001a). The World Bank is promoting participatory poverty assessments to inform development strategies, and Urban Global Observatory initiative of the UN Centre for Human Settlements (www.UNCHS.org) is establishing a hierarchy of urban observatories spanning from local settlements to city- and national-level institutions. This global initiative aims to stimulate broad-based consultative processes to help identify and integrate urban information needs; build capacity to collect, manage, analyse and apply urban indicators; provide information and analyses to all stakeholders for more effective participation; evaluate policies and practices; and share information, knowledge and expertise using modern ICT. As statistics are about people, the local-level picture is critical in constructing a city-wide, national or global understanding of urban poverty. The Local Urban Observatory in Victoria Falls, Zimbabwe, facilitated by the Shack Dwellers Association, resulted in community mobilization, increased involvement in decision-making, and increased confidence and negotiating power (Homeless International, 2001).

The benefits of participatory communication include the empowerment of communities, with an increase in the capability to confront their own ideas of development as well as those of the NGO and public sectors. Effective two-way communication flows have the potential not only to inform people about the world around them, but also to enable them to influence the world. Communication cuts across issues of power and identity by involving the human subjects of social change in the political process of development. Participatory communication practices, which owe a great deal to Paulo Freire (1967), are differentiated from more commercial ones in the following terms (Dagron, 2001):

- horizontal versus vertical
- process versus campaign
- long-term versus short-term
- collective versus individual
- with versus for
- specific versus massive
- people's needs versus donors' musts
- ownership versus access
- consciousness versus persuasion.

By adopting the thinking and practices of participatory development, information and knowledge systems can be mapped, ranked, defined, analysed and assessed in a manner that enhances understanding among a wide range of stakeholders. The well-known constraints and problems associated with participatory research and development serve as a reminder that there is no 'magic bullet'. Information and knowledge sharing is rarely an end in itself, rather a means to an end, which is why the need for impact assessment remains a critical challenge. Nonetheless, the establishment of a baseline of understanding of local information assets, flows and gaps can support development initiatives to set goals and plan actions to improve existing information-sharing systems, in order to enhance livelihood options.

CONCLUSIONS

The diversity of information and information sources for many people continues to increase, yet for the millions of people living in absolute poverty, lack of choice and inequitable distribution of information and knowledge assets remains a significant dimension of their poverty. There is a risk that the poor will become excluded from the growing wealth of information accumulating in rich sectors of society. The role of development agencies is about more than providing information – it is about accessing and making use of information throughout the complex process of exchange and development they aim to facilitate. Many of the problems related to urbanization, such as poverty, inadequate shelter or facilities, insecurity, underemployment and impermanence, could be lessened with improved access to information on technological, social and political innovations and solutions, particularly by the grassroots.

Information needs are similar in many low-income settlements, but priorities clearly differ depending on the context. There are a multitude of organizations generating and providing information on development issues, innovations and potential development solutions. Such information can often be in the wrong place or not in an appropriate format, or become unintentionally or deliberately blocked before reaching the intended beneficiaries. By considering the types of information flows, channels, media and institutions concerned, it is clear that language, literacy and technological capability are important constraints to accessing new information and knowledge assets. Numerous communities still operate largely within the oral traditions of information exchange and rely on first-hand experience and personal exchange as a means to meeting their livelihood needs. Alternative forms of communication, and a communication continuum linking media and actors at all levels, are important to those who are supporting grassroots initiatives, in order to exchange information among themselves and with other sources in the South and North, and thereby increase horizontal and vertical information flows as well as ensuring sharing between the two. Critical information providers exist within low-income communities, and interaction with them enables development agencies to understand better how to strengthen these key points of leverage for pro-poor change.

The adoption of the Sustainable Livelihoods Framework (DFID, 1999) in modelling KIS of poor urban women and men deliberately aimed to put knowledge and information assets at the centre. The KIS research reported here demonstrates that it is possible to adopt participatory approaches and mapping techniques in order to better understand indigenous knowledge processes and products, as well as advantages and limitations of information flows within low-income neighbourhoods and the wider world. Breaking down research activities and analysis to focus on specific areas created an understanding of local information flows. Nonetheless, efforts to model information flows have been full of frustrations for some researchers, especially those operating in hostile political environments. Modelling practice is evolving, and different approaches have been tried. Developing the capacity of community-based development agencies to understand and analyse the impact of KIS will require an investment in knowledge and skills development.

Participatory approaches to urban development are already employed in informing and affecting behavioural change among popular, public and NGO institutions. The support mechanisms and assistance required to develop information dissemination capacity among and between poor people in developing countries need to be increased. The public sector lacks information and knowledge management capacity, but remains critical in building local capacity to embrace and support information flows with the most marginalized and disadvantaged sectors of society. The NGOs and CBOs are key intermediaries.

Processes have not generally been developed to assess the impact of information dissemination initiatives, nor to identify possible areas of further research to produce needs-based information. Much of the evidence for the impact of dissemination activities is anecdotal, and few attempts have been made to analyse why certain approaches can be considered to have been successful and others to have failed. For credibility and effectiveness reasons, it is important that more attention and resources be invested in systematic participatory impact assessment at the community level.

CHAPTER THREE

The hi-tech gift economy

Richard Barbrook

'. . .when [Ben Slivka] suggested that Microsoft consider giving away its browser, à
la Netscape, [Bill] Gates exploded and called him a "communist". . .'

(Wallace, 1997: 266)

THE LEGACY OF THE NEW LEFT

The Internet is haunted by the disappointed hopes of the 1960s. Because
this new technology symbolizes another period of rapid change, many contemporary commentators look back to the stalled revolution of over 30
years ago to explain what is happening now. Most famously, the founders of
Wired continually paid homage to the New Left values of individual freedom and cultural dissent in their coverage of the Internet. However, in their
Californian ideology, these ideals of their youth were going to be realized
through technological determinism and free markets. The politics of
ecstasy had been replaced by the economics of greed (Barbrook and
Cameron, 1996).

Ironically, the New Left emerged in response to the 'sell-out' of an earlier
generation. By the end of the 1950s, the heroes of the anti-fascist struggle
had become the guardians of Cold War orthodoxies. Frustrated with the
recuperation of their parents' generation, young people started looking for
new methods of cultural and social activism. For instance, the Situationists
proclaimed that the epoch of the political vanguard and the artistic avant-
garde had passed. Instead of following the intellectual elite, everyone
should instead determine their own destiny.

'The situation is . . . made to be lived by its constructors. The role played by a passive . . . "public" must constantly diminish, while that played by those who cannot
be called actors but rather . . . "livers" must steadily increase.'

(Debord, 1981: 25)

These New Left activists wanted to create opportunities for everyone to
express their own hopes, dreams and desires. The Hegelian 'grand narrative' would culminate in the supersession of all mediations separating
people from each other. Yet, despite their modernism, the Situationists

believed that the future was – paradoxically – a return to the past. Within Polynesia, tribal societies still organized themselves around the potlatch: the circulation of gifts. Without needing either the state or the market, individuals successfully worked and lived together (Mauss, 1990). According to the Situationists, the New Left revolution had to recreate this idyllic condition. Commodity relations must be completely supplanted by potlatch culture: *anarcho-communism* (Gombin, 1971: 99–151; Katsiaficas, 1987: 204–212).

During the decades following the 1960s, this utopian vision has continued to inspire radical media activists. For instance, in the late 1970s and early 1980s, 'free radio' stations in France and Italy were created through gifts of time and money from their supporters (Downing, 1984). In recent times, activists within do-it-yourself (DIY) movements have also identified themselves with the participatory spirit of the 1960s. Direct action and free parties are still the antidotes to political apathy and commercial culture. Once again, the gift is about to replace the commodity (Brass et al., 1997).

THE INTERNET AS REALLY EXISTING ANARCHO-COMMUNISM

Although also a child of the 1960s, the Internet should have little in common with the utopian dreams of the New Left. For this is a technology developed by computer scientists sponsored by the US military. Yet the Internet was – and still is – constructed around the gift economy. Although funded by the Pentagon, the inventors of this computer network built the system for themselves. Within universities, the gift economy has long been the primary method of socializing labour. Funded by the state or by donations, scientists do not have to turn their intellectual work directly into marketable commodities. Instead, research results are publicized by 'giving a paper' at specialist conferences and by 'contributing an article' to professional journals. The collaboration of many different academics is made possible through the free distribution of information (Hagstrom, 1982: 29).

Within small tribal societies, the circulation of gifts established close personal bonds between people. In contrast, the academic gift economy is used by scientists who are scattered across the world. Instead of creating intimate relations between individuals, their gifts are used to acquire intellectual respect from their peers through citations in articles and other forms of public acknowledgement. Scientists can obtain personal recognition for their individual efforts only by openly collaborating with each other through the academic gift economy. Although research is increasingly being commercialized, the giving away of findings remains the most efficient method of solving common problems within a particular scientific discipline.

From its earliest days, this free exchange of information was firmly embedded within the technologies and social mores of cyberspace (Geise,

1996: 126–132). Above all, the founders of the Internet never bothered to protect intellectual property within computer-mediated communications. On the contrary, they were developing these new technologies to advance their careers inside the academic gift economy. Far from wanting to enforce copyright, the pioneers of the Internet tried to eliminate all barriers to the distribution of scientific research. Technically, every act within cyberspace involves copying material from one computer to another. Once the first copy of a piece of information is placed on the Internet, the cost of making each extra copy is almost zero. The architecture of the system presupposes that multiple copies of documents can easily be cached around the network. As Tim Berners-Lee – the inventor of the Web – points out:

> 'Concepts of intellectual property, central to our culture, are not expressed in a way which maps onto the abstract information space. In an information space, we can consider the authorship of materials, and their perception; but . . . there is a need for the underlying infrastructure to be able to make copies simply for reasons of [technical] efficiency and reliability. The concept of "copyright" as expressed in terms of copies made makes little sense.'
>
> (Berners-Lee, 1996: 11)

Within the commercial creative industries, advances in digital reproduction are feared for making the 'piracy' of copyright material ever easier. For the owners of intellectual property, the Internet can only make the situation worse. In contrast, the academic gift economy welcomes technologies that improve the availability of data. Users should always be able to obtain and manipulate information with the minimum of impediments. The design of the Internet assumes that intellectual property is both technically and socially obsolete (Kleinman, 1996).

Even though it has expanded far beyond the university, the Internet remains predominantly a gift economy. From scientists through hobbyists to the general public, the charmed circle of users was slowly built up through the adhesion of many localized networks to an agreed set of protocols. Crucially, the common standards of the Internet include social conventions as well as technical rules. The giving and receiving of information without payment is almost never questioned. By adding their own presence, every user contributes to the collective knowledge accessible to those already online. In return, each individual has potential access to all the information made available by others within the Internet. Everyone takes far more out of the Internet than they can ever give away as an individual.

> '. . .the Net is far from altruistic, or it wouldn't work. . . Because it takes as much effort to distribute one copy of an original creation as a million . . . you never lose from letting your product free . . . as long as you are compensated in return . . . . What a miracle, then, that you receive not one thing in value in exchange – indeed there is no explicit act of exchange at all – but millions of unique goods made by others!'
>
> (Ghosh, 1998: 10)

Despite the commercialization of cyberspace, the self-interest of Internet users ensures that the hi-tech gift economy continues to flourish. For instance, musicians are using the Internet for the digital distribution of their recordings to each other. By giving away their own work to this network community, individuals receive free access to a far larger amount of music in return. Not surprisingly, the music business is worried about the increased opportunities for the 'piracy' of copyrighted recordings over the Internet. Sampling, DJ-ing and mixing have already blurred property rights within dance music. As demonstrated by the popularity of Napster, more and more people are now swapping MP3s of their favourite tunes. However, the greatest threat to the commercial music corporations comes from the flexibility and spontaneity of the hi-tech gift economy. After it is completed, a new track can quickly be made freely available to a global audience. If someone likes the tune, they can download it for personal listening, use it as a sample or make their own remix. Out of the free circulation of information, musicians can form friendships, work together and inspire each other. As one practitioner explains:

'It's all about doing it for yourself. Better than punk.'
                                                              (Lillington, 1998: 3)

In recent years, software development has also been transformed by the hi-tech gift economy. Many users had long been frustrated by the inflexibility and unreliability of proprietary programs. With the spread of the Internet, they began collaborating to develop their own software. Unlike commercial products, these programs can be modified, amended and improved by anyone with the appropriate programming skills. Closed code becomes open-source. Instead of being paid, individuals are rewarded for donating their labour to these projects by gaining access to software made by their fellow developers and by achieving recognition among their peers. Alienated work becomes participatory play (FSF, 1996; Raymond, 1998). Like the music industry, commercial software companies are increasingly threatened by the vitality of the hi-tech gift economy. For instance, Bill Gates admitted that Microsoft's biggest competitor in the provision of web servers comes from the open-source Apache program (Porterfield, 1998: 2). Anarcho-communism is now the alternative to monopoly capitalism.

Within the developed world, most politicians and corporate leaders believe that future prosperity depends on the commodification of information. Over the past few decades, intellectual property rights have been steadily tightened through new national laws and international agreements. Even human genetic material can now be patented (Frow, 1996). Yet, at the 'cutting edge' of the emerging information society, money–commodity relations play a secondary role to really existing anarcho-communism. For most of its users, the Internet is somewhere to work, play, love, learn and discuss with other people. Unrestricted by physical distance, they collaborate with each other without the direct mediation of money or politics. Unconcerned about copyright, they give and receive information without thought of payment. In the absence of states or markets to mediate social bonds, network communities are instead formed through the mutual obligations created by gifts of time and ideas.

> 'This informal, unwritten social contract is supported by a blend of strong-tie and weak-tie relationships among people who have a mixture of motives and ephemeral affiliations. It requires one to give something, and enables one to receive something. . . . I find that the help I receive far outweighs the energy I expend helping others; a marriage of altruism and self-interest.'
>
> *(Rheingold, 1994: 57–58)*

On the Internet, enforcing copyright payments represents the imposition of scarcity on a technical system designed to maximize the dissemination of information. The protection of intellectual property stops all users having access to every source of knowledge. Commercial secrecy prevents people from helping each other to solve common problems. The inflexibility of information commodities inhibits the efficient manipulation of digital data. In contrast, the technical and social structure of the Internet has been developed to encourage open cooperation among its participants. As an everyday activity, users are building the system together. Engaged in 'interactive creativity', they send e-mails, take part in listservers, contribute to newsgroups, participate in online conferences, and produce web sites (Berners-Lee, 1998: 5). Lacking copyright protection, information can be freely adapted to suit the users' needs. Within the hi-tech gift economy, people are successfully working together through '. . .an open social process involving evaluation, comparison and collaboration' (Lang, 1998: 3).

THE 'NEW ECONOMY' IS A MIXED ECONOMY

Following the implosion of the Soviet Union, almost nobody still believes in the inevitable victory of communism. On the contrary, large numbers of people accept that the Hegelian 'end of history' has culminated in neo-liberal capitalism (Fukuyama, 1992). Yet, at exactly this moment in time, a really existing form of anarcho-communism is being constructed within the Internet. When they go online, almost everyone spends most of their time participating within the gift economy rather than engaging in market competition. Because users receive much more information than they can ever give away, there is no popular clamour for imposing the equal exchange of the market place on the Internet. Once again, the 'end of history' for capitalism appears to be communism.

For the hi-tech gift economy was not an immanent possibility in every age. On the contrary, the market and the state could only be surpassed in this specific sector at this particular historical moment. Crucially, people need sophisticated media, computing and telecommunications technologies to participate within the hi-tech gift economy. A manually operated press produced copies which were relatively expensive, limited in numbers and impossible to alter without recopying. After generations of technological improvements, the same quantity of text on the Internet costs almost nothing to circulate, can be copied as needed and can be remixed at will. In addition, individuals need both time and money to participate in the hi-tech gift economy. While a large number of the world's population still live in poverty, people in the industrialized countries have steadily reduced their hours of employment and increased their wealth over a long period of social struggles and economic reorganizations. By working for money during some of the week, people can now enjoy the delights of giving gifts at other times. Only at this particular historical moment have the technical and social conditions of the metropolitan countries developed sufficiently for the emergence of digital anarcho-communism.

'Capital thus works towards its own dissolution as the form dominating production.'

(Marx, 1973: 700)

The New Left anticipated the emergence of the hi-tech gift economy. People could collaborate with each other without needing either markets or states. However, the New Left had a purist vision of DIY culture: the gift was the absolute antithesis of the commodity. Yet anarcho-communism exists only in a compromised form on the Internet. Contrary to the New Left's analysis, money-commodity and gift relations are not just in conflict with each other, but also co-exist in symbiosis. On the one hand, each method of working does threaten to supplant the other. The hi-tech gift economy heralds the end of private property in 'cutting-edge' areas of the economy. The digital capitalists want to privatize open-source programs and enclose social spaces built through voluntary effort. The potlatch and the commodity remain irreconcilable.

   Yet, on the other hand, the gift economy and the commercial sector can expand only through mutual collaboration within cyberspace. For instance, the free circulation of information between users relies on the capitalist production of computers, software and telecommunications. This miscegenation is also found within most Internet projects. For instance, a website can be constructed as a labour of love, but still be partially funded by advertising and public money. Crucially, this hybridization of working methods is not confined within particular projects. When they are online, people constantly pass from one form of social activity to another. In one session, an Internet user could first purchase some clothes from an e-commerce site, then look for information about education services from the local council's site and then contribute some thoughts to an ongoing discussion on a listserver for fiction writers. Without even consciously having to think about it, this person would successively have been a consumer in a market, a citizen of a state and an anarcho-communist within a gift economy. Far from realizing theory in its full purity, working methods on the Internet are inevitably compromised. The 'New Economy' is an advanced form of social democracy.

At the beginning of the twenty-first century, what was once revolutionary has now become banal. As Internet access grows, more and more ordinary people are circulating free information across the Internet. Far from having any belief in the revolutionary ideals of May 1968, the overwhelming majority of people participate within the hi-tech gift economy for entirely pragmatic reasons. Sometimes they buy commodities from e-commerce sites. However, they usually prefer to circulate gifts among each other. Internet users will always obtain much more than will ever be contributed in return. By giving away something that is well made, they will gain recognition from those who download their work. For most people, the gift economy is simply the best method of collaborating together in cyberspace. Within the mixed economy of the Internet, anarcho-communism has become an everyday reality.

'We must rediscover the pleasure of giving: giving because you have so much. What beautiful and priceless potlatches the affluent society will see – whether it likes it or not! – when the exuberance of the younger generation discovers the pure gift.'

(Vaneigem 1972: 70)

CHAPTER FOUR

The role of communication in urban communities

Norma V. Madrid

INTRODUCTION

Looking at the current trends in the development field and the underlying political philosophies, community participation has become imperative to development practice during the past two decades (see e.g. Midgley et al., 1986; Stiefel and Wolfe, 1994). The active participation of local-level groups, often named 'communities', has become seen as the most desirable and efficient way of solving place-related problems facing low-income urban settlements in developing countries, such as those associated with housing, solid waste management, health, etc. (Abbot, 1996; Beall, 1997a,b; Moser, 1989).

The term 'community participation' (or 'community-based action') is often used by Southern and Northern non-governmental organizations (NGOs) and other agencies involved in development, including larger international funding bodies, bilateral and multilateral aid agencies, and states. The findings of some World Bank studies on participatory Bank-financed projects, for instance, have shown that the community involve-ment in decision-making was 'the single most important factor in determining success' (Narayan, 1996: 12). Likewise, it has also been shown that among the critical factors that have hindered the success of these Bank-financed projects is the lack of participation among group members of community associations and cooperatives (Rietbergen-McCracken, 1996).

Although many agencies and NGOs tend to work with pre-existing com-munity or local-level organizations, there are many projects that have included the creation of new community-based organizations (de Berry, 1999). However, neither pre-existing nor newly created community organ-izations necessarily imply the actual participation of all their community members, and neither assures the existence of a 'sense of community' in the locality.

DEFINING COMMUNITY

The concept of community is not always clear, and definitions often ignore some relevant factors and circumstances that can enable a group of people to have a sense of community or not. A sense of community, however, is a primary condition for an individual to be willing to voluntarily participate in any action that will benefit the collective rather than just the self.

Ethnicity, religion, nation and gender are some of the conditions that foster the conformation of diverse communities, as these have been considered fundamental principles of cultural self-definition, sources of meaning and social identity. Nevertheless, individuals who live in the same area do not naturally share similar values or conditions, especially in the case of urban dwellers who have migrated from different rural regions or countries. In fact, they may have no shared beliefs or cultural features and, in many cases, have completely different social backgrounds.

The term 'community' still denotes a social entity with common ties but does not refer to the ties themselves (Azarya, 1985), whereas 'social networks' refer to individuals, the links between them and the multiple relations that can exist among them (Monge, 1985). A network is a social web of connecting points of interaction, defined by a group of relatives, neighbours, friends and colleagues to which an individual, family or group is related (Johnston et al., 1986). Usually, although not always, networks are based and co-exist within geographically defined groups.

However, a too often romantic, naive and 'mythical notion of community cohesion continues to permeate much participatory work' (Guijt and Shah, 1998: 1). Portney and Berry (1997: 633) have argued that:

> 'People's sense of community, their sense of belonging to a neighbourhood, their caring about the people who live there, and their belief that people who live there care about them are critical attitudes that can nurture or discourage participation.'

Nonetheless, other social theorists have acknowledged that place-bound communities *do* act.[1] Castells (1997), for example, cites several examples of poor local communities around the world which have organized, acted and engaged in collective survival (see also Moser, 1989).

Whether local communities act or not is only part of the problem. *Why* or *when* they act, and the cleavages and conflicts within these communities, are also important issues that can make any number of groups in the same neighbourhood act separately instead of acting together as a single community. 'They may interact *conflictually*, instead of acting *cooperatively*' (Davis, 1991: 5). Moser (1989: 127) argues that in most low-income settlements 'there are often more conflicting interests than similarities between neighbours'.

'Cooperation' is the term used to describe the kind of pro-social behaviour underlying collective action and is found when 'two or more people come together to work toward a common goal that will be beneficial to all concerned' (Schroeder et al., 1995: 20). Raven and Rubin (1983, cited in Schroeder et al., 1995: 20) emphasized the mutual dependency of cooperative relationships and defined *cooperation* as:

'[a] relationship between two or more persons who are positively interdependent with respect to their goals. That is, the movement of one person toward achieving a goal will increase the likelihood of the other person reaching his or her goal.'

A better understanding of the conditions under which the collective action of territorially based communities occurs, or does not occur, would allow more appropriate and effective impacts in thousands of projects, programmes and policies which are based on community-driven action. In this chapter it is proposed that *communication* is at the very core of the sense of community, and that it is actually a prerequisite for collective action. Communication is presented here as an essential element that allows neighbours to share ideas and interests, and creates actual relationships and social networks. In that sense, we explore the most common ways in which neighbours communicate with each other, and the most common barriers to communication between poor urban inhabitants of a common area are explored.

THE SENSE OF COMMUNITY IN URBAN SETTLEMENTS

Many concepts of community may be found in the literature. The term here, however, refers to the

'. . . social complex of shared meanings, sentimental attachments, and interpersonal networks of recognition and reciprocity that are slowly established among the proximate inhabitants of a common territory.'

(Davis, 1991: 12)

Usually, such a common territory is known as a neighbourhood or locality, and it is important to note that there is a substantial difference between the terms 'community' and 'neighbourhood'. The terms cannot be interchanged. While the latter has connotations of 'physical, spatially defined sites where bonds of sentiment and solidarity may or may not be present' (Davis, 1991: 12), community implies the existence of at least some kind of kinship or social connections which provide the resources – information, pooled labour, trust – that make collective action more likely (Wilson and Musick, 1997).

Traditionally, resolving the common problems of rural communities has been the subject of many development projects worldwide. During the 1950s, for example, community development was promoted mainly in British colonies with a rural 'productive' orientation, as the emphasis on the rural sector was a development priority necessary for economic growth (Moser, 1989: 90). The expertise of many development planners, field workers and agencies is based on multiple rural development projects and programmes. Therefore the literature on development abounds with successful examples and case studies relating to community participation in the resolution of rural place-related problems (e.g. Rietbergen-McCracken, 1996).

Nevertheless, urban settlements have progressively become a main issue for development purposes and social policy-making, as the developing world's urban population has dramatically increased in the past few years. By the year 2015, 'the majority of the world's absolute poor will live in cities of the Third World' (Beall, 1997a: 2). Therefore development policy-makers and practitioners are bound to foresee what the particular characteristics of the poor urban settlements are at present, and what they will be in the coming years. Increasing urban poverty in developing countries is not only a problem in itself, but also brings with it complex social consequences in terms of psychosocial environment, general social behaviour and interpersonal relationships that influence the ways in which individuals interact and behave within their habitat.

A number of sociologists have written about the differences between the rural and urban environments, emphasizing the fact that rural or 'traditional' communities have more cohesion and lamenting the lack of shared values in modern communities (e.g. Sandel, 1984; Gilbert and Gugler, 1992; Portney and Berry, 1997). Gilbert and Gugler (1992: 167) comment on the 'disorganization argument', which suggests that 'urban dwellers are no longer effectively integrated into a community: no longer subject to informal social controls over their behaviour, without a firm commitment to community values'. Marx and Engels, a century ago, noted the 'loss of moral certainty' that came with the development of urban industrial society, and used terms such as 'collection of selfish individuals' and the '*loss of community*' to describe the urban society (Barnett, 1988).

Both Durkheim and Weber saw the 'modern era' as 'the social birth of the *individual* as a relatively free agent' (Webster, 1990: 48), far away from rigid, traditional patterns of norms and beliefs. In fact, the *individual* and *collective* facets of human nature have been discussed by experts in almost every discipline, in attempts to establish how human nature determines the evolution of humankind and how humankind itself can influence and accelerate its own development (Webster, 1990). Certainly, even the most different and initially opposite political philosophies, such as classical social democracy and conservatism, seem to be closer over the past decades and concur, after lengthy debate, that modern societies are becoming more individualistic (Giddens, 1998: 3).

Giddens points out that 'socialism began as a body of thought opposing individualism' (Giddens, 1998: 3), and that later on 'collectivism became one of the most prominent traits distinguishing social democracy from conservatism, which ideologically placed a much stronger emphasis upon "the individual"'. However,

> '. . .much of this has been going into reverse since the late 1970s. Social democrats had to respond to the challenge of neoliberalism. . . [and] have struggled to accommodate to the rising importance of individualism and lifestyle diversity.'

> *(Giddens, 1998: 34–35)*

Urban neighbours do not always have the sense of community required to initiate sustainable collective action. Davis (1991: 4) says that:

> *'Several generations of sociologists, for example, in contrasting . . . the modern urban neighbourhood with the . . . "pre-modern" village or clan, have concluded that urban neighbourhoods no longer contain the primary bonds of kinship and sentiment that make community – and community action – possible.'*

Intensive, daily contact between people of the same tribe or ethnic background generates 'thick trust', considered the essential ingredient of mechanical solidarity (Newton, 1997: 578). The classic examples are tribal societies or small homogeneous communities in rural peripheries or remote islands. Modern society is based on the 'thin trust' associated with the organic solidarity of 'looser, more amorphous, secondary relations' (Newton, 1997: 578).

The role of communication in collective action

Collective action depends to a large extent on the kind of networks in which inhabitants are embedded. In recent sociological and development literature, great importance has been placed on bonds of kinship, social networks and trust in relation to participation, as these are considered 'resources' for social mobilization (Coleman, 1988; Putnam et al., 1993; Janoski and Wilson, 1995; Wilson and Musick, 1997). Also, the norms learned through the various agents of socialization, such as family, friends, school, churches, etc., are acknowledged as key features leading to voluntary action in cooperative exchanges (Janoski and Wilson, 1995).

> *'Social ties . . . supply information, foster trust, make contacts, provide support, set guidelines and create obligations. They make volunteer work more likely by fostering norms of generalized reciprocity, encouraging people to trust each other and amplifying reputations.'*
>
> *(Wilson and Musick, 1997: 695)*

The concept of social capital encompasses those resources and sees them as useful tools for individuals to engage in collective action. As outlined by Robert Putnam (1993), social capital refers to 'features of social organization, such as networks, norms and trust that facilitate coordination and cooperation for mutual benefit', and is a concept that has entered into development thinking and discourse as the recipe for a 'robust collective life' (Beall, 1997b).

Coleman (1988) argues that social capital is defined by its function: 'It is not a single entity but a variety of different entities, with two elements in common: they all consist of some aspect of social structures, and they facilitate certain actions of actors . . . within the structure.' Social capital inheres in the structure of relations between actors (Coleman, 1988).

Although neighbourhood residents are not always organized in formally structured groups, features such as trust, loyalty and reciprocity in community-based projects have proved to be key for resource mobilization, and to keep transactional costs low for both beneficiaries and agencies (Narayan, 1996). Also, social capital has been associated with economic development and good government by some authors who argue that identical institutional forms, development strategies and decentralization programmes may yield dramatically different practical results, depending on the social context into which they are introduced (Widner and Mundt, 1998).

'The theories suggest that where people of different backgrounds talk to one another more, trust their neighbours, and share norms that support openness and compromise, we are also more likely to observe better government and higher levels of economic development.'

(Widner and Mundt, 1998: 1)

Cooperation is possible only when people are able to communicate with one another and discover or feel that they share similar characteristics or a common fate. Research on cooperation has indicated that groups in which subjects are able to talk among themselves showed higher rates of cooperation than those who were not allowed to discuss the problem faced. Thanks to interpersonal communication, 'the group may develop a sense of belongingness and affiliation with each other [which] may be accompanied by a shift of focus from self-concern to heightened concern for the well-being of the group as a whole' (Schroeder et al., 1995: 225).

Schroeder et al. (1995) record that several research results show how even a few minutes of communication can duplicate the amount of cooperation in a group. In terms of the biological characteristics of the human being, some experts argue that altruism and prosocial behaviour are attained through communicative genes, not altruistic genes, as the latter do not exist (Schroeder et al., 1995). However, research results also indicate that simply talking with others and becoming acquainted with other group members does not appear to be enough to generate concern for the common good. Instead, it has been suggested that cooperation is the result of effective communication and shared cultural perspectives (Schroeder et al., 1995). Findings relating to the common obstacles to participation in 48 World Bank-supported projects showed that poor communication about the purpose and obligations of the groups' participation was one of the five main obstacles (Schmidt, 1996).

It is puzzling to try to define 'effective communication', as communication is a term commonly used in a wide array of contexts by experts and ordinary people with a wide range of viewpoints; hence there are hundreds of definitions throughout the literature. Porter and Samovar (1988) see communication as:

'. . .a dynamic . . . process in which sources and receivers . . . produce messages that they transmit through a channel in order to induce or elicit particular attitudes and behaviour.'

There are many types of sources, receivers, messages and channels, and hence there are many forms of communication. For instance, the diverse forms of communication that can slowly nurture social bonds go further than just talking with others. 'Communication is both verbal and non-verbal in form' (Hall, 1992). Two common aspects of communication between neighbours are explored below, and some of the forms that might be more directly linked to the relation between communication and the sense of community are briefly examined.

INTERCULTURAL AND SUPPORTIVE COMMUNICATION

Intercultural communication

Communication is intimately linked to the notion of culture. Several theoretical perspectives argue that communication and culture are so interlinked that they can almost be considered the same thing. Depending on the perspective within which these two terms are treated, as found in current literature on intercultural communication, culture can adopt several forms or means of expression. Three such forms are: culture as *community*, culture as *conversation* and culture as *code* or a system of values (Hall, 1992).

In the light of the traditional perspective of intercultural communication, culture is:

'the deposit of knowledge, experiences, beliefs, values, attitudes, meanings, hierar-chies, religion, timing, roles, spatial relations, concepts of the universe, and mate-rial objects and possessions acquired by a large group of people in the course of generations through individual and group striving.'

(Samovar et al., 1981: 24)

Culture provides the 'sense of place' in one's social world. This sense of place is invoked and constituted through community-specific ways of speaking, facilitating a sense of shared meaning and a coordination of action among members of a social group (Hall, 1992). In other words, communication and interchange between inhabitants can nurture the building of an indi-vidual sense of place and sense of belonging to a particular social group. Those communities whose solidarity is raised from the social relations of race, ethnicity, nationalities or religion (who share cultural patterns) are commonly acknowledged as culture-bound communities. However, inter-cultural communication is not the only interaction between members of a group (racial or otherwise), as group membership does not guarantee shared knowledge or values. Instead, and from another perspective, culture can be seen as an 'ongoing creation of the everyday activities of its members . . . [which] contains diverse . . . expressions of lived experiences', or *conversation* (Hall, 1992: 53). Culture

'. . . allows a group of people to create shared meaning, participate in the emotive world of a community, and coordinate potentially diverse lines of action by integrating named entities into a recognizable whole.'

(Hall, 1992: 55)

Therefore effective communication between neighbours may be seen as the starting point for the creation of cultural bounds between people who live adjacent to each other. It might allow 'localities' to become actual communities, creating social ties as strong as those shared, for instance, by culturally bound groups.

Supportive communication

The study of social support came from epidemiological studies suggesting that social ties had significant effects on both physical and emotional health and wellbeing (e.g. Burleson et al., 1994). Increasingly, social support is seen as a fundamental interpersonal communicative process occurring within the structures of people's relationships and life events, and is a primary means by which interpersonal relationships are created and sustained (Albrecht et al., 1994; Burleson et al., 1994; Schroeder et al., 1995). It also influences the way in which individuals view themselves and 'coordinate their actions in support-seeking and support-giving encounters' (Albrecht et al., 1994: 421).

For poor people, supportive actions of neighbours, such as small loans, caring for children, and sharing food or other goods, are often major means of economic survival (Rabrenovic, 1994). Such actions are genuine non-verbal ways to communicate positive messages of affinity and affection between residents, and can promote very strong social ties and constitute the basis for supportive networks.

Supportive networks are the foundations for the support communities. 'One of the most potent . . . consequences of the communication of social support may be the creation of culturally shared value systems that promote supportive, prosocial conduct on a community wide scale' (Burleson et al., 1994: xxvi).

Chatting with neighbours is likely to be the most common way of communication within a locality. Face-to-face communication allows the creation of a high proportion of friendships in an area, and is an important source of social support in a neighbourhood. 'People develop positive feelings about their neighbourhood. Positive feelings influence mental and physical well-being, make residents less fearful of crime, decrease their residential mobility, and increase their local political involvement' (Rabrenovic, 1994: 79). Recent studies on social capital in Africa have yielded results that directly relate the recentness of settlement of people in some districts of Uganda to very low levels of social capital and poor political participation (Widner and Mundt, 1998).

In project design and implementation, it is important to give voice to the disadvantaged (Schmidt, 1996). This is true not only for agencies to obtain genuine feedback, but also to allow discussions and chatting between local people in order to provide a suitable environment for the sharing of ideas and interests, to promote the building of new relationships and to strengthen existing ones.

COMMON BARRIERS TO COMMUNICATION IN URBAN AREAS

Having explored the most common ways of communication between neighbours, it is worth analysing some characteristics of the urban scenario in the developing world that might become barriers to communication and constrain the formation of communities.

Barbero (1994) argues that some years ago the cultural map of developing countries was composed of hundreds of culturally homogeneous communities, strongly homogenous but dispersed and isolated. Today there is another map, characterized by a huge rural–urban migration that is not merely quantitative, but indicates the birth of a heterogeneous urban cultural fabric composed of a huge diversity of forms, practices, lifestyles and narrative ways (Barbero, 1994: 35). This heterogeneity challenges current theoretical frameworks and notions of culture, community and city.

One of the major factors affecting people's lives in the cities of developing countries is poverty. Urban poverty is seen as a multifaceted, complex process which embraces not only economic issues, such as levels of income and expenditure, but also social, political and ecological factors. People's unfulfilled basic needs (e.g. employment at unreasonable levels of pay; lack of health and education facilities), exclusion, sense of helplessness (Moser, 1996) and distressing environmental conditions dramatically affect the physical and mental wellbeing of urban dwellers (Hart, 1996).

In addition, there are other social factors associated with urban poverty, such as high degree of inequality, vulnerability, social diversity and household breakdown (Wratten, 1995; Moser, 1996; Beall, 1997a). 'Vulnerability' is a concept that intends to capture the dynamic nature of poverty, and refers to 'the insecurity of the well-being of individuals, households, or communities in the face of a changing environment' (Moser, 1996: 2). Therefore the survival strategies of low-income populations generate an intense individualism that is contradictory to the solidarity necessary for community-based action (Moser, 1989: 127).

In addition to poverty, there are some other factors related to the personal background of poor urban dwellers, especially migrants from rural areas or another country. Language, for instance, or ideological differences, might be considered the strongest barriers to communication as they refer directly to the constitutive elements of the communication process (different codes; opposite messages). Research in Africa by Widner and Mundt (1998) found that Tororo District, in the eastern part of Uganda, was a poor performer in terms of social capital due to the co-existence of people from five different ethnic groups whose languages are mutually incomprehensible. In Tororo, linguistic diversity prevented people from talking to one another (Widner and Mundt, 1998: 1).

There are, however, many other aspects of city life for those living in slums that commonly constitute substantial barriers to communication, and which can be related to three main dimensions: uncontrolled city growth; lack of time; and the psychosocial environment.

Uncontrolled growth of cities

The lack of planning and disorganized growth of urban space is one of the main issues to be considered in relation to urban settlements. Most cities in developing countries have no control over squatter settlements, which inevitably develop into unplanned slums. Such low-income urban settlements are characterized by poor housing, lack of public services (water supply, sanitation, solid waste disposal), health hazards and overcrowding (Wratten, 1995). There is virtually no space left for social interchange in such situations.

Furthermore, city planners seem to be trying to 'order' the urban chaos from the 'informational paradigm' (Barbero, 1994: 36). The kind of communication that appears to predominate in the planning of cities today is based not on interpersonal relations, but on the 'flow' of vehicles, people and information. Public places within neighbourhoods, such as squares, parks and boulevards, that traditionally have allowed the encounter of neighbours, are being progressively substituted by streets (to benefit the 'flow') and new unplanned settlements (Barbero, 1994). Also malls, cable television and the Internet (Portney and Berry, 1997) have replaced the traditional common places that allowed interpersonal face-to-face communication.

Barbero (1994: 41) illustrates this phenomenon with the following example:

'Comparing communication practices in a supermarket with those in a popular street market in Bogota, we could verify the substitution of the communicative interaction by the textual information. Selling and buying in a town square means to get involved in a relationship that demands talking. It is a communication, which arises from the space expression. . . In contrast, you can shop in the supermarket without talking to anybody. . . In the supermarket there is only the information transmitted by packages or advertisements.'

Lack of time: long working days and distances

Poor people's jobs usually involve very long working hours, and the leisure or socializing time of the poorest dwellers in urban areas is constantly being reduced. Informal economy activities, an increasing practice in cities of the South, are undertaken mainly by low-income people and are usually carried out both during business hours and after work. Also, slums are usually located on the periphery of the city, while factories, businesses, markets and other workplaces are usually either in the city centre or in particular industrial areas far from residential sectors. This involves very long journeys to and from home, particularly after work when work at home is also waiting to be done. Such circumstances certainly reduce the time for socializing (face-to-face communication) in poor neighbourhoods, at least on working days.

Psychosocial environment: crime, violence and vulnerability

Crime and other types of violence affect everyday lives and lifestyles, and the relationships and attitudes of many city inhabitants. People tend to avoid being on the streets at particular hours of the day, which reduces their willingness to participate in activities other than their jobs (see, for instance, Moser, 1996). The common policy of fixing security bars and locks on dwellings tends to cause people to remain inside. Giddens (1998: 86) argues that 'as they withdraw physically, they also withdraw with roles of mutual support with fellow citizens, thereby relinquishing the social controls that formerly helped to maintain civility within the community'. Throughout the process of adjusting and adapting themselves to a hostile climate, people become progressively more apathetic and inward-looking.

Vulnerability due to changing economic conditions also seems to be a key barrier to collective action. It has been suggested that severe economic crises in the South have affected the extent to which people become involved in voluntary action, especially in cities, where the negative impact of economic crises has been higher (Moser, 1996). In Moser's study, female dwellers in four urban communities of the South report their decreased involvement in voluntary community activities due to difficult economic conditions. In 1992, after a severe economic crisis, fewer women were actively involved in community-based organizations, and they attributed the declining participation to their increased need to earn an income and survive.

CONCLUDING NOTE

Is it not a paradox that while urban space and city dynamics progressively hinder interpersonal communication between city-dwellers and neighbours, place-bound communities are increasingly expected to cooperate and act collectively? The spatial characteristics of slums and squatter settlements, coupled with features of their particular psychosocial environment (such as increasing violence and crime), are far from facilitating social interchange and face-to-face communication. On the contrary, these conditions may generate barriers to communication and hence to place-based social development.

In the long term, urban planning and management, development policy-making and research should observe the relevance to existing communities of communication, and the need for strengthening social capital for development purposes. There are many organized initiatives, such as those based on street theatre, for example, whose main purpose is to foster communicative processes between inhabitants of the same locality. Such activities should be taken into account, promoted and supported by development agencies and governments and – why not? – included in project design and implementation for solving both place-related problems and other social development issues that must involve community participation. Seen either as input into development projects, or as a process whereby poor people can gain influence and access to resources for improving living standards, participation is definitely a major and useful tool for development policy and practice.

Effective communication should be regarded as an important 'prerequisite' for collective action. Fostering the various forms of communication which have been analysed between locality members will hopefully increase the likelihood of cooperation and reduce conflict, differences and diversity, whether through long-term policies in terms of both infrastructure and social issues, or through short-term projects and programmes. At the least, boosting communication can create a suitable environment for people to express their demands, needs and interests which, after all, constitute the main purpose of many participatory community-based actions.

CHAPTER FIVE

Facilitating information dissemination and exchange through formal and informal networking

Otto Ruskulis

BACKGROUND

Social networks are interconnected groups of people who are in a two-way communication with one another and share information or knowledge of some sort, addressed at meeting specific needs or interests. Networks are also 'a social web composed of groups of relatives neighbours and friends to whom an individual or family is related, often by shared values and goals' (Johnston et al., 1986).

Networks can be found within poor communities, and are important sources for the poor to gain advice, information and support from network members. They are also a principal asset in relation to the livelihoods of poor communities. Hence social networks have an important role in communicating for development, and their contribution is now being recognized to the point that donor funding has sometimes allowed their establishment in various development-related fields. As networks are a relatively new subject in development, substantive research is required to assess their impact.

Networks are a means of collaboration between organizations and groups in both the production and dissemination of outputs of a project. Networks may involve organizations coming together and agreeing to cooperate on particular actions or projects. Such organizations may include local authorities, private companies, non-governmental organizations (NGOs), community-based organizations (CBOs) and research organizations.

In addition to being a means of information exchange between organizations with common objectives, networks may also have other functions, such as lobbying, representing members' interests or generating capacity-building.

Communication exchanges and activities within networks may be undertaken either through formalized channels and procedures, or in an informal and unstructured way. Many networks allow both approaches to a greater or lesser degree. There are usually some basic formal ground rules relating to membership and objectives that must be observed. Formally constituted meetings and other joint operational requirements are also important to maintain cohesion within the network. Network members operate in different ways. For example, network members may occasionally meet during the course of a project, or regularly exchange information through informal meetings, by post, e-mail, phone, fax or through a common Internet or intranet site.

Networks may have particular objectives, such as the production of specific research – developing a wider market for cooperatively produced goods might be one such example – or they may be contributing in a specific way to a general development aim. Network activities may be time-limited if they are undertaken to produce a particular output, or they may be more-or-less continuous if a network has a broader, development-related goal. Much of a network's development, the achievement of its aims and the benefits realized by the individual network members are obtained through ongoing informal exchanges.

COALITIONS AND ALLIANCES

Coalitions are collections of networks, organizations or even individuals sharing common goals or visions. Coalition members usually interact with each other more loosely than through a network. Coalitions often have a prominent lobbying or empowerment role.

Coalitions may operate at a local level, or be nationally, regionally or globally based. Locally based networks are likely to be concerned with relevant local issues and exchanges between members that take place on an informal, person-to-person basis. Global or regional networks are likely to be more formally structured, with printed or electronic outputs being used to a significant extent in communications between members. A number of networks and coalitions related to building and shelter exist today. The majority focus on housing rights and are nationally or regionally oriented, although their activities also encompass other objectives. However, networks from other development fields, such as those related to the field of agriculture, have been in existence longer and have developed further. Most research on networks has been undertaken in fields outside shelter and the built environment.

Alliances are constituted in a similar way to coalitions, but generally have a longer-term relationship and wider set of objectives.

NETWORK DEVELOPMENT

The main drive behind the development of NGO-based networks is based on the view that lack of access to relevant knowledge is a critical factor hampering NGOs' work, and this lack is perceived as surmountable through the sharing of ideas, experiences and information in an organized way (Engel, 1993). The desire to coordinate and avoid unnecessary replication of research activities and outputs can also be a factor. The reason for establishing a network may be based on the recognition that a particular approach has failed to achieve its purpose and requires re-evaluation and the consideration of alternative approaches; or that the task to be undertaken is too great for a single organization to cope with alone.

Other networks, with a lobbying or advocacy purpose, may be established in response to threats to livelihoods, sustainability and the environment, or to a particular vulnerable group. Such threats might come from powerful vested commercial interests or restrictive global or national policies.

The decision to develop a network is usually taken by a small number of initiating members. They have to agree on the objectives and modes of operation of the network, membership criteria and commitments, and how the network is to be sustained in order to achieve its objectives. During its operational phase, there will be opportunities to assess or evaluate the network, modify its focus, and create openings for new members to join and contribute to the activities. The activities of a network may be significantly expanded or curtailed by specific events, for example: the network achieving its objective; funding constraints; a change of leadership; a change in external events; or the identification of new opportunities. Such factors will alter the direction a network takes, and networks unwilling to change direction in response to external factors are likely to lose relevance, influence and purpose.

The final stage of a network is its cessation, or the decision to take the network in a new direction. Ideally, cessation will occur after a network has achieved all or most of its objectives or, in less favourable circumstances, due to significant funding difficulties, loss of interest of the members or arguments over the direction the network should take.

MANAGEMENT AND OPERATION OF A NETWORK

The key to the sustainability of a network is whether its members believe the benefits of membership outweigh the cost and time commitment of contributing to the network. Ultimately, enthusiasm for networking activities will depend on how useful the members believe the objectives of a network to be, and whether they consider such objectives to be achievable.

The level of commitment that members are willing to make to a network will determine the level of information exchange between members and how such information exchange is managed. Other factors to be considered in determining how a network should be managed and operated include:

- geographical spread of the members

- number of network members
- level of synergy between the objectives and activities of the different members
- resources – financial, staff and access to communications media available to network members
- whether the purpose of the network is principally to enable information exchange between members or to achieve more wide-ranging outputs
- whether the network includes different types of organizations – so-called vertical networks made up of research organizations (e.g. NGOs and grassroots); or is built on organizations of similar type (horizontal networks of NGOs only).

Networks may also be classified as 'hard' or 'soft'. Hard networks impose a set of agreed conditions or ways of working on their members. In soft networks, activities are undertaken on a much more informal and less systematic basis – generally as the needs for such activities arise. Most networks, even the softest, do have some form of structure, although this structure might be unwritten and based on a level of common understanding.

Once established, a network will have to decide whether it requires a formal management secretariat or intends to adopt an alternative management approach such as:

- no formal management
- management tasks divided among the members
- management undertaken by members on a rotating basis.

Management tasks may include:

- fund-raising and donor reporting
- organizing meetings and planning future activities
- publicizing the network
- monitoring progress against objectives
- introducing new members
- training of members
- representing members' interests to official bodies
- undertaking other network-related activities such as production of a newsletter
- settlement of disputes
- development, in collaboration with the members, of procedural arrangements for undertaking joint activities
- ensuring the network is officially registered and recognized, if such registration is deemed necessary.

Network members will have to decide how important these various management functions are, and whether they are capable of handling them themselves or whether a formal secretariat is required.

As well as information-sharing between the network members, the activities of a network may include:

- training and capacity-building of members or intended beneficiaries
- lobbying and advocacy
- publications and other dissemination activities
- research projects
- development projects
- consultancies
- exhibitions, trade fairs, conferences and other organized events
- organization of exchange visits
- provision of advice and information
- sharing information on local actions undertaken towards broader, regionally based or global objectives.

The level to which individual members of a network pursue these activities would depend on how relevant they are to their own objectives and their own capacities.

INFORMATION EXCHANGE THROUGH NETWORKING

In successful networks, members communicate with each other frequently as the need arises, although formal meetings are also important to ensure that the development of the network is planned, and that members are kept up to date with the latest details relating to network development and activities. Some members of larger networks may be on the fringe of active involvement, and attending formal meetings might be their main means of keeping up to date. Also, sub-groups within a network may take the opportunity of presenting their outcomes to other network members at formal meetings. Formal meetings for network members are expensive in terms of both time and travelling costs, especially if a network operates globally; but such meetings need to be held at least on an annual basis if they are to represent a meaningful and useful channel for information exchange.

Smaller networks are easier to manage than larger ones because, when networks become too large, regular person-to-person interaction (probably the most useful aspect of networking activities) becomes more difficult to achieve.

Newsletters are another means of communication. However, unless a network is very large, a newsletter produced specifically for the network may be viable only if there are also interested subscribers outside the network. A minimum of 100 recipients is considered to be a viable number to justify a network newsletter.

Contact lists, regularly updated and sent out to members, are also an important means of communication within networks. Such lists may contain names, addresses, details of activities, specializations and the interests of members. Such lists are particularly important in large networks or coalitions, where the members do not all know one another or where membership comprises mainly individuals as opposed to groups or organizations.

The Internet is becoming increasingly important as a means of communication between network members, especially if the network is internationally oriented. Communications may be increased through the development of a network website, which would need to be managed and possibly linked to an intranet facility for the sole use of members, through personal e-mails or e-mail discussion groups. The advantage of a network maintaining a website is that external parties will have access to it.

One of the principal benefits of the Internet is its relative cheapness and speed compared to mail, phone or fax. A website, or managed electronic discussion group, allows anyone who is interested to gain simultaneous access to information. While its main advantage is that information does not have to be posted out to members individually (which is costly and time-consuming), a critical disadvantage is that members from the South may have difficulty accessing it.

An important aspect of networking activities is the dissemination of results, messages and outputs to organizations or individuals outside a network. Outputs of a network may include promotional or advocacy materials specifically produced, network demonstration projects, seminars, courses or workshops, the participation of network representatives on policy-making bodies, press articles and media events, and the organization of cultural events and exchange visits.

IMPACT ASSESSMENT OF NETWORKING ACTIVITIES

An assessment of the impact of networking activities is very difficult to undertake with any degree of certainty, except possibly for assessing improvements in skills, knowledge and the ways in which member organizations work. It would be difficult to isolate the impact of networking from other possible influences on the work undertaken by organizations, such as a change in funding levels, a change of management, project staff undertaking training courses, or the organization developing a new product or service. The positive impact of particular aspects of networking may also be assessed to some degree. Such aspects include:

- sharing of work and avoidance of duplication (cost- and resource-saving)
- the work of a particular organization reaching a wider audience through networking activities (more contacts)
- activities may be undertaken by a network as a whole which are beyond the capacity of its individual members (members are able to partake in a wider range of identified activities)
- members have the possibility of increased access to useful information (increase in the physical information resource and its utilization)

- individual members may have improved access to donor funding through belonging to a network (increased resources and range of activities)
- individual member organizations may be better able to assist other NGOs and CBOs through improved training or the provision of information as a result of network membership (greater range of training and information materials provided, and more people trained)
- individual members and their contacts may have increased opportunities to be innovative (increase in number of identified innovations).

The costs and commitments of belonging to a network must be offset against the benefits. It is likely that an organization with little active involvement in a network will receive little benefit from membership, and might consider that the cost and commitment outweigh the benefits and eventually decide to leave the network.

Members may become inactive due to geographical isolation, dissatisfaction with the aims and objectives of the network, lack of resources or a change in direction.

But it is likely that active members will consider the benefits outweigh the costs. Some members may also be willing to take leading roles in the development of a network and may, for example, find funding for network development, or provide specialist inputs such as the production of a newsletter or development of a website.

Such members may willingly make a greater commitment to a network than any benefit they may possibly gain from it, and should such leading members withdraw their services, a network may cease or its activities may be severely curtailed. A successful network which provides a high degree of beneficial impact will probably have most of its membership actively involved in the network's activities – individual members taking a lead in some activities and supporting others, with numerous complementary activities and a high level of active information exchange taking place. Ultimately, such a network might also have a significantly beneficial impact on the target beneficiaries with whom its members work, although in ways that would not be easy to assess or quantify, nor to separate out from a range of other possible influencing factors.

SOME EXAMPLES OF NETWORKS

Agevi (1998) presents a number of networks that are active internationally in the housing and shelter fields.

Habitat International Coalition (HIC)

This is a global coalition of NGOs and other organizations involved in shelter and human settlements. It is particularly active in housing rights and related issues, such as opposition to eviction, women and housing, and housing and environment. The coalition has influenced housing policy at the UN, but is not directly involved in housing projects.

Habitat for Humanity

This is a large NGO organizing housing projects in over 30 countries. It is perhaps not a true network, more a series of field projects with offices in a number of countries belonging to the same organization, with some degree of information-sharing between them.

Asian Coalition for Housing Rights

This coalition principally lobbies for housing rights in Asia. It perhaps has greater links to the grassroots than HIC, although professionals generally run it.

Homeless International

This is a British-based NGO supporting local initiatives and capacity-building in relation to improving shelter. It focuses particularly on removing the constraints to improved shelter by encouraging community-based housing finance schemes, and encourages information exchange between the projects it supports.

Shelter Forum

This is a network of some 600 grassroots organizations from Kenya and other East African countries concerned with improved shelter and housing rights. It focuses on empowerment of the poor and disadvantaged, especially women, and provides advice and information to its members as well as taking a proactive campaigning role on locally relevant issues.

The Mutirao 50 Network in Brazil

This is a grassroots-focused project operating in shanty towns in Brazil. It seeks to mobilize and involve a broad range of groups with differing interests and specializations in the building and shelter field concerned with the improvement of human settlements. Such groups include the communities themselves, the private sector, universities and local authorities. The network organizes not only housing projects, but also projects on micro-enterprises and the provision of social amenities.

Zone One Tondo Organization Network (ZOTO)

This is a Philippines-based organization of community groups, with around 100 member organizations representing over 60 000 low-income residents from the city of Tondo. ZOTO acts very much in a representational role for the residents and communities, and at times is in conflict with the government and other powerful vested interests.

Building Advisory Service and Information Network (BASIN) (Wishart, 1996)

This is a network of specialist organizations on housing and appropriate building technologies – five from the South and four from Europe. Its principal role is the dissemination of information relating to the suitability of building technology and community-based approaches in housing. BASIN also has a significant advocacy role through some of the membership – principally Shelter Forum and Intermediate Technology.

Building and Social Housing Foundation

This is not strictly a network, but operates along similar lines to a soft network. The organization gives an annual prize – the World Habitat Award – to a project which is considered to offer the best solution to a housing problem, and is viable and sustainable. Entries for the annual awards are described in detail and widely disseminated.

La Red and Duryog Niravan

These are networks of organizations and groups involved with disaster mitigation in vulnerable regions – La Red in South America and Duryog Niravan in South Asia. The improvement of dwellings to reduce disaster vulnerability is only one aspect of the work of these networks, which take a holistic approach to disaster mitigation.

The above examples are by no means an exhaustive list of networks and coalitions involved with work on building and housing, but they illustrate the diversity of networking approaches which have been developed in response to particular problems, opportunities or issues to be tackled. Some of the above networks have been established in response to local concerns, while others operate on a more global scale and are concerned with broader issues related to building and housing. The objectives of such networks and coalitions also vary, but there is a high degree of information-sharing between members in all of them.

SPECIAL TYPES OF NETWORK

Nested networks (Carley and Christie, 2000)

Networking activities that attempt to involve a great diversity of stakeholders, from the grassroots to governments and policy-makers (networks that are heavily biased towards verticality), risk becoming unmanageable, having their objectives diluted or that particular stakeholders may become excluded. One approach to overcoming such problems and increasing the effectiveness of networking activities is the development of nested networks. Such networks operate mainly horizontally at different stakeholder levels, but with common objectives. They provide an approach that establishes a practical application of the adage 'think globally, act locally'.

Thus there might be networks of grassroots organizations, researchers, NGOs, local authorities, funders and policy-makers working towards a common goal. The members of the network at different levels would interact to a great extent with their own peers. However, there would also be vertical linkages between individual members rather than at network-wide level. One example would be a particular local authority working with numerous other local authorities in a common network, which has links and works with several particular CBOs in the area under its control. These organizations would then become incorporated into the wider nested network. The strength of links and relationships established many times on an individual basis between the different levels of a nested network could be a critical factor in determining at what level the objectives are achieved.

Global initiatives, for example on environmental sustainability (Agenda 21) and urbanization (Habitat II), are to a degree organized as nested networks. These provide the means to involve ordinary citizens in global initiatives through organizing and implementing actions at a local level in the places where they live and work.

Social networks

Social networks may be considered as 'social capital' (Dasgupta and Serageldin, 2000; Woolcock, 2000) because they are an important asset in the reduction of poverty and vulnerability. Additionally, although personal contacts are important for almost everyone, they are particularly so for most poor people in developing countries. Many such people cannot afford radios, televisions or even newspapers or books. A significant proportion are functionally illiterate – and many more lack literacy in English, the language most used in the production of printed materials. Facilities such as community notice-boards, community-based newsletters and the production and distribution of leaflets to households, as is frequently the case in the North, are largely absent from poor urban communities in the South. As a result, many poor people are almost wholly dependent on talking to other people to get news and information to help them manage their lives.

Poor people in urban areas have or develop social links based on:

- kinship (to extended family members or people originating from the same rural area)
- employment or trade
- use of facilities such as shops, markets, bus stops, water points, etc.
- association, for example by joining mothers' clubs, sports clubs, religious institutions, development committees, etc.

■ neighbourliness – especially important for women, for many of whom other women from the neighbourhood are their principal source of social contact.

These types of contact are important not only for accessing information, but also for undertaking activities based on reciprocity. Examples of reciprocal arrangements include repairing a leaking roof in return for receiving help to fill out an application form; cooking food in return for fetching water; and looking after children in return for repairing clothing. Reciprocity is an important component of the survival strategies of many poor people, especially women, who have little or no cash available to pay for services.

People who are fortunate enough to have a range of contacts within each of the above five areas have a diversity of people to approach, should they require favours or information. Some people, however, have few personal contacts and are at a significant disadvantage. The poorest groups, including the elderly, sick and disabled, and households headed by women, fall into this category. Their social networks would include small numbers of people in a similar situation to themselves, who are unable to help significantly in reducing poverty and vulnerability or in identifying and developing new opportunities.

In a research project entitled 'Strengthening poor people's knowledge and information systems' (funded by the UK Department for International Development and undertaken by the Intermediate Technology Development Group (Schilderman, 2001)), the importance of social networks in the daily lives of poor people was recognized. This research indicated that, although some poor people in informal settlements do have access to media such as radio, television and newspapers, word of mouth is by far the most important information medium. However, information provided by other media, which is considered to be interesting or useful, is often passed on to others by word of mouth.

It was also found that 'key informants', people especially well informed in certain areas or well connected to influential or knowledgeable people, are key factors in transferring knowledge or information to communities. Some examples identified through the research include stonemasons and hardware shop owners in Peru, who provide information on building and house repairs; a local councillor in Zimbabwe, who provides information on community development issues and dealing with local authority bureaucracy; and an NGO in Sri Lanka willing to provide help and advice on setting up a community-based waste-management project.

Involving key informants in community-focused action projects is important in improving their capacity to transfer and disseminate knowledge and information. This may be accomplished by strengthening their capacity and ability to find information from NGOs, public libraries, local authorities and government departments. This is in line with other reports which emphasize that in order to achieve development objectives, the community's social capital should be linked to institutions outside the community, such as local authorities or NGOs.

Issues of importance relating to information needs may be broadly grouped into eight different categories:

- getting places
- illness
- money
- school
- water
- waste
- security
- shelter/housing.

In different settlements, different priorities may be identified which are relevant to particular local conditions. In Sudawelle in Colombo, Sri Lanka, for instance, security was an important issue, both within the settlement and in obtaining the necessary passes and clearances to be able to travel outside it. In Epworth near Harare, in Zimbabwe, housing was the most important issue. In Galle in Sri Lanka, waste management was the greatest concern, which was addressed through a community-based waste-management project in collaboration with an NGO. For information relating to particular concerns in each area, different key informants were involved.

In relation to strengthening key informants to enable them to become more proactive in obtaining information, there is a need for institutions holding information to become more effective in disseminating information. This could be accomplished by identifying and working with key informants in communities and, at the same time, becoming more proficient in using a range of different types of media – especially radio, drama, video and posters or illustrations – in conjunction with participatory community methods.

CONCLUSIONS: THE INFORMATION EXPLOSION AND THE FUTURE

Numerous development-related projects and activities have been undertaken on the basis of collaboration through networks or coalitions in a number of fields, including shelter. Networks can be an effective means for organizations to exchange information, share work, scale up outputs and disseminate information. However, networks are not always successful in their objectives. In some cases the reasons for this are apparent, and may include resource constraints or over-ambitious objectives; but in other cases they are not. Undoubtedly, members' personal considerations and levels of motivation are important contributory factors. Little research has been undertaken into factors that contribute to the success or failure of networks, and the lessons that may be learnt to enable networks to operate more effectively and achieve greater impact.

Networking activities may be generated by formally constituted organizations or institutions, and also by community members through social networks, although the basis on which these activities operate differs considerably. Closer links between these types of networks could provide a means for poor people to participate more actively in research and implementation projects, and to increase the range of information they have access to, which would also increase the possibility for them to undertake a greater range of independent actions. Key informants, people within or linked to communities who have a relatively wide range of information, contacts and influence, could also play a more significant role in helping to link poor peoples' social networks to more formally constituted networks of institutions.

The rapid and continued development of information and communications technology (ICT) over the past decade is likely to create new opportunities for networking, especially at the international or global level. Significant developments have taken place in telecommunications infrastructure, especially satellite-based links, increased computing power and accessibility to computers, data and information storage, equipment for sending and receiving faxes, document scanners, computing software and particularly in Internet-related developments – e-mail communication, Internet and intranet websites and electronic discussion groups. The accessibility of ICT is still much greater in the North than in the South and, although this situation is likely to change and become less North-biased over the coming years, many countries in the South are likely to remain severely under-resourced in these facilities for many years to come.

Although there has been a significant increase in Internet-based facilities over much of Asia – especially South-East Asia and Latin America – ICT is still severely under-resourced in many countries in sub-Saharan Africa, particularly outside the administrative and business districts of the main cities. Information dissemination is increasingly undertaken in textual or electronic formats, which increasingly marginalizes those who are computer- and text-illiterate, or have restricted or unreliable access to ICT-based services and infrastructure. In particular, poor and vulnerable people in urban informal settlements are likely to become increasingly marginalized in the level and type of information they have access to.

Many organizations in the South, especially smaller ones based in a single location or those working closely at grassroots level, are likely to have limited access to the Internet or, in some cases, to have e-mail only. Many local authorities are in a similar position. The focus of networks towards the grassroots can be an effective way of increasing the involvement of poor people in action research, at the same time strengthening their ability to obtain and manage information, as well as to develop skills and knowledge. However, in networks moving rapidly towards electronic information dissemination and knowledge-sharing, there is a risk of grassroots-based organizations being excluded. A role would still exist for the better-resourced members to repackage and redistribute information to their local contacts. Newsletters, radio broadcasts, information leaflets and manuals, and frequent face-to-face meetings and dialogue will still be important. Key informants within communities will still have an important role to play in disseminating information and knowledge more widely. The closer linking of key informants to the established network activities of organizations will greatly increase their access to information. Considerable practical difficulties will, however, have to be overcome to establish and maintain the links between key informants and networks.

CHAPTER SIX

Cultural differences and legibility[1]

Nabeel Hamdi with drawings and captions by Ripin Kalra

INTRODUCTION

Knowledge and learning are key themes in development planning today, part of a new agenda designed to promote sustainability. Much of this knowledge and learning is disseminated through training, capacity-building, guide books, manuals, databases and websites, and directed largely at improving efficiency – whether of urban management, water supply, sanitation and health, shelter provision or the use of appropriate technologies. These so-called depositories of best practice are largely instrumental in the pursuit of goals set nationally and internationally, according to methods which are assumed to be value-free and universal in application. In the main part, our conventional models of learning and dissemination are in conflict with political and ethical rationales, and traditional wisdoms. Some argue that traditional wisdoms 'have become dysfunctional because they have not yet confronted that new complexity which is the challenge posed to them by modern science and technology' (Goulet, 1995), or by the new demands of cities.

Undoubtedly, times have changed, and so have needs and aspirations. This chapter assumes that the key to sustainable development is access to new wisdoms. It argues that knowledge and learning, through reflective practice, are the means by which traditional wisdoms can be adapted to the new challenges of cities, and new ones can be discovered. It assumes that 'the getting of wisdom' (Edwards, 1996) is the process by which knowledge is internalized and made culturally specific to the logic and habits of communities and organizations, through carefully considered methods of assimilation, and in this way becomes sustainable.

In this respect, improving access to knowledge and information through appropriate interpretative techniques is instrumental to the getting of wisdom in ways which are adaptive and legible.

ETHICS, WISDOM AND REFLECTIVE PRACTICE

Pick up any of the profusion of handbooks or manuals available, and their formats, language, rationale and logic will be variants of a familiar routine: sort out the problems; assess your strengths and opportunities; figure out your options; evaluate your risks; acquire the necessary resources; establish a programme for monitoring progress; then get the job done. The whole will be 'branded' with words that reflect today's development priorities and which open doors to donor funds – sustainability, stakeholder participation, gender equality, enabling policy, poverty reduction, public/private partnership, civil society and the like. The texts will typically include case studies and precedents describing how it was all done elsewhere, what worked and what did not, and why; hints on how to do and what to watch out for as work proceeds; checklists on charts and process diagrams ensuring good linkages between this phase and that, between key people and levels of organizations, and between sectors; all cross-referenced to logical frameworks, project-cycle management and other advice worked out in London, Brussels or Washington, and placed in the appendices.

The best of these guide the user through a network of routines and interpretative techniques in a process of self-discovery about means and ends, which are recognized as contextual in time and place. They recognize that, in practice, most ends are confused and uncertain. They have to be sought in action, articulated and agreed, and then often corrected or modified as work proceeds. The worst are prescriptive, instrumental and heavy-handed. They will assume a rationale biased in favour of alternatives which can be easily verified or measured, and argued with 'hard logic'. They will be either ignorant or disdainful of local practices, skills, abilities and attitudes, and will adopt notions of efficiency based on absolutes, and on criteria that are substantially economic and technical. They will fail to acknowledge that, in many societies, 'people calculate economic and technical efficiency in ways which 'internalize' such values as religious duties, kinship obligations, artistry and recreation' (Goulet, 1995). It is intrinsic practical wisdom, for example, that leads us to understand that for many societies, *friendship* not *stakeholder participation* is the basis of good partnerships and getting things done. Optimal rather than absolute efficiency is key – routines that are 'efficient enough' to do the job and appropriate to the circumstances, not according to a prescribed model, but according to the wisdom and judgement of those doing and thinking on the ground. The worst manuals and guide books offer 'good conscience to the rich and spiritual solace to the poor', while promoting the careers of development academics and the profits of private entrepreneurs.

In real life, it seems, 'we are bound to an epistemology of practice which leaves us at a loss to explain or even describe the complexities to which we now give over-riding importance' (Schon, 1983). This demands competencies that enable development practitioners to cultivate responses to the change, diversity, uniqueness and uncertainty which are the norm today.

What we need is a new code of conduct based on mutuality between technical, political and ethical rationalities – a code which is culturally legible, which recognizes cultural differences and offers an alternative to technical rationality based in nurturing new wisdom through reflective practice. We do need the capacity to operate effectively through new skills, information, routines, procedures and techniques. But we also need wisdom, the capacity of 'judging rightly in matters relating to life and conduct – a soundness of judgement in the choice of means and ends' (*Oxford English Dictionary*).

The key question must be: to what extent does the knowledge that we consider essential for good practice also enable traditional wisdom to adapt to the new circumstances of cities, to new technologies, and to agreed international standards on justice, equity and rights? And, in this respect, what moral imperatives are implicit in the rationale adopted – the primacy given to professional knowledge, the value assumed, the relationships implied between people and organizations, assumptions made about whose knowledge and expertise is best or more advanced, whose selective view of reality counts most, whose moral standards are more just, about the universal value of practices put forward as best and about 'absolutized ideology' or some alleged efficiency imperative?

In place of technical rationality and reductive thinking (reducing reality to parts that can be easily managed and measured), and in search of new wisdom, is Don Schon's concept of reflection-in-action – of 'thinking about doing something while doing it' (Schon, 1983). He argues that much reflection-in-action hinges on surprise when making mistakes in 'open learning'. We want to reflect on things that go very well or very badly, in order to apply corrective measures as our plans proceed, or to modify the norms and methods of enquiry and action for next time. Reflective practice qualifies or disqualifies the assumptions we make and the values we apply when defining problems, setting priorities or evaluating appropriate alternatives. It tells us about the value and appropriateness of the norms and standards we apply, the procedures we adopt, patterns of behaviour we assume to be correct or acceptable, and prevailing attitudes – about wisdom and good judgement. Reflection nurtures wisdom and is a 'corrective to over-learning' in schools. It relies strongly on shared or participatory patterns of enquiry which often lead to a restructured understanding about needs, desires and goals, as well as about the nature of problems, the aspirations of people, and the constraints imposed by the culture politic and those who hold power. It is a process intrinsically technical in character and substance. It follows the 'Freirian concept of conscientization, calling for raising the self-reflected awareness of people rather than educating or indoctrinating them, for giving them power to assert their voice and for stimulating their self-driven collective action to transform their "reality". . .' (Rahman, 1995: 25).

Given these three integrally related themes of ethics, wisdom and reflective practice, how can we structure a code of conduct that improves access to knowledge and makes its dissemination more effective?

To these ends, various questions need answers. What is to be disseminated, by whom, to whom, where and how? Who will control the lines of access and filter what is deemed appropriate or good practice? How is this to be decided? What are the constraints to improved access, and how can they be removed? What methods of access are appropriate given the diversity of physical, technical, linguistic, geographic and cultural settings to which these models will have to respond? What is the value of any specific body of knowledge or information, to whom should it be targeted and for what purpose?

In devising models of access to knowledge and information appropriate to the large diversity of interests, settings and circumstances, a number of questions are worth thinking about.

What are the aims of dissemination?

The assumption is that learning through the progressive dissemination of knowledge and information is key to sustainable development. The purpose of dissemination is therefore to enhance opportunities for more learning – that is, to assimilate rather than emulate new routines, technologies, techniques or good practice. Dissemination, in other words, is about unblocking lines of access to more learning and wisdom, not just more information. Stimulating thought and informing about available choices is key to effective dissemination.

Figure 6.1 The purpose of research is best served when some effort is made towards two-way communication

Figure 6.2   Stimulating thought and informing about available choices is key to effective dissemination

In addition, there will be questions about the principal aims and objectives of dissemination. Will it be to change behaviour among administrative, institutional or professional staff in order, for example, to adopt new planning routines which are more participatory, more adaptive or more decentralized? Or is it to persuade people such as managers to adopt standards or development controls? Is it to inform on the latest methods, techniques or technologies? Is the intent to stimulate thought about needs, objectives or priorities, or to motivate action where there is intransigence? Or will it be to change attitudes and shift paradigms about the delivery of housing, services, utilities or appropriate technologies (Pretty et al., 1995)?

Which way is the information going? What or who is getting in the way?

Figure 6.3 identifies lines of access and actors. It reveals complex and intricate relationships to which dissemination media, technologies, techniques and institutional arrangements must respond.

- The strongest line is from those at the top, centre or North to local or regional organizations. Dissemination usually takes the form of publication or training using case studies and examples of good practice reflecting national or global interests.

- From community-based organizations (CBOs), non-governmental organizations (NGOs) and local practitioners, whose knowledge about practice – about what works, what doesn't and why – is passed up to policy-makers and strategic planners in the interest of devising 'enabling' policy. The question is: how to tap and disseminate the wealth of innovation and wisdom implicit in the minds and practices of those working and coping on the ground? Conferences, evaluation and monitoring are typical media.
- From one community to another, or from one region to another, pooling wisdom, sharing experience, mostly on an informal basis. Local and regional network organizations and other grassroots associations are typical, and examples are increasing: the People's Dialogue in South Africa; the Asian Coalition of Housing Rights; Solidarity for the Urban Poor in Cambodia; Slum Dwellers International, among others. Exchange programmes between these groups are increasing, and are a 'root strategy for education and communication of the poor by the poor' (ACHR, 2000).

Are participants convinced they need it? Are they motivated?

Those at whom research is targeted will, in the first place, need to be convinced that they need its outputs. The questions are: who is doing the convincing, and in whose interests? Counterparts (local research institutes,

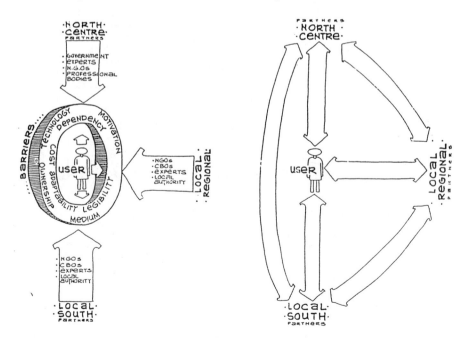

Figure 6.3 There are many barriers to good communication between actors

governments, NGOs, communities) will need to be motivated on the basis of shared interests or mutual reliance to believe they will be better off than before after assimilating the information or new techniques. Converging the interests of stakeholders is, therefore, a key to learning. This demands processes that are intensely participatory at all levels of acquisition and dissemination.

Lack of motivation is one of the main reasons why learning fails, and this may be due to a variety of causes.

- It may be that new knowledge or information is forced on those whom outsiders think need it.
- Participants may not be clear how this new knowledge or routine will change their lives, whether they are managers or community leaders.
- Participants may be uninvolved due to the style of culturally unfamiliar media, which may not be easy to follow or read.
- Some will know it all from before; others may be suspicious or resentful of the material or the organization the disseminators represent.
- The language and style could be demeaning, illegible or even threatening, given the context in which it is disseminated. In Cambodia, for example, to many people community participation was reminiscent of 'collective work' imposed by the Khmer Rouge – something to avoid rather than embrace.

Figure 6.4   In order to solicit criticism and open up discussion, the objectives of the project and its impacts must first be communicated

Most research is initiated and funded from 'outside' and by outsiders. That first level of convincing, therefore, usually takes place with professional counterparts in the host country, who may go along with the priorities and objectives of the proposals because of the prestige of working with the lead (Northern) institutes, for the benefit of their own careers, or for promotional or travel opportunities. Local 'host' counterparts will have to convince government officials of a need, and they, in turn, will go along with the proposals as much for the spin-off advantages as for their inherent benefits. By the time the project arrives at the community level it will be encumbered with agendas reflecting priorities, routines, standards, rationales and customs that may threaten the status quo locally, either among government officials or community leaders. Communities will also go along with this outside agenda in the expectation that they will get more if they do than if they don't.

All parties will spend as much effort in pushing their agendas and defending their ground as in assimilating the outputs of the research. It is worth noting that since development is a competitive enterprise, there is pressure on donors, development organizations and individual development professionals to use publications as proof – both of their productivity and innovation capability, where those publications may not be the best medium for dissemination. The result, very often, is that research outputs as embodied in guidebooks, manuals and other publications wind up on shelves, in cupboards or in learned journals, rather than in the hands of those who need them. And, given that much of their content will have been devised by researchers (outsiders) for other researchers or donor clients, very little of the knowledge they contain will reach those on the ground. This leads to the fourth question.

Are those who need information involved in producing and disseminating it? Do they own it?

Various constraints lie in the way of ownership, which together contribute to clogging the flow of knowledge and information and, therefore, to learning. They can be grouped into three categories: lack of resources; inappropriate media; and dependency-inducing behaviour. All three determine the level of control and dependency of one group or another and the level of assimilation that is possible.

Lack of resources

Resource constraints are the most familiar and are relatively easy to identify. They are also relatively easy to resolve if there is the political will. Each system, for example, will have instant costs relative to the technology, materials or equipment it demands. Each system will demand its own level of infrastructure, and each will demand its own type of expertise or human resources to get it going and keep it going.

Inappropriate media

The medium of documentation and dissemination must also be culturally familiar and legible. These issues are discussed further below. Suffice it to say here that cultures which typically disseminate information through oral testimony, for example, will not easily assimilate information through books, charts or diagrams, or through information technologies. And if the setting for dissemination is unfamiliar (government offices, conference centres, lecture halls, workshops, games or role-play), this may reinforce the gap between 'them' and 'us', the 'haves' and 'have-nots', and may serve to threaten the authority of managers, the patronage of elders, or the legitimacy of community leaders.

In India, not long ago, the author and his team used participatory rural appraisal (PRA) methods during an action planning workshop on improving conditions in a Delhi slum. A fairly conventional planning routine was followed, identifying problems, setting goals and priorities, exploring options for solving problems, and so on. Flip-charts with yellow Post-it notes were the medium of documentation, along with group work and modelling. Bits of paper and card with notes and ideas all informally layered onto large cardboard cut-outs of streets, houses and public spaces served to brainstorm problems and ideas. The informality of the model was emphasized because it sat on the floor of the community centre where work was taking place, and made it necessary for people – community leaders, men, women, children, officials from the planning authority – to kneel and crawl to work with the material. It was to be a participatory event where barriers between 'them' and 'us' would be broken down so that decisions could be made equitably. Later, in round-table discussions set up to break down barriers and improve communications, carefully selected groups debated issues and problems in order to decide the way forward.

Figure 6.5   People's capacity to articulate needs through self-expression is greatly influenced by the familiarity of the setting in which dialogue is conducted

Significantly, in the team's enthusiasm to empower the poorest and most vulnerable, the PRA exercise served to alienate public officials and potentially made things worse in the long term. Those who did work with the models were instructed to do so by elders and officials standing on the fringe – eager to show willingness to their enthusiastic guests, but eager also to ensure that the status quo was zealously safeguarded. The modelling exercise itself assumed free-and-easy relations between men and women, young and old, officials and others – relationships which were observed to be awkward and formed barriers to learning. Both modelling and round-table discussions were perceived as too informal – even disrespectful of elders and others with status acquired by reputation, age or cast – who would traditionally assume the very leadership roles that many of the exercises sought to undermine. The end images themselves – a cardboard and collage model, a flip-chart covered in Post-it notes – failed to match expectations or to capture people's aspirations. The setting itself threatened the authority of managers because it gave local leaders status over publicly appointed officials and, worse, was ignorant of patronage patterns, a more traditional basis for participatory work. The 'Post-it' format for group work gave status to those who could read and write, when most could not.

Overall, the exercise was token or therapeutic at best – something, the hosts felt, that it was necessary to go through in order to please outsiders and secure development funds.

Dependency-inducing behaviour

Perhaps the most complex block to dissemination is implicit in the behaviour of those whose job it is to acquire and disseminate – usually the researcher or expatriate practitioner – who may, inadvertently or otherwise, deny the wisdom and intuitive know-how implicit in the routine of everyday actions because they are difficult to model or make explicit. To deny action as an integral part of research is to risk irrelevance. The assumption here is that 'much of the knowledge relevant to practice is inherent in intelligent action' (Schon, 1983), rather than derived through conventional theory–method–practice routines. The question is: how to get at it, and then how to disseminate it? Schon (1983) suggests:

> *'Once we put aside the models of technical rationality, which lead us to think of intelligent practice as an application of knowledge to instrumental decisions, there is nothing strange about the idea that a kind of knowing is inherent in intelligent action. Common sense admits this category of know-how, and it does not stretch common sense very much to say that the know-how is in the action. . . . Although we sometimes think before acting, it is also true that in much of the spontaneous behaviour of skilful practice, we reveal a kind of knowing which does not stem from a prior intellectual operation.'*

Figure 6.6   Involvement of users and their knowledge in the process of research will ensure the outcome of research is well understood by the users

What we seek to respect is knowledge and information derived by people who think about doing something while doing it, and in active partnership with others who may already be engaged in 'time-honoured action'. What we need are settings for dissemination where information about the negative impacts of our proposals or findings are not withheld from other stakeholders; where assumptions can be tested publicly; and where negotiation about priorities, responsibilities and possible courses of action are conducted in open forum. The objective is to learn about what is most likely to work, rather than to push through pet ideas, outside agendas or idealized situations.

Instead, the culture of dependency and defensiveness pervades professional behaviour because experts are dependent on a 'problems industry' for livelihoods where to be in control is to be professionally competent. What we do, instead, in response to the uncertainties of practice is to seek security through a repertoire of defences. The risk of surprise, of being wrong or ignorant, admitting uncertainty, changing your mind or admitting the value of non-expert know-how, encourages at best, more specialization; at worst, more jargon and abstraction. This approach sometimes encourages oversimplification, reducing complex problems and issues to single objectives, standards and criteria; rejection of situations which are not easy to explain or put into manuals or databases, excluding knowledge and information from those outside professional circles; or normalization, denying the unique, the one-off, the locally specific, transforming and incorporating problems into safe, well-established disciplinary routines in the interests of 'universal' or global legibility, at the expense of local or regional value.

This leads to the fifth question.

Are the outputs legible? Are they adaptive?

Five considerations are worth noting which, together, offer a broad-based understanding of legibility.

Social legibility

It is well known that different social groups assimilate and interpret information in different ways and at different rates. Much clearer differentia-
tions are therefore needed when preparing and disseminating research
outputs between, for example, age, gender, ethnicity, class, caste, income
and vulnerability. The source of information and channels for dissemination will have some influence on how acceptable it is, based on patterns of
patronage, trust or influence.

Familiarity of context will also influence receptiveness to knowledge
transfer and new ideas. For example, training workshops and, in particular,
workshop facilitators may not 'correspond with any understood model of
social relationship' (Dudley, 1993). In addition, large group sessions where
training is usually conducted can place constraints on expression and can
block learning.

Cultural legibility

The language and media of expression are key in respect to cultural legibility, as are literacy levels, pride, suspicion, expectations and the dominance

Figure 6.7   Good communication aims to involve everyone

Figure 6.8   In hierarchical communities, presenting an opinion may be seen as a sign
of dissent

Figure 6.9   The manner in which authority finds expression when arranging meetings

Figure 6.10   Role models versus experts

of the articulate or politically powerful. Prevalent belief systems will place significantly different values on information or routines. Methods such as gaming, role-play and theatre will lack professional credibility for some, as in the example above, or may demand relationships among actors which are unfamiliar or unacceptable. Books, posters, maps or sophisticated diagrams may block rather than facilitate dissemination, depending on the target and content. Technologies, with all their implied differences in behaviour and process, may not fit the needs, desires and aspirations of people, whatever their practical advantages. On the other hand, modern or 'respectable' imagery, although sometimes unfamiliar, may be more acceptable because it represents what could be in the future, rather than what is now. This barrier to legibility can be removed through the use of local language and icons. The quality of communication can be enhanced if it encourages local responsibility.

Economic legibility

The knowledge of possible gains and losses involved in the communication, design, implementation and operation of a development idea is

Figure 6.11   Postcard designed for UNICEF to promote oral rehydration treatment (ORT)

critical to maintain the interest of the user. Information as 'trade-offs' to enable participants to internalize cost-effectiveness in terms of their own social and cultural value will be important in judging the value of ideas, programmes or projects being proposed.

Graphic or visual legibility

Diagrams, cartoons and speech bubbles may be familiar media of expression to one party (for example, urban communities with access to TV, comics and advertising), but not to another (for example, rural). Similarly, managers, architects or builders will probably read the same information in quite different ways. Diagrammatic abstractions can be easily misunderstood by communities – literal or caricatured images can also distance readers from the subject matter. Too much graphic information can confuse and distract. The key to good graphic legibility at the community level is: clear target; essential information; literal representation.

Verbal legibility

Clarity of language – which should be simple and jargon-free – is essential. The use of the local vernacular is key. While one group may well understand bus stops as 'communication nodes', others will not! Extended captions are not easy to link to graphics. It is always preferable for texts to feature in the local language. Levels of literacy will have to be assessed, and the word communicated by either written or oral means. In this sense, which medium would be the most appropriate – book, radio, TV, poster? Formatting is key – should it be narrative, instructive or tabulated?

Figure 6.12   The absence of daily wages from community meetings

Figure 6.13   The relationship of disseminated knowledge with the standards and codes of practice of the target group must be made explicit

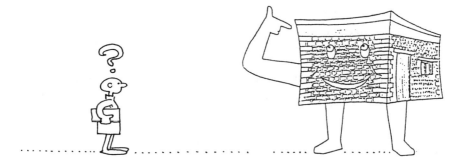

Figure 6.14 The ability to understand cartoons is a largely urban experience

Figure 6.15 Training is needed to be able to read abstract representations such as charts, flow diagrams, plans and sections clearly

Figure 6.16 Diagrams are developed by people to express concepts in their own terms

Given the variety of factors involved in making knowledge legible, there is a need to make communication more adaptive to local conditions. Every partner and place may have a unique form of communication using their own signs, symbols and codes. The task is to ensure that their vernacular is at the core of communication methods, in the interests of effective assimilation. This leads to the sixth question.

Figure 6.17   Researchers need to bridge the gap between the working language of researchers, and the languages and concepts understood by the participants and end-users of research

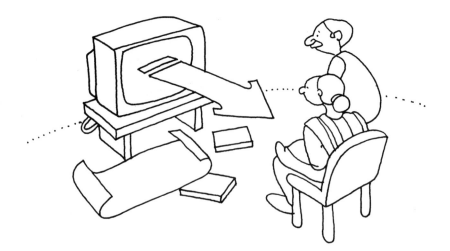

Figure 6.18   Indirect assimilation through simulations and equipment only

What methods of assimilating new knowledge are appropriate?

At the core of making information legible is the use of simulations or interpretative techniques. Simulations can be used to express the views of all partners, highlight issues, inform about development, present options for development in practice and encourage the participation of all partners.

It is part of the process of assimilation to ensure that simulations necessary for all people (participants) to express themselves, make themselves heard and understood, and visualize the full impact of the project on their lives or work, have been identified and provided.

Figure 6.19   Assimilation without simulation and equipment

Figure 6.20   Assimilation through interpersonal interaction and a body of simulations and equipment

Roles and limitations of interpretative techniques

The presence of a partner provides an opportunity for the other to ask free-form, spontaneous questions. The discussion can be done at a pace and in settings that suit all the people involved.

Simulations and equipment such as slides, videos, drawings and sketches help in the discussion or may represent the ideas of a person who is not present. They may be used to document the responses and present themselves to be manipulated by the participants.

Figure 6.21   Assimilation through interpersonal interaction and a body of simulations and equipment (which help to record, process and project new choices)

Figure 6.22   The skills and resources required to use equipment may not be present in all places

Figure 6.23 Each form of simulation is relatively useful in what it can convey

Figure 6.24 The capacity of end-users to understand reality through simulation may be very limited

Figure 6.25 These aids, which sometimes depict the final product like a building, may need to be manipulated in order to accommodate new ideas

Figure 6.26   Conceptual ideas about economy, society and culture are hard to present legibly without the use of visual codes or representations

SUMMARY CHECKLIST – THINGS TO THINK ABOUT WHEN DECIDING A MODEL OF ACCESS

- Is it flexible in structure, can it be adapted to a variety of situations?
- Is it cost-effective?
- Does it involve those who will be directly affected by its content in preparation and dissemination?
- Are its purpose and target clear?
- Are counterparts convinced they need the output – are they motivated by its content?
- In which direction is the information to go and, in each case, what is the best setting? Who decides? Who controls?
- Are local resources available to implement its findings?
- Is the medium for its dissemination appropriate?
- Is it legible – socially, culturally, graphically and verbally?
- Do the process and method embodied in the documentation encourage improvisation and chance learning?
- Are the content and procedures sensitive to differences in age, gender, class, income, geography, ethnicity?
- Are the examples used to illustrate text identifiable and tangible to users? Do they embody progress?

CHAPTER SEVEN

Communicating desire

Robert Brown

'You know what you're talking about.'

The above comment came from a resident living on a local authority housing estate where a master plan for regeneration was being developed. The estate was similar to much inner-urban social housing (also referred to as affordable or subsidized housing) built in the UK in the post-war era; after many years of broken promises and failed initiatives, the residents were highly cynical and suspicious, making the resident's comment all the more surprising. A rather congratulatory note of support, it suggested that from the resident's viewpoint, at least, something positive was happening in how community participation in the design process, and communication itself, was being realized.

Several years after the resident's comment was made, and from the activities which prompted the comment, it is easy to note the inherent optimism and the sense of conviction held at the time that the approach taken to community participation offered a viable way forward. The distance of time, however, now offers a valuable perspective for reconsideration of that approach. The context of the procurement of social housing has changed markedly in even that short time; additionally, architectural practices new to this work are being given the opportunity to bring a fresh approach to participatory design. Recent developments in education practices have provided additional insights into the nature of working with groups. It is with these considerations in mind that preparing this chapter presents an opportunity to re-examine the philosophical stance, as well as some of the methodology utilized, in following this direction.

Contextually, this chapter is set within the practice of participatory design in social housing in the UK over the past 12 years, working on behalf of the architectural firm Levitt Bernstein. This text does not argue the value of community participation per se. It assumes that the reader subscribes to both the goals and benefits of such involvement. Nor does it set out to offer a panacea. Its primary intent is to examine an underlying problem that impedes communication in participatory design, and examine one approach for achieving more effective communication, drawing on the experience of that approach in practice, and relevant discourse to consider its merits.

WHAT GAP?

Effective communication is recognized as central to the success of community development. But just as the primacy of effective communication is well recognized, so too is the conflict that often exists between the community and professionals. Both have commented on the dissatisfaction encountered in their supposed working relationships (e.g. Anon., 2000a; Hugill, 2001). This relationship too often degenerates into a power struggle, with each vying for control of the project; communication in such a scenario typically becomes one-way. Consequently, the resulting design process is led by one party or the other: one yields a paternalistic approach led by outsiders (e.g. the architects), which will not engender the feeling of ownership necessary for a community's sustainability; the other a community-directed approach which may not make effective use of the skills and knowledge that the professionals have to offer.

But why does this divide between community and professionals exist? The reasons are identifiable: in the UK, on community development projects, there is typically a decided difference between the two, marked by distinctions in education, economic and employment status, social class, race, ethnicity, life experiences and vocabulary. The professionals generally have greater access to and familiarity in interacting with existing power structures. Additionally, they have experience of engaging with technical and managerial conditions of development and working with other professionals. Each of these can contribute to a feeling of a gulf between the community and the professionals, and particularly in the case of the latter two distinctions, a sense of one side (the professionals) having a greater degree of power and control over the other. Combined with a sense of suspicion, and sometimes hostility, that has built up among the community towards professionals (an understandable reaction given the recent history on most social housing estates of years of poor housing management, lack of investment, broken promises and failed initiatives), it too often is a confrontational relationship.

Apart from the ill-feeling this engenders, criticisms exist that this inequality in power and control results in a coopting of the community by the professionals. The inevitable outcome is the imposition of one group's values on the other – typically, the professionals' (middle-class) values on the community (working class) (Chesterman and Stone, 1987).

Much of the available discourse on participatory design focuses on the need to establish effective communication, and on techniques for doing so (Allesbrook et al., 1988; Allen et al., 1993). Central to this has been the notion of identifying a common vocabulary. While such efforts are worthwhile, they alone do not resolve the situation. Indeed, problems are still experienced in practice, with the community and the professionals appearing to be going in different directions and pursuing different aims. In light of this experience it becomes clear that the focus on shared words and related techniques for communication does not recognize or address more profound obstacles in the exchange of ideas and concepts. What is too often overlooked, or indeed even acknowledged as an issue, is how people relate to the built environment, and how this gives rise to a disparity in principle that underlies the divide between the professionals and the community. As long as this disparity remains unaddressed, it will continue to impede effective communication and an effective working relationship.

Over the past 40 years there has been a significant amount of research in the field of environmental psychology. This research has found that there is a fundamental disparity between architects and non-architects in how each perceives, interprets (gives meaning to) and values the built environment, and how they communicate that experience. Owing to their professional education and experience, architects emphasize perceptual values and the representational meaning of the built environment; non-architects give emphasis to its associational and responsive meaning (Groat, 1982; Rapoport, 1977, 1982a; Hershberger, 1988; Devlin, 1990). In designing the built environment, architects tend to focus on visual qualities such as the use of materials, geometric proportions and the concepts these can embody. Non-architects, on the other hand, do so more in terms of the way of life they associate with the built environment (the image of the built environment is seen as a symbol for a way of life), and the values associated with that way of life. What is significant in this discussion is that, while both are exposed to the same environment, they place emphasis on different aspects of it. Thus the community and the architect each bring to the participatory design process their own way of relating to the environment, which in turn informs how each approaches and considers its design.

With their initial reference points being so dissimilar, the assumption that shared words have the same meaning for each group is inevitably mistaken, and can lead to a relationship where each tries to impose (consciously or unconsciously) on the other their own subjective definitions and values. Even with the best intentions, and using recognized models of practice, failure to recognize and discuss the difference in how each relates to the built environment can, in turn, lead to a rupture in the relationship that is (apparently to both sides) only solved through compromising one's own goals and beliefs. Such a result is far from satisfactory for either the community or the architect.

It is in this climate that architects and local communities often find themselves working. It is a situation based on 'mutual ignorance' (Gibson, 1987). But is there a way of overcoming this dilemma? Can this condition be resolved, or will it remain as a divide between the community and the professionals?

BRIDGING THE GAP THROUGH MUTUAL LEARNING

In order to fully bridge this gap, it is vital to address the fundamental disparity underlying it. By first acknowledging this disparity, an understanding of each other's values can develop and common ground be identified. To paraphrase Amos Rapoport, what is being suggested is not only looking at the *what* and *how* of the proposal, but also looking at the *why* – it is about understanding the motivations and values behind the what and how (Rapoport, 1982b). It is through an approach based on mutual learning that this is achieved.

Bill Halsall, architect for the acclaimed Eldonian Village in Liverpool (Owens, 1988), has spoken of how a shared vision can develop from mutual learning. Through shared experiences, the community and the architect can begin to define to each other how they relate to the environment and what they value in it. From this dialogue, designs can develop, free of mis-understandings and bias. 'The key aspect of this process is that it links indi-vidual and group learning to community learning, providing a forum for experimentation' (Ventriss, 1987).

What primarily distinguishes this approach from other participatory design methods is the attitude behind it. The prevailing norm has too often been for professionals to see it both as their responsibility and as a neces-sity to 'educate' the community. In this context, the learning is one-way. While contributors to the field (Allesbrook et al., 1988) have spoken of ending such a paternalistic approach, in practice such attitudes have remained, with the professional 'leading' the process. Mutual learning, on the other hand, is based on the principle that the learning, and directing of this learning, goes both ways – the community and the professionals are learning both from each other and together.

Mutual learning is about more than just the transfer of knowledge. The typical outcome in much participatory design is one where the commu-nity tells the professional what their needs are (generally in pragmatic terms), and the professional advises them whether or not the required outcome is possible, while simultaneously trying to convince the commu-nity of what they should have (as seen by the professional). Any learning that occurs through this is just a surface-level exchange of factual infor-mation. Mutual learning, as applied here, is based around a consideration of values. By addressing and considering together each other's values, each is prompted to reflect on their existing views. Such an approach enables deeper learning to occur, with potential for a transformation in their respective world views.

A valid concern regarding this approach, and a common criticism of par-ticipatory design in general, is the marginalization of the architect/profes-sional. It is important to reaffirm that this exchange can, and should, go both ways. Contributing to *The Scope of Social Architecture*, Geoffrey Broadbent notes that '. . .people's horizons of expectation are always limited by what they know' (Broadbent, 1984). One of the obligations of the professional is not only to inform the community of what is and is not possible, but also to raise their awareness of new possibilities. The archi-tect, due to education and experience, has knowledge to contribute, and it is of value to the community to understand this knowledge. When this knowledge is considered, it allows the opportunity for the community to know and understand both the possibilities of choice and the nature of the choice (Conan, 1987).

Mutual learning allows the design process to begin non-commitally, with no decisions being made. It provides an opportunity for the sides to get to know each other (Gibson et al., 1986). Through a shared experience, common ground is established based on a mutual understanding of the issues involved and of the other's goals and aspirations. During this time alternatives are explored, both to raise an awareness of what is possible and to define this common ground.

Although viable in theory, how does this take place in practice? Such an approach runs contrary to the image of practice as offered by the profession and architectural media, in which the architect acts alone, having a right to singular control over the design (Cuff, 1998). Breaking through the boundaries of this myth calls for new ways of working. The experience of working with local communities on the regeneration of housing estates in inner London suggests some possibilities.

PUTTING MUTUAL LEARNING INTO PRACTICE

The process starts with the community, beginning with where they are, and not where the professional is. Hester (1987) refers to this as identifying how the community experiences the place where they live, and not starting with how the professional experiences it. Or as one resident put it to us, 'we are experts at living on the estate'. They have a wealth of experience at living and coping with life in their environment; considering that experience can begin to reveal what the community thinks not only about their existing environment, but also about their desired environment.

Examining the community's existing environment takes place in many forms: personal interviews; group discussions; walking visits around the estate with residents; mapping exercises which map both local landmarks and preferred routes, etc. An exploration of the residents' ideal environment parallels consideration of the existing environment. Residents are prompted to reflect on and discuss their desires, although this is approached laterally. For example, residents might be asked to bring or draw a picture of their ideal home. The aim is not to identify a particular image they want – *what* they want to live in – but rather to identify in qualitative terms *how* they want to live. Through a series of non-leading questions, what emerges is their feelings on the *way* of life they value. As an illustration, on one project this discussion revealed the following:

■ a sense of place, with a definable character giving a sense of identity to their community

■ a dwelling whose external appearance suggests shelter, having a feeling of warmth; something that looks like home, and yet is open to personalization by the resident
■ internally, a sense of light and openness going through the dwelling.

This information then provides a frame of reference against which proposals may be considered and measured.

An obvious criticism of this methodology is that it might elicit unrealistic expectations – that the residents' ideal home might be beyond the economic and political parameters of the scheme. But research has shown that people generally do not have unrealistic expectations. One such study examined the public's image of the ideal home. Using photographs of existing homes, residents were asked to identify their preferences and why. Generally, what was identified as the 'ideal home' was that which the public considered to be (socially) acceptable, affordable and familiar, and not some fantasy (Hardie, 1988; see also Rapoport, 1977; Devlin and Nasar, 1989). In the experience of practice discussed here, it has been found that the local community typically aspires to what is next up on the social ladder (e.g. private housing across the street from their social housing), and not to some unrealistic expectation.

Simultaneous with this exploration is an examination of existing environments having some degree of relevance to the residents' own community. Raising residents' awareness of how architects approach the design of the built environment – the fundamental principles that inform their design strategies – augments this. Through this, and critically through the discussion this exploration prompts, both residents and professionals can broaden their knowledge of potential ideas and begin to assess these in the light of existing views. From this, a synthesis of shared aspirations begins to emerge.

The design process is then moved forward by putting this all into play (quite literally). Tony Gibson, developer of the 'Planning for Real' participation method, has noted that in the participatory design process the relationship must not be just a talking one, but a working one as well (Gibson et al., 1986). Developing this thought further, the working relationship must also be an unthreatening one, accessible to the non-professional. Accordingly, when possible alternatives begin to be explored, this is done in the form of user-friendly 'design games'. In these, the residents themselves have a go at developing proposals, from the scale of the entire estate down to the individual dwelling, with the use of 3-D models. This allows them the opportunity to see for themselves both the limitations and potential of what is possible, and how their preconceived ideas work. It also reveals their preferences and values for their community. Throughout this process, residents are encouraged to take the lead. With little prompting they begin to look at and discuss each other's ideas, evaluating these in light of their own, and vice versa. During this process, individual residents, perhaps those with greater familiarity with the issues, begin to offer assistance to others in the group. The dialogue or 'teaching' among residents that this game-playing fosters is then carried over into other activities.

When the time comes to test the alternatives in detail, the residents already understand the design process, what is possible and what is not. This enables them to make judgements free of their preconceptions and/or a sense of myopia overshadowing consideration of the needs of the greater community. Perhaps more significantly, they are able to see some of their own ideas in the design proposals, not only providing a greater understanding of the proposal, but also engendering a sense of ownership. (For a further description see Brown, 1998.)

More recently, this approach has been developed into a more formal structure for dissemination through the Housing Corporation's Best Practice programme (Partners in Charge, 2000). The intention of this programme, set within a participatory format, is to enable social housing landlords to work together with their residents to prepare them for participation in residents' panels in order to appraise proposed housing developments. While exposing residents to new knowledge and working with them to develop new skills for assessing proposals, the programme also examines how designers approach design, and encourages residents to reflect on and evaluate both their existing and ideal environments. Reflection on these issues by the residents elicits feedback, and an opportunity for learning by the landlord.

DISCUSSION

As the critique at the beginning of this chapter suggests, there is an inherent optimism in the description of this approach. A review of discourse on participatory design suggests this is not uncommon, particularly when those advocating that particular approach are the authors. Yet experience, and observations by those outside the process, suggest that things are not always so successful or simple. For example, feedback on the art and architecture practice Muf's Southwark Street public consultation project was very positive according to Muf, but mixed according to Southwark (Michell, 2001). Given this, is the optimism regarding mutual learning justified? There are a number of questions worth considering, which are briefly examined here.

How does mutual learning address long-standing criticisms of community participation in general?

There are a number of long-standing criticisms that question the very nature of community participation. Some of these are not addressed here, and include the quality achieved through this process in design terms, as viewed by the mainstream of the architectural profession (Schuman, 1991); identifying what is meant by community and determining who actually constitutes that community (Sennett, 1996); how extensive the consultation should be, interacting primarily with the community directly affected versus reaching out to the wider community ('How Far Participation?', unpublished paper, R.B.); whether those participating in the process are representative of the community (Goodlad, 1990); and balancing local need against a common good and who has the responsibility to make this decision – the community directly affected, or the professionals charged with acting on behalf of the greater community (Gregory, A., untitled paper on public involvement in the planning and development process, 1998). These are complex questions that require full consideration, and have been addressed in other publications to varying degrees, but they are beyond the scope of this chapter.

Another long-standing view criticizes bringing the community into the decision-making process, as they lack the necessary skills and knowledge (Ventriss, 1987; see also Turner, 1987). From this perspective, it is felt that at best they may be misinformed; at worst, myopic vision will stand in the way of their taking the community as a whole into consideration. The principle of mutual learning explicitly aims to address these concerns. Experience of practice, as illustrated in the discussion on design games, suggests that approaching community participation from this base provides a foundation that enables a community to make an informed decision.

Other long-standing concerns include the parallel constraints of time and money. The current condition in which design and development occur, especially within the field of social housing, is one in which there is considerable pressure to complete a scheme quickly. In this context, participatory design is usually hard-pressed to keep pace within a condensed programme. This can give rise to considerable conflict, as those new to the process (the residents) often feel that decisions are being forced on them without there being sufficient time to gain a full understanding of the issues before decisions have to be made. What is necessary is a way of achieving the desired result within the time period available. In the experience considered here, it was possible to develop a master plan viable to both the community and the professionals within the realities of the time (and cost) constraints faced today.

A final long-standing criticism, notable for the process of mutual learning described here, is what incentive is there for people to share their knowledge? This is especially relevant given the history of much of what is often called community participation. The result of this has too often been the co-option of the community by the professionals or relevant authority. In this scenario, the community is asked to contribute their time, energy and hard-earned experience, only to see their input normalized into prevailing outcomes and without being able to gain any measurable role in determining their future (Ventriss, 1987). Intrinsic to mutual learning is the 'opening-up' of the design process to the community. Yet this should not be considered as a relinquishing of 'power'; rather, it is about two parties too often divided coming together to share both responsibility for decisions and their respective knowledge and experience. Used in tandem, this can be both a powerful and effective approach in achieving an environment that is responsive and meaningful to the community, one that they feel is 'theirs' and of which they feel in control. To be most effective, the participatory design process should be part of a more holistic approach that includes parallel initiatives in community development and resident participation in management; such efforts will enable the community to take on an even more tangible role in determining their future.

Is such an approach viable within today's changing context of legislation and social housing initiatives?

How applicable is mutual learning in light of both recent legislation and housing guidelines, given the significant shifts in government policy in recent years? The Local Government Act 2000 empowers local authorities to promote the economic and social wellbeing of their community. Accordingly, they are charged to prepare local strategies to address local problems, all in consultation with the community (Local Government Act, 2000). Linked to this are the New Best Value Indicators issued by the Department of the Environment, Transport and the Regions (DETR), now the Department of Transport, Local Government and the Regions (DTLR), setting key performance targets for local government to achieve, including more community involvement (Anon., 2000b). Another initiative, the New Deal for Communities, places equal emphasis on community participation. Intended to help regenerate the poorest communities within the UK, the initiative is founded on the idea of partnership, involving local people and organizations as well as regional and national services (DETR, 1998).

The documentation issued under these various pieces of legislation does not prescribe how these aims are to achieved – a challenging task in face of the wide range of complex and interconnected issues. An approach based on mutual learning suggests a possible way forward. The principle of mutual learning is compatible with the principle of community participation incorporated in the new legislation: through its sharing of existing information and exploration of new ideas, people begin to communicate and work in partnership.

Have others in the field adopted or developed similar approaches?

The validity of mutual learning is also interesting to consider in the light of current trends in contemporary architectural practice in the UK. Two such practices, Fluid and Muf, each express a vision of establishing a 'shared ground' with the community. For Fluid, this begins by '. . .assembling a picture of a place as experienced by local residents. . .' (McAdam, 2000). Likewise, Muf's strategy is to '. . .instigate a two-way process of negotiation and proposition which makes space for other forms of knowledge to influence the design process, for example, the experience that comes with living someplace for twenty years or the experiences of a child' (Hill, 1998).

Is this approach relevant outside the UK?

Outside the UK, the principle of mutual learning also forms part of the strategy for integrating the community and professionals. Publications by those practising in the Southern context cite the use of the same fundamental principle. Dr Kevin Wall, discussing the experience of community development in South Africa, notes that in this work there is a significant risk of the community and professionals talking at cross-purposes, which can lead to a breakdown in communication. This breakdown arises from differences in language, knowledge, experiences and values. Vital to success in the face of these obstacles is identifying not only a common language, but also an understanding of each other's values and shared concepts (Wall, 1993).

These concerns form part of the evolving approaches to development being taken in the developing world by Western-based organizations such as the UK's Department for International Development (DIFD) or Oxfam. Integral to their initiatives are the principles of developing an understanding of conditions from the community's point of view, and building on this knowledge and the community's own strategies in order to achieve a more sustainable livelihood for the inhabitants.

Does mutual learning have possibilities for application in other fields of development?

The principle of mutual learning has wider applicability beyond participatory design. Some lessons drawn from education illuminate its validity for use in addressing a wide range of issues. Underlying mutual learning is the concept of learning as a tool for developing dialogue and understanding, as well as a shared sense of vision. Looking at learning in general, current thinking and research in higher education and adult learning has moved towards a similar approach. Recent developments have shifted education away from the paternalistic model of teaching that has previously dominated over learning as a more shared exploration (Nicol, 1997).

In the work illustrated in this chapter, several key strategies have been employed, based on the principle of mutual learning. They are listed below, and their relation to developments in education is outlined in the following paragraphs.

- Start with where the community is.
- Heuristic learning – learning by doing.
- Group learning.

Start with where the community is

As noted previously in the description of how mutual learning was applied to participatory design, it begins with where the community is. Dialogue is initiated by exploring how the community thinks and feels about the environment. By starting with what members already know, and respecting their unique experience, the community is able to proceed from familiar and hence more comfortable ground in what could otherwise be an intimidating process full of all sorts of new information. While easing the introduction and exploration of new ideas, its accessibility also helps to encourage greater participation. This existing knowledge and experience then becomes a point of reference against which new information can be assessed and synthesized.

The above methodology parallels current education thinking on experiential learning. These initiatives encourage students to reflect on their own experience and existing knowledge; such an approach is found to be more effective in engaging students and prompting them into more active, self-led learning (Entwistle et al., 1992). Equally, building on previous experience and knowledge can prompt students to reassess the preconceptions that underpin their thinking and beliefs: '. . .central to adult learning . . . is the process of reflecting back on prior learning to determine whether what we have learned is justified under present circumstances' (Mezirow, 1990).

Heuristic learning – learning by doing

A key component in applying mutual learning to participatory design is the use of games. As noted, community members participate directly by having a go themselves. Instead of listening to professionals 'tell' them, they experience new knowledge and skills first-hand, and are able to synthesize this with their existing views and capabilities.

Recent research on learning has demonstrated that the most effective way of learning is not through the 'transmission' model (telling), used so often in the past in education and participatory design (Allesbrook et al., 1988). Rather, it is better to 'interact' with new knowledge and skills, transforming them into one's own and thereby making them meaningful (Nicol, 1997). Further research supports the link between the level of involvement and knowledge gained. If we read something, we remember 10 per cent; if we hear something, we retain 20 per cent; if we see and hear something, this figure moves to 50 per cent; saying something yourself increases it to 70 per cent; but if we say and do something, what is subsequently remembered rises dramatically to 90 per cent (Wilsing and Wilsing, 2001).

Group learning

In participatory design, what can too often happen is that the exchange of knowledge becomes focused – and dependent – upon the professional. While it is understandable, given the architect's likely greater familiarity with the process and knowledge about the various issues, this focus can limit dialogue. Group learning is based on the idea that knowledge (and learning) can and should go in any direction, especially within the community, so that they learn from each other. To enable this, residents are prompted not only to take an active role in leading discussions and in engaging in games, but additionally to take on the role of 'teacher' themselves. Having one of their 'own' as the teacher not only helps to make the process more accessible to the 'learner', but also prompts the teacher to critically consider the information they are presenting, and to find effective ways of communicating this to others. Through the dialogue that emerges, community members begin to share thoughts and define their needs and aspirations, not only as individuals but also, more importantly, as a community.

Again, recent education research has identified that such collaborative learning is highly effective in developing critical thinking, and has extensive social benefits as well. It provides a more supportive learning environment, less stressful and more accessible. In this context mutual respect emerges, leading to the development of a shared sense of goals. From this, an enhanced sense of responsibility and self-efficacy can grow (Nicol, 1997).

SOME FINAL CONSIDERATIONS

The approach towards community participation set out here is not intended to be all-inclusive. Indeed, there is a danger in adapting a dogmatic approach. This chapter tries to avoid prescribing certain methods; instead, the emphasis is on examining the philosophical underpinnings of the approach and particular methods that have been found to be successful in following that philosophy.

Integral to these thoughts is that the approach has to be flexible and adaptable to each situation, for example to the cultural context. A particular methodology used in one situation will not necessarily work in another. It requires the community and the professionals working together to explore and agree the methods for how they might do so. It is the principle, and not any set definitive method, which is crucial here and will allow mutual learning to adapt to a variety of contexts.

Another significant factor to consider is the need for an understanding of the 'political' context in which the development is occurring. If the project is having to proceed against hidden agendas, whether held by the community, the architect or the client/funder, then progress will be problematic no matter what the approach. Effective communication, and hence a positive working relationship, will occur only when the process is transparent. As such, mutual learning, or any other participatory approach, will be viable only if all parties are committed to it.

CONCLUSIONS

While communication between the community and professionals is recognized as vital in participatory design, it is not always achieved. The emphasis of much guidance on how best to achieve it has been on specific techniques and, while useful, these do not guarantee success. The fundamental shortcoming in this emphasis is that the disparity in how architects and non-architects relate to the built environment, and hence how they approach its design, is overlooked.

Given this disparity, it should be no surprise that communication, and hence working together, can be so problematic. In order to move forward, it is necessary first to examine the disparity in how each relates to the built environment. This shared examination of the others' meanings and values not only enables an understanding of each other and a common language to develop, but more significantly, a shared ground can be identified from which work can begin. It is important therefore that each is contributing fully to this learning process.

Mutual learning is not a prescriptive process; inherent within this principle is a sense that the form of communication and working relationship will grow out of this dialogue. Developing theories within higher and adult education support distinct practices that have been found to be effective; these theories advocate the benefits of learning drawn from prior experience, learning by doing and group learning. These lessons suggest that mutual learning has applications beyond participatory design.

The viability of mutual learning as a tool in establishing effective communication is borne out by the experiences of others in practice. There are many engaged in social housing in the UK who work to principles in common with mutual learning; others working outside the UK subscribe to similar fundamentals. Recent legislation in the UK sets out goals conducive to using a mutual learning approach.

The approach of mutual learning suggests a way forward for developing effective communication, and hence a positive working relationship in community development. It is not a specific process, but rather a philosophy and an adaptive vehicle for achieving this. It is a movement away from a paternalistic approach, and calls for an attitudinal shift towards collaborative working, based on mutual respect in which both sides value the experiences of the other and recognize that they can learn from this experience.

'Both parties in the collaboration need to learn from each other; the potential user brings to the table matters of everyday life which are ignored in traditional architectural discourse. However, the acceptance of the everyday is not seen as a collapse of the lofty ideals of the profession but as the opening up to a productive realm in which both architect and user enact reciprocal transactions between the simple realities and the highest dreams.'

(Till, 1998)

CHAPTER EIGHT

Barriers and gaps in the communication process

Catalina Gandelsonas with drawings by Bill Erickson

This chapter discusses various ways in which the transfer of knowledge to urban poor communities might be improved. Communicating knowledge and best practice information has never been particularly easy or successful and, although a practice may be clearly the best in one particular context, it does not follow that it will suit another. People from different cultures have different languages, values, beliefs and perceptions that condition their behaviour, and as a consequence, recommended practices may not work in practice. Differences in the physical, social, economic and political context will inevitably influence and determine the degree of success.

It is argued here that, in order to communicate effectively, knowledge and good or best practices should be framed in ways that are sensitive to specific cultural and behavioural contexts (Schneider and Barsourx, 1997). This should permit them to be interpreted or mediated through mechanisms that allow communities to adapt knowledge to suit their particular circumstances. The successful communication of knowledge and good or best practices requires a broad understanding of the knowledge transfer process, and a critical awareness of how early knowledge transfer models failed to give proper recognition to the significance of cultural factors in the process.

This argument draws on recent research in 'Communication for Urban Development' and 'Localizing the Habitat Agenda for Urban Poverty Reduction' (Max Lock Centre, 2001a, 2002).[1] It basically elaborates on the hypothesis that the transfer of knowledge of good or best practice is more effective when related to communities' needs and culture, and when channelled 'horizontally' through networks and partnership arrangements. To elaborate on this, the chapter focuses on the understanding of communication aspects of knowledge transfer which involve action in four key areas, as follows.

- Understanding the mechanics of communication processes and knowledge generation to overcome communication barriers and gaps.
- Identifying existing social networks (formal and informal) at the community level, which are able to codify their tacit knowledge and make it explicit.

- Applying knowledge management tools for the communication of explicit and tacit knowledge in the implementation of best practices, and exploring how the key members of social networks could help in codifying practices to make them more communicable to communities.
- Creating partnerships with strategic stakeholders in the urban development process and drawing on networks at various levels – for example international and national associations of municipalities, non-governmental organizations (NGOs) and community-based organizations (CBOs) – to guarantee that these approaches will be implemented and capacity-building will be accomplished.

COMMUNICATION MODELS: THE LOGIC AND MECHANICS OF THE PROCESS

Communication theory describes the mechanics of communication models as a cycle that includes 'factors' and 'actions'. Factors include: the *people* involved in the process (including a *sender* and the *receiver* of a message); a message or *knowledge*/best practices to be communicated; a vehicle or medium for transmitting the message; and the effect the message has on the receiver. Actions include the coding[2] and decoding[3] of the message, and the acknowledgement of its receipt by the recipient (Watson and Hill, 2000; Figure 8.1).

The communication process begins when a sender (anyone) sends a message (information, knowledge or best practices[4]). The message is then translated into one or several signals (it is encoded), and transmitted through a medium or channel (networks or media) to another person (the receiver of the message; in this case, the urban poor) (Figure 8.2).

After the message has been sent from the sender to the receiver, the receiver transmits a signal to let the sender know that the message has been received. The communication process will be completed when the receiver interprets the message (or decodes it) in accordance with his/her cultural values, beliefs and reference systems, and then returns a signal (the effect), which in some way confirms that the message has or has not been understood (Max Lock 2001b). Visualizing the mechanics of the communication

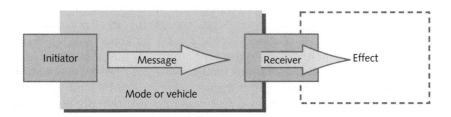

Figure 8.1 A simple, linear model of communication

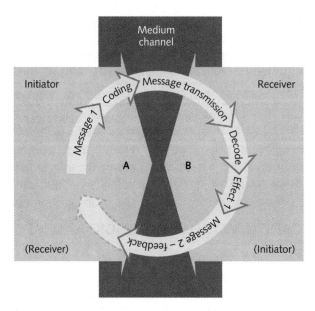

Figure 8.2   After the message is sent from A to B, the receiver (B) then transmits a signal or feedback, letting the original sender (A) know whether the message is understood

process allows one to understand why barriers and gaps are likely to occur, as there are many situations in which the coding and decoding of the message sent will be blocked.

THE PEOPLE INVOLVED IN THE COMMUNICATION PROCESS

Senders, receivers and decoders of the message are interest groups, referred to as stakeholders, including groups or institutions that are potentially involved in development processes (ODA, 1995). The urban poor, their social networks and community organizations are key stakeholders, and a primary target of the communication process in development. Intermediaries or strategic stakeholders include CBOs, NGOs, consultants or professional groups, etc., who are strategic in that they code and decode messages or knowledge. Such organizations are in direct contact with urban poor communities, as they share the same language and reference systems. They can therefore translate and communicate knowledge provided by researchers and academics, and may be involved in negotiation and development activities. Supporting stakeholders include research communities such as universities and research centres, private sector firms, journalists and donors. These may be based locally or elsewhere, and support development in various ways. Any of the above stakeholders may communicate or transfer knowledge or information, or initiate the process. The various stakeholders involved in communicating knowledge for development may have different cultures and reference systems and may possibly speak different languages or dialects, all of which explains why communications are an arduous and difficult process.

WHAT ARE THE MESSAGE, KNOWLEDGE OR BEST PRACTICES?

Traditional communication theory combined with contemporary business management theory provides explanations for some of the barriers and gaps that hinder the transfer process (Max Lock, 2001b).[5] In recent years a great deal of international research has been undertaken and applied by the business management sector in relation to knowledge management.[6] This theory pays particular attention to the importance of the message or 'knowledge',[7] a key concept in the understanding of communication

Nonaka and Takeuchi use 'knowledge' as the basic tool in analysing company behaviour. Knowledge has specific dimensions that may be explicit and formal,[8] or tacit and informal[9] (Polanyi, 1966; MacDonald, 1999; Brooking, 1999).

In Nonaka's theory explicit and tacit knowledge complement each other and generate a dynamic, which creates new knowledge that can then be communicated and translated into a best practice.[10]

Nonaka believes that knowledge can only be transferred when new knowledge is generated. Additionally, knowledge is best generated when those with explicit and those with tacit knowledge interact. This interaction generates four stages or modes of knowledge conversion: socialization, externalization, combination and internalization (Nonaka and Takeguchi, 1995) (Figure 8.3). Socialization is the sharing of tacit knowledge with others by means of mentoring (sharing internal knowledge, skills and insights). Externalization is the process of converting tacit knowledge into explicit knowledge, which creates conceptual knowledge. Combination is a mode of knowledge conversion, which involves a combination of different types of explicit knowledge; this happens when people exchange knowledge via documents, telephone, meetings, etc. Internalization reconverts explicit knowledge into tacit knowledge. It consists in learning-by-doing, a process that occurs when the previous modes of knowledge conversion (socialization, externalization and combination) are internalized or absorbed in people's minds as tacit knowledge, which is represented by mental images or models.

These four modes of conversion are represented by Nonaka in a diagrammatic knowledge spiral (Figure 8.4), which indicates how knowledge may best be transferred in development.

This knowledge generation process can best be accomplished when people get together, meet up and communicate face to face in favourable settings (Davenport and Prusak, 1998: 93).

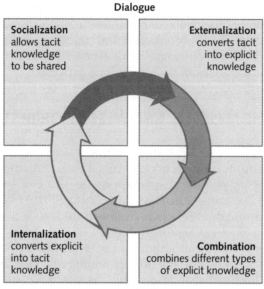

Figure 8.3   Conversion of knowledge (adapted from Nonaka and Takeuchi, 1995)

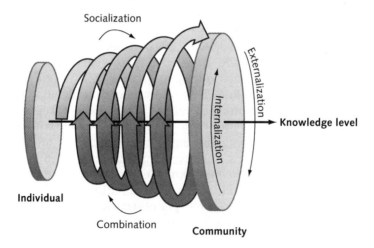

Figure 8.4   The knowledge spiral (adapted from Nonaka and Takeuchi, 1995)

Once the communication process has been initiated, crucial questions may be raised in relation to the message, knowledge or best practices. Have the receiver's needs, cultural circumstances, context, language and reference system (values and beliefs) been taken into account? Messages that are insensitive to people's reference systems (cultural background, beliefs, values and traditions) affect a recipient's willingness to decode and understand them. Knowledge management theories have several interpretations[11] all based on Nonaka, whose theory was found to be the most useful for transferring knowledge in the management context (Gandelsonas and Lloyd-Jones, 2001).

THE BEST VEHICLES FOR COMMUNICATING THE MESSAGE

In addition to the message and people involved in the process, a successful communication cycle requires a mode or vehicle for transmitting the message between sender and receiver, and vice versa. Social networks, intermediaries and media are such modes or vehicles for channelling information.

Social networks

Social networks are the ideal vehicles for achieving 'knowledge capture, knowledge building and knowledge dissemination' (Earl, 1998: 10). Networks can be identified in terms of the special social relationships which generated them. Those relationships may be given by similar gender or age, kinship associations, religious and ethnic origin-based networks, politically-based networks, neighbourhood-based groupings, credit groups, employment-based networks, and linkages with NGOs and other organizations (Phillips, 2002). Social networks may influence people's behaviour as much as the physical environment, ideology, climate and residence (Johnston et al., 1986).

The importance of networks is highlighted in the Sustainable Livelihoods approach (DFID, 2000b) and in Chapters 1, 2, 4 and 5 of this book. It is also embodied in the concept of social capital – one of the key assets that people draw upon in their livelihood activities.

Social networks in urban areas are more diverse than in rural areas, and relationships in urban areas are formed around short-term reciprocity centred specifically on money, and the longer-term reciprocity of food, water, space, childcare (Moser, 1996) and labour (Beall and Kanji, 1999; Rakodi, 1999). Social network functions include leadership, management, and practical and emotional support. These functions give network members a sense of affiliation, confidence and emotional support and, more than anything, a sense of common purpose. Such functions make networks the ideal vehicles for transferring knowledge, best practices and capacity-building. Positive aspects and opportunities brought about by networks include richness of social contacts, and sharing common struggles and adversity. However, networks in urban areas may suffer from a number of inhibiting factors (see Chapter 4). The social capital generated by them is weaker because of the mobility and heterogeneity of the population. In order to obtain basic resources for survival, the poor are sometimes forced to engage in relationships that may be highly exploitative. This type of social capital is sometimes referred to as 'negative social capital', and the resulting networks are very unlikely to provide a vehicle for transferring knowledge geared towards alleviating urban poverty (Phillips, 2002).

Intermediary organizations

Intermediary organizations are the key stakeholders bridging the communication gap between researchers and local communities (Max Lock Centre, 2001a). They may be NGOs, CBOs, local universities, media and other agencies, or groups that share the language and reference systems of urban poor communities. Because of their closeness to the local context, combined with an ability to speak the same language, play an advocacy role, interpret the local culture and conduct technical research, intermediaries have a strategic role in the transfer of knowledge.

The capacity that intermediaries have for transferring knowledge is not guaranteed in every situation because the communication and transfer of information involves a number of stages, which may lead to potential distortions or delays. Therefore the usefulness of the information transferred will depend on the quality of the links between intermediaries and grassroots groups. Intermediaries that are related to social networks should, furthermore, be used to improve access to and transfer of knowlege to communities.

Media

The media provide the channel by which a message or knowledge is transferred. There are a wide range of media technologies available, and different opportunities and constraints are associated with each. There are also many different ways in which such technologies may be used.

Communications media must be accessible and legible, or they have no purpose. To that end, it is important to understand how different types of media may be combined to put a particular message across, to reach a particular audience and/or to improve communications between groups of people. Characteristics and types of media are explained in Chapters 1 and 2 and the importance of legibility is examined in Chapter 6.

Networks, media and intermediaries are crucial in the communication process because they help to deliver the message. They may all act as coders, decoders or translators of the message, especially in those cases where messages (knowledge, best practice) are delivered to communities with different cultures, language, beliefs and reference systems.

THE EFFECT OF THE MESSAGE

Changes in the behaviour of communities, which may have resulted from transferred messages or knowledge, should be monitored or assessed to make sure that the communication cycle has been completed. This is an important aspect that should not be overlooked, as if no changes occur it means that the message has not been decoded or understood by the receiver (Watson and Hill, 2000). The effect or understanding of the message is conditioned by two factors: velocity and viscosity (Davenport and Prusak, 1998). These factors help to determine whether the message or knowledge has been transferred or not. Velocity relates to how quickly and widely knowledge is disseminated. Viscosity refers to the richness and complexity of the knowledge transferred. The more complex the message is, the more difficult its transfer will be. Thus, high levels of viscosity will determine how much of the knowledge transferred has been absorbed and applied. Complex messages obviously have this particular quality, which means that special monitoring and assessment will be required to verify that this type of knowledge really has been absorbed.

BARRIERS AND GAPS IN THE COMMUNICATION CYCLE

The complexity of the communication cycle explains why – and at what part of the communication process – barriers develop and gaps occur. They are basically the result of failures in coding and decoding the message.

Barriers, which are defined as specific obstacles to the transfer of knowledge, usually produce gaps in the communication process. Cultural differences may create specific barriers in the transfer of knowledge, as barriers appear when values, language, beliefs, reference systems, education, income, gender and age differ. Gaps are defined as the lack of connection between senders and receivers of knowledge, and result from existing barriers. Gaps may occur in the following contexts.

- When the initiator's coding does not relate to the receiver's ability to decode the message. This occurs when the message is not properly generated and coded due to cultural and language factors that have not being taken into account, and the message is therefore alien to the values of a particular community (Schneider and Barsourx, 1997; Davenport and Prusak, 1998; and Chapters 6 and 7).
- When the hierarchy of needs[12] of a particular community may have been over- or underestimated. Thus the knowledge conceived may not be relevant to the needs of the community, and the receiver may therefore be unwilling to decode the message (White et al., 1994).
- When there is a lack of consideration for the receiver's local tacit knowledge (White et al., 1994; Davenport and Prusak, 1998).
- When there is a lack of access to common media compatible with the community's culture and reference system, or the wrong media have been used (Max Lock Centre, 2001a).
- When there is a lack of monitoring and assessment of changes in behaviour, which may have resulted from the transferred message (O'Dell and Grayson, 1998).

- When links and interactions of networks are broken (Watson and Hill, 2000)
- When there is a lack of appropriate settings (e.g. meeting places) and inadequate time for the transmission and assimilation of knowledge (Davenport and Prusak, 1998).
- When senders of a message believe that receivers lack absorptive capacity. This may have resulted from a belief that knowledge is the privilege of particular groups. It may be overcome by encouraging non-vertical hierarchical approaches to knowledge, and the acceptance and reward for creative errors (Davenport and Prusak, 1998: 98).
- When tacit knowledge may be transferred only through a sequence of tutorials or lengthy apprenticeships (Davenport and Prusak, 1998: 102).
- Finally, lack of trust is a major deterrent in the transfer of knowledge. To overcome this problem it is recommended that relationships be built through face-to-face meetings (Davenport and Prusak, 1998: 93).

If barriers and gaps are eliminated, communicating knowledge between researchers and communities will be more successful. The next important step will be to try always to combine communities' 'tacit knowledge' with researchers' 'explicit' skills or knowledge. This will only happen if people are encouraged to meet to discuss ideas and generate new knowledge, which will be more compatible with what they need and understand. A good example of the application of this process is given in the following case study relating to Shack International.

SHARING GOOD PRACTICE AND LEARNING LESSONS – A CASE STUDY[13]

The experience of Shack International is of particular interest as it is a good example of how a wider international network of CBOs may operate, communicate and share knowledge and good practices.

Shack/Slum Dwellers International (SDI) is an international network of organizations of the urban poor who share ideas and experiences, and support one another in gaining access to adequate land, infrastructure and housing. SDI brings together poor men and women from urban settlements through national and international exchange visits, exhibitions and meetings in order to enable the rapid transfer of knowledge, experiences and skills directly between organizations of the urban poor.

The strength of SDI lies in its combination of local and global dimensions. Communities gather information about their own settlements and use this to explore collective, community-led solutions to the needs which they identify as most salient for their communities. These local federations, supported by a professional local NGO, have become part of a global network of similar local organizations facing similar challenges. 'Communities learn to see their own situations in a new light, to share their own knowledge and to learn from the experiences of others. The lessons learnt are then adapted to the local context' (www.homeless-international.org).

SDI network members meet regularly through exchanges to share ideas and offer support to each other. Their exchange process represents a commitment between organizations of the poor 'to communicate with each other to examine their problems' . . . then 'evaluate proposed solutions, refine them and spread them around'. Clearly, only a few members of each community can make this type of visit, so the SDI knowledge management strategy focuses on how the lessons learned from these experiences and exposure to practice elsewhere can be injected into the fabric of what is happening at home. This is done in part through a reporting-back process, through meetings, story-telling, reports and videos. In the longer term, ideas begin to be applied practically and, gradually, as they begin to make sense to the community, they become absorbed in the larger practice of the group. Local networks have an important role in this whole process, amplifying and building on the experience of the broader international network.

The way that new knowledge is shared between SDI members involves a conversion process of socializing (meeting other people with similar problems); externalizing (speaking from their perspectives and reference system); and combining (mixing their tacit knowledge with the new knowledge and skills seen and experienced), which allow them to internalize new knowledge generated from this process.

The SDI network encourages community members to see and experience best practices implemented in other countries directly from their own cultural perspective and reference system. Seeing and observing through face-to-face meetings, or horizontal exchanges, are powerful experiences that give visiting community members insights which allow them to internalize new knowledge. Exchanges with similar communities create a solidarity that simulates and enables a more efficient transfer of development knowledge from one poverty context to another.

CONCLUSIONS

An understanding of the mechanics of the communication cycle and knowledge generation, codification and transfer may help to explain what barriers may be encountered during the communication process. These concepts apply equally to the transference of knowledge and good practices in development as, only when the receiver's culture, tacit knowledge and needs are taken into account by consultants, researchers or donors, will new explicit knowledge be transformed and then transferred.

The knowledge thus produced, in conjunction with a community, will then relate to the receivers' needs and specific culture. This will ensure that knowledge transferred is useful and that communication barriers are avoided from the beginning of the process.

The empowered receivers will trust knowledge generated in this shared manner, as it will be suitable for their specific community context and needs. It has been found that direct contact between researchers and communities is essential to build rapport and eliminate barriers created through lack of trust. Such types of contact should be encouraged and supported in order to achieve better communication. Trust, however, can only be built over time through an adequate number of meetings. Finding effective ways for people to talk and listen to one another through spontaneous exchanges can produce an effective transfer of knowledge. Thus, face-to-face meetings are by far the most important channel for knowledge transfer and casual conversations should, therefore, be included as a means of reflecting, learning and exchanging knowledge, which may then eliminate gaps that previously could only be bridged through intermediaries or networks.

Pilot programmes reflecting the application of these concepts should be encouraged and evaluated through qualitative and quantitative measurements to check and correct the implementation of these ideas.

Finally, although these techniques may improve communication as a result of the application of new methods, little will happen if good governance and partnerships are not implemented to support this type of knowledge generation and transfer.

CHAPTER NINE

Improving communication in Amazonia: examining the environmental imagery of Amazonian indigenous life

Kathleen Richardson

INTRODUCTION

Communication is concerned with human relationships. There is a desire by development professionals to improve communication, not for its own sake, but to facilitate development practices. The proposal that communication is technically and socially important is beyond dispute, although achieving 'good' communication is beset with difficulties. In one respect, 'bad' communication can be likened to two people talking on a noisy phone – if only the lines were clear, it is argued, good communication could ensue. But this simple analogy clouds an important issue that requires further investigation: even when lines are free from interference and all the actors are talking in the same language, communication can still break down – why is this? Communication is always part of a complex web of agendas, so different actors pursuing different agendas can all assume a common language and yet have different aims, intentions and needs. And what is the point of promoting communication if the demands are ignored or considered by those asking the questions to be unpalatable.

This chapter assesses the problem in relation to representations of indigenous peoples in Amazonia. In the past two decades, the growing concern for the Amazon forests by Northern development organizations has coincided with the aims of indigenous peoples' demands for land rights. This has led to popular images of Amerindians as ecologists and against forms of economic practice such as mining, dams or infrastructure development (Cummings, 1990). The representations of Amerindians as against development often serve to disguise the real complexities of life in Amazonia, where the image of Indians as 'natural ecologists' is often manufactured by outsiders. In Amazonia there is a marked difference between the image of the Indian generated by environmental campaigners and development organizations, and the reality of the demands and desires of particular Amazonian groups. This is a paradox. Development practitioners are critical of past practices where development initiatives were imposed on communities. This chapter argues that this situation still occurs, as illustrated by the case of Amazonian communities.

ECO-INDIAN IMAGERY

The Amazon is a contested domain and is a site of battle for various groups. Northern ecologists and environmental groups have promoted campaigns to preserve the forest and protect its resources (Maxwell, 1991; Chernela, 1995); on the other hand, indigenous groups are facing legal and developmental conflicts in their territories. This has led, at times, to a convergence between indigenous peoples and Northern environmental organizations. The dynamic interactions between developers, ecologists and indigenous activists has promoted the examination of mythical reformulation of themes as diverse as 'noble savages', 'pristine forests' or 'primitive ecology', all which have come to life in Amazonia.

In Amazonia there are more than 200 Amerindian groups, population estimates for which vary from 200 000 (Rocha, 1999) to 300 000 (Rabben, 1998). The quantification of indigenous persons in Amazonia became politicized in the late 1980s, with the rise of New Social Movements and the accompanying legal changes in indigenous status.[1] Of the numerous indigenous groups, none has featured so regularly in the international discourse about Amazonia as the Kayapo and the Yanomami of Brazil; ironically, these groups have now become an annoyance to the environmental movement. The trends that deselected the Kayapo and Yanomami are interesting to consider. Brazil has only a small percentage of indigenous population, and the Kayapo and Yanomami are fewer in number than their Jivaro neighbours on the Peru/Colombia/Ecuador border. The centrality of the Brazilian rainforest to the narratives of environmental disaster is key to understanding the prevalence of these two groups (Rabben, 1998; Ramos, 1998).

The relations between environmentalists and indigenous groups are consistently tangled, so it is not possible to examine development as a separate theme in environmental narratives (Redford and Stearman, 1993; Adams, 1995). The agendas of the different groups are discursive and ambiguous (Ramos, 1998; Turner, 2000). Northern environmentalists are motivated by a desire to preserve the forests, and justify this cause on the basis of scientific evidence that establishes a link between Northern productive systems and environmental depletion.[2] For Western scientists, the Amazon is home to extensive natural resources and great biodiversity of plant and animal species. But what is a 'resource'? Something that is a resource in one circumstance might not be in another. Coal lay in the earth for millions of years before its discovery as a fuel. Uranium, a useless metal in one set of circumstances, in another becomes a powerful source of atomic energy. There can be no sense of a 'resource' in the abstract, and resources from nature are continually given form and value by human societies.

Ecological groups argue for the protection of the forest resources, regardless of their potential uses for Amerindian and non-Amerindian groups (Maxwell, 1991; Chernela, 1995; Brosius, 1999; Posey, 2000).

This tension has generated both conflict and consensus with indigenous peoples whose physical and cultural survival is dependent on the forest. Since the late 1980s, environmental/indigenous relations were promoted around the theme of environmental protection. Campaigns by Northern environmental groups to block international and national development programmes such as mining, dam-building and road construction have been mediated through concern for indigenous groups in the region (Coomes, 1995; Conklin, 1997; Brosius, 1999; Turner, 2000). Indigenous groups have served as an example to environmentalists of cultural systems that can exist in the absence of resource-depleting and environmentally damaging economic modes of production (Redford and Stearman, 1993).

Thus the Amazon has become a site for the appropriate management of rational knowledge. The desire of environmental groups to preserve the natural resources of Amazonia has resulted in a rethinking of natural and human development. Since Stockholm in 1972, there have been over 1200 multilateral and bilateral treaties and other agreements on environmental matters. Virtually every country in the world has some form of environmental legislation or agency, although the developed countries have made the most progress in these areas (Halpern, 1992).

Environmental and indigenous discourse was given life in the 1980s, when the Kayapo, with the support of environmental NGOs and anthropologist Darrel Posey, met with World Bank officials to criticize potential plans to build a dam in Kayapo territory. As a result of this meeting, the World Bank cancelled a US$500 million loan to the Brazilian energy sector (Rabben, 1998). These interactions have led international institutions to interpret Amerindian practices as ecological, and in 1988 Yanomami activist Davi Kopenawa received the United Nations Global 500 Award for his contribution to defending the environment (Rocha, 1999: 29). In 1989 indigenous groups hosted the Altimira conference. The meeting, a protest against the prospective dam-building project in the region, was attended by 400 indigenous representatives and over 500 Brazilian and international media, as well as numerous environmental groups, human rights organizations and development agencies (Cummings, 1990; Rabben, 1999; Rocha, 1998; Turner, 2000). Conklin (1997) has noted the subversive dimensions of Altimira, where she is critical of environmental groups and the media for generating particularly selective images of the Indian as ecological.

'ECOLOGICAL' INDIANS AND LAND RIGHTS[3]

The campaigns between indigenous peoples and Northern development organizations have repeatedly taken the form of struggles over land rights. The specific language employed depends on the context in which it is expressed, and the interpretation of phenomena is always translated through the conceptions and categories of the 'culture' involved in rendering the meaning. Non-Amerindians play a determining role in relation to land rights for indigenous groups, as it is the state institutions that sanction, enforce or reject claims. In Brazil, the state first initiated arguments in favour of land rights in the 1960s, on advice from the Villas Boas brothers. The Xingu National Park was established in 1961 (Villas Boas and Villas Boas, 1973).

The concept of reservation, or reserve, or National Park is an alien concept to pre-colonial Amerindians, and acts as a compromise between the states and indigenous peoples. It also, implicitly and explicitly, signifies and structures a set of socio-legal relations. While claims for land rights and reservations are supported by indigenous communities, and this is seen as a vehicle for self-protection, reserves and national parks are the result of externally related constructions for preserving and protecting indigenous areas.

The demand for land rights is a recurrent theme for indigenous groups. According to the Foundation of Indigenous Peoples (FUNAI), only half the indigenous land in Brazil has been demarcated, and for around one-fifth the process has not yet started. Hence ecologically framed arguments can help promote the alliances and agendas of indigenous groups and environmental organizations. This is illustrated in the case of land rights. Greenpeace has supported both Kayapo and Yanomami land rights claims, and is now supporting the Deni people of the north-east Brazilian rainforest. The following letter from the Deni in 2001 illustrates this point:

> We want to demarcate our lands.
> The land of Apurina people was already demarcated.
> The land of the Paumari peoples was already demarcated.
> The land of the Jarauwara people was already demarcated.
> Suruaha people have demarcated their land.
> All of the populations of our region have already demarcated their own land.
> We are the only ones left.
> Now we want to demarcate our land, this year, 2001.

> (Greenpeace Briefing, August 2001).

The fact that the Brazilian state is so reluctant to recognize land rights has resulted in environmental groups taking the lead role. Hence their alliances with indigenous communities act as mutually beneficial arrangements (Redford and Stearman, 1993). This association has also created the format in which issues are discussed, framed and translated for state institutions and international development institutions. Examples of statements such as the following are prolific in international development literature:

> 'Indigenous Peoples have the right to maintain and strengthen their spiritual relationship with their traditional land, waters and resources for future generations.'

> (UN, 1993, Part 6, Article 25)

And the Inter-American Commission on Human Rights Organization of American States, 81st Session on Indigenous Culture and Ecology, asserts:

> *'Recognizing the respect for the environment accorded by the cultures of indigenous peoples of the Americas, and considering the special relationship between the indigenous peoples and the environment, lands, resources and territories on which they live and their natural resources. . .'*

(IACHR, 1997).

The Centre for the Development of Indigenous Amazon Peoples, Lima, Peru says this:

> *'Our work is motivated by the necessity to reclaim the indigenous people's Common Law right to the territories and natural recourses that, since time immemorial, have been the base of their physical and cultural existence. These communities, of which we understand little, are the only peoples who have succeeded in maintaining large territories of the Amazon in conditions of equilibrium with the rich biodiversity, thanks to their harmonious relationship with the environment.'*

(Garcia, 1997).

Ecological categories are routinely deployed in descriptions of Amerindian life. These practices not only exist in the abstract in particular theoretical discourses, but form the framework for interpreting the practices in Amazonia. The themes 'special relationship', 'spiritual relationship' or 'harmony' correspond to values based on a range of assumptions, often highly debatable (Alvard, 1995; Hill, 1995) but nonetheless now rendered in international official language, and are integrated as part of the discourse of development. Turner (2000) has argued that the Kayapo, for instance, while they do impute certain forms of spiritual force or magical power, tend to think of such power in practical terms as sources of danger to be guarded against or of power to be appropriated by those with the special knowledge and skills to do so, not as grounds for mystical identification, production or respect. He continued:

> *'. . . whole set of attitudes and ideas presupposes and experience of the natural world as a system far beyond the power of human techniques to alter in any general way, and thus collectively impervious to human exploitative activities.'*

(Turner, 2000)

The Kayapo and their alliance with Northern environmental groups had their territories recognized by the Federal Government in the 1980s and 1990s. With the help of the Rainforest Foundation, the Kayapo became internationally known in their campaigns to gather support for their land demarcations. Their territory is mostly contained in six reserves that cover a combined area of some 100 000 km². In 1991, the Yanomami campaigned with the support of anthropologist Alcida Ramos and environmental groups to extend the reservation's territory. The passage below is worth examining in some detail as it illustrates how the lives of Amazonians are translated by their supporters, and how legal causes are justified in employing imagery of the Amerindian life-world that reproduces and reinforces environmental meanings – an extract from a speech given in 1989 to the Attorney General of Brazil by Alcida Ramos to support land demarcation for the Yanomami.

> *'The way in which the Yanomami exploit their natural resources is the result of a long tradition passed on through countless generations and has attained a point of equilibrium in spite of extremely poor soils, so that they have succeeded in sustaining a growing population without depleting the forest. It is unquestionable that the Yanomami in Brazil need a territory of over nine million hectares; not only to maintain an economic, social and political standard of living that has proved its efficiency in the preservation of rainforest for centuries but also to guarantee the necessary space for future generations to provide continuity to their culture. All of these considerations show very clearly not only that the Yanomami are capable of extracting a sustainable livelihood from the environment, but also it is they who can adequately protect the ecological stability of their territory.'*

(cited by Rocha, 1999: 31)

The extract is useful in assessing a range of ecological values and themes attributed to Amerindian peoples. The argument that Amazonians practise conservation despite poor soils is a theme examined by Meggers (1971) and subsequently criticized by Nugent (1981) and Johnson (1982). Here the assumptions made depict the practices of Amerindians of possessing 'eco-foresight', and suggest that over time this has resulted in a static set of circumstances where forest resources are maintained. Studies have suggested that the particular use of soils, game and forests may be a by-product of the lack of technology and small population in the regions, rather than any conscious attempt to prevent the depletion of natural resources (Hill, 1995; Turner, 2000). It has been proposed that a conservation ethic is not practised in these areas, so challenging this argument (Redford and Stearman, 1993; Alvard, 1995).

Ramos argues that the Yanomami have been practising their form of existence for thousands of years. But if it has existed for thousands of years, why is it framed in the language of contemporary development policy? The struggles for indigenous land rights have been translated into categories by international development institutions, and Amerindian systems are recast as 'sustainable livelihoods' or 'sustainable development'. Both sustainable livelihoods and sustainable development are dominant models of environmental development (Adams, 1995; Chernela, 1995; Coomes, 1995; Henrich, 1997), and both imply a form of economic practice that does not rely on the 'unsustainable' use of forest resources.

But to what extent have conflict and ambiguity always featured as an ongoing part of the eco-Indian discourse? Redford and Stearman (1993) raise concerns as to the roles of indigenous peoples and biodiversity. They reprint an article that was first published in *Cultural Survival Quarterly* in 1989 by the Coodinadora de las Organizaciones Indienas de la Cuenca Amazonica (COICA). COICA represents about 229 native Amazonian groups, comprising

1.2 million people in Peru, Bolivia, Ecuador, Brazil and Colombia. The issues that concern these indigenous groups include the following.

> 'We are pleased and encouraged to see the interest and concern expressed by the environmentalist community for the future of our homeland. . . . We recognise that through these efforts, the community of environmentalists has become an important political actor in determining the future of the Amazon Basin. . .
>
> Our concerns: we are concerned that you have left us, the indigenous peoples, out of your vision of the Amazonian Biosphere. The focus of concern of the environmental community has typically been the preservation of the tropical forests and its plant and animal inhabitants. You have shown little interest in its human inhabitants who are also part of the biosphere. . . . Whilst we appreciate your efforts on our behalf, we want to make it clear that we never delegated any power of representation to the environmentalist community nor to any individual or organization within that community.
>
> What we want: we want you, the environmental community, to recognise that the most effective defence of the Amazonian biosphere is the recognition of our ownership rights over our territories and the promotion of our models for living within the biosphere.'
>
> *(Redford and Stearman, 1993: 249–50)*

This is an interesting issue. Not only northern environmentalists are promoting ecological claims about Amerindian practices – this document serves as one example (of many) where Amazonian groups also employ the language of environmentalism. This is a paradox, and has caused great anxiety in the region. On the one hand, Amerindians have clearly promoted their causes by employing environmental imagery and language; on the other, many have subsequently engaged in practices which are antithetical to the environmental movement, such as logging timber or mining. The ideology of environmentalism serves as a powerful frame in which divergent groups can express their concerns. According to Redford and Stearman (1993), if indigenous peoples have presented themselves uncritically as 'natural conservationists', is it only because they recognize the power of this concept in relaying support for their struggle for land rights, particularly from important international conservation organizations. Hill (1995) argues that, regarding indigenous conservation practices, she sees 'no empirical evidence' of conservation practices. Hill also has this to say:

> 'Although native knowledge of the forest is indeed impressive and important, the native secret of sustainable use lies simply in low population densities and low levels of technology. Natives often know less about long-term sustainable use than the average student of conservation biology. They frequently care little about the long-term ecological impact of their subsistence activities because they have no history of experience with the problem. Nevertheless, native peoples can rapidly come to appreciate conservation concepts and are likely to be major allies of international conservation organisations because they have some goals in common with such groups.'
>
> *(Hill, 1995: 806)*

This statement is interesting, as it challenges many contemporary notions promoted by anthropologists and ecologists (Warren et al., 1995; Posey, 2000) that indigenous peoples have 'ecological' knowledge about their environments. The extent to which environmental groups will continue to support Amerindian land claims will be based on how these current problems and disputes are reconciled. Finally, this material can also have the inadvertent effect of being used in the promotion of anti-indigenous political agendas. To challenge notions of 'ecological noble savages', as Rajinkra Puri argues:

> 'Policy makers unfamiliar with the issues might mistakenly decide to exclude all native peoples from national parks and conservation areas or to over regulate their use of resources rather than leave control to "traditional" means because of the fear that they are contributing to species extinction.'

> (Puri, 1995: 810)

Many native peoples have been cleared off lands for the protection of conservation parks,[4] demonstrating how the constructions and continued existence of Amerindian life-worlds are still greatly dependent on relations that are external to them, and that these relations are continually and potentially transformed by socio-economic relations of the states and institutions of dominant societies. In some areas of the world, indigenous peoples are increasingly being moved off the land to make way for conservation areas. This demonstrates how the fragile relations between environmentalists and indigenous groups should remain an area of interrogation for development workers.

THE ENVIRONMENT – THE NEW BATTLEFIELD

The difficulty with negotiating indigenous land rights in environmental language cannot be underestimated. While international support for indigenous communities may be secured, this support correspondingly structures the forms of development that recipient groups are expected to practise. The representations of indigenous life-worlds as incompatible or hostile to development have also been contested by Joseph Henrich (1997). Henrich challenges two prevalent ideas about indigenous groups. First, he argues that environmental degradation is caused by 'externally-imposed political, legal and market strategies', which compels indigenous peoples to pursue 'short-term, unstable economic strategies'. Second, he challenges the notion that, if given territories, indigenous peoples will implement their 'traditional knowledge in conservation resource management practices'.

Joseph Henrich's work in the Peruvian Amazon among the Machiguenga Indians is an interesting account of the desire for market integration felt by indigenous peoples who, while having the opportunities to retreat from areas where the market is operable, still prefer to live and work in these sites. Moreover, it is not that these development practices have recently occurred due to 'new' globalized relations. Cleary (2000) begins to illuminate the historical complexities of indigenous and non-indigenous interactions. Cleary disputes the notion that 'Indians' are opposed to mining, farming and commercial interests. He highlights several cases among the 'Mundurucu, the Yanomami, and the Macuxi' which encouraged some to 'return to their home areas and set up indigenous mining operations on a small scale from the 1960s onwards'.

The rise of environmentalism, combined with a 'global' indigenous movement, has begun to underscore a number of debates that appropriate the ecological mythology of the Indian life-world and hybridize these representations by promoting 'essentialisms' for political and strategic purposes (Fisher, 1997). Conklin (1997: 711) examines the role of body painting and dress employed by indigenous activists in their confrontations with state officials and international institutions. She says that 'native costume took on new meanings in the 1980s with the rise of environmentalism', because the

'nature of contemporary eco-politics – especially its dependence on global media – intensified pressures for Indian activists to conform to certain images.'

(Conklin, 1997: 712)

The displacement of indigenous clothes from ceremonial contexts to public confrontations with the state, media and international community is a conscious strategy of particular activists. On the other hand, it is a procedure that is necessary in a world obsessed with sound-bites and the media. Turner (2000) has argued against the romanticization by Northern environmentalists of Amazonian Indian peoples as 'primitive ecologists'. He claims that indigenous peoples are depicted as representing 'a spiritual feeling of kinship for everything natural'. This argument, he suggests, is promoted by 'certain anthropologists' (such as Posey, 2000) that the Kayapo possess and practise a highly sophisticated 'science' of forest 'management', through which they have virtually created the forest through a kind of ecological gardening (Turner, 2000). Ramos (1994) has argued that environmental development organizations are interested in Amerindians as long as these groups serve ecological agendas. She examined a conflict between the Tukano of the upper Uaupés region and the development organizations. The Tukano had signed agreements with a mining company and the military. The Paranapanema mining enterprise presented the Indians with the service of controlling illegal gold prospectors from their land in exchange for mineral exploitation on an industrial scale. The military promised the Indians schools, hospitals and funding from economic development, in exchange for a huge reduction of their traditional lands in the Uaupés region (Ramos, 1994: 154). This agreement, according to Ramos, cost the Indians a long and bitter ostracism by the indigenous community. After two years the Paranapanema abandoned the area, arguing that the resources

were not worth the investment, and reneging on their commitment to provide schools, hospitals and resources for community improvement. When
the Tukuno later approached a Brazilian NGO to support their case for
compensation, they were castigated. Ramos suggested that external NGO
influence in the region has led to the bureaucratization of indigenous goals
and forms of organization, creating an image of the Indian which was
hyperreal, and an Indian imagery that absolved them of their contractions,
ambiguities and complexities. In recent years these tensions have become
increasingly marked, as Turner explains:

> '. . . some environmentalists and ecologists have reacted to recent cases of indige-
> nous groups who have permitted ecologically destructive practices like mining or
> logging on their land in exchange for fees. The Kayapo again have served as a lead-
> ing example, this time as villains rather than heroes.'

> *(Turner, 2000)*

According to Headland (1997), the Kayapo are no longer interested in serv-
ing as natural conservationists for Northern environmental groups. In
1993, US$15 million was earned from selling the natural resources on their
land – logs, gold and certain plants (the latter to the Body Shop). Of the
3500-member Kayapo nation, many are reported to own cars, city apart-
ments, video cameras, televisions and aeroplanes. Hill argues that support
for indigenous land rights should rest on two assumptions. The first is that,
regardless of whether peoples behave as conservationists, they should have
inalienable rights; and the second, whether native peoples practised conservation in the past is unlikely to be relevant to whether they practise it in
the future (Hill, 1995).

The narrative of environmentalism is employed as a strategic vehicle by
the Yanomami, Kayapo, Deni and other groups to promote agendas that are
ambiguous in meaning. There are three positions that aim to explain this
eco-Indian phenomenon.

One argument suggests that the representations of Indians as ecological
is of eurocentric origin. Indigenous groups have been forced into this
mould by powerful agendas of Northern institutions, and hence indigenous
groups have exploited the narratives of environmentalism to support their
own agendas (Redford and Stearman, 1993; Conklin, 1997; Ramos, 1998).
Conklin typifies this argument:

> 'Western images of Indians are the product of Western discourses. These images
> often say more about Westerners than about Indians and tend toward simplistic
> notions that do not encompass the complex realities of most native lives.'

> *(Conklin, 1997)*

While this argument undoubtedly has some merit, it does depict indigenous peoples as passive victims in the environmental debates.

The second argument is proposed by environmentalists who claim that
Indian groups have falsely gained their support in land right campaigns,

only then to introduce a market economy in their areas. This argument may be subdivided. On the one hand, many think this is outright manipulation of environmental agendas; but on the other, some suggest that indigenous peoples have acted 'unconsciously' due to the impact of global pressures. Thus, when given land, instead of protecting it they allow its destruction in exchange for money.

The third argument is expressed by Turner (2000), who sees no conflict between the Kayapo's use of environmental language in their campaigns to acquire larger reserves as well as logging and mining for fees. Turner explains that partnerships formed between commercial companies and the Kayapo are conducted within the parameters of Kayapo lifestyles:

> 'Logging in the Kayapo area has been almost exclusively for mahogany, the most valuable of the tropical hardwoods, but one for which the Kayapo has no indigenous uses. Mahogany grows sparsely, with individuals trees scattered at wide intervals through the forest. The logging roads that must be cleared to take out the huge trunks cause more damage to the forest than the cutting of the individuals trees, but even so, damage to the forest ecosystem from mahogany logging operations is minimal. . . Most Kayapo therefore do not regard the mahogany logging operations of their Brazilian concessionaries as serious threats to their environment, despite their temporary damage and negative effects such as driving off game. By Kayapo cultural standards, they are not ecologically deleterious to anything like the extent of the massive dams or gold mines against which they have mobilised militant actions.'

> *(Turner, 2000)*

Turner imaginatively tries to reconcile the selective economic exploitation of Kayapo land within the frame of non-market logic, although even here he is selectively recounting indigenous development practices. Mining is considered one of the official 'anti-indigenous' activities, yet evidence suggests that indigenous peoples joined mining organizations during the 1960s and continue to have contracts with them (Ramos, 1994). Additionally, indigenous groups have become better organized and more able to deal with commercial and legal institutions, who, in the past, would not have given them any consideration.

CONCLUSIONS

This chapter has sought to address the theme of communication, ironically, by examining bad communication practices. The case of Amazonia illustrates that there can be no set formulae for communication, decided in the abstract and imported into each and every situation, as each circumstance and set of issues needs to be addressed afresh. What the cases do express is that dominant agendas still frame practices. In this case, the dominant agenda is the environment, and this agenda itself is continually framing relationships between groups and development institutions. In many respects, indigenous groups have employed ecological language in order to gain land rights and support, because this language has the most listeners and, correspondingly, the greatest resources. If Amazonian groups use environmental language one minute and buy cars and aeroplanes the next, this means that they are using development language to obtain the resources they want and need. Development practitioners should ensure that indigenous groups are allowed to express a range of development objectives, free from the influence of the latest fashionable development agendas. This will only result from better communication practices.

CHAPTER TEN

Making differences: cities, NGOs and the cultural politics of development discourse

Carl O'Coill

'So geographers in Afric maps,

With savage pictures fill their gaps

And o'er uninhabitable downs

Place elephants for want of towns'

Jonathan Swift[1]

The field of development has produced a vast and multifarious body of knowledge about 'Third World cities'. The topic unites texts from disciplines as diverse as economics, political science, public administration, sociology and anthropology, as well as planning and architecture. This covers everything from cultural determinants of architectural form to the practicalities of urban waste management. Not surprisingly, academics outside the field often react with suspicion when confronted by the 'irreducible untidiness' of development studies (Hulme and Turner, 1990: 8). How can such an apparently disparate set of research interests constitute a coherent body of knowledge?

In the literature on cities and development, we find very little to justify the general field of discourse. If the geography of the 'developing world' is defined at all, it is usually defined unproblematically in terms of national economic statistics. Sometimes the controversy surrounding terms such as 'Third World' or 'developing country' is acknowledged. Generally, however, difficulties of definition are quickly dismissed, and research is justified by reference to the supposedly self-evident reality of the cities and countries specified within the investigation. Gilbert and Gugler maintain they use the category 'Third World' merely as a 'convenient shorthand' to denote the nations they list in Africa, Asia and Latin America (1992: 6–7). Similarly, Hardoy and Satterthwaite may criticize development's many 'inaccurate generalizations and conceptions', but it seems that they do so not in order to reject its terminology, but merely to validate their own claims to discover 'what is actually happening in Third World cities' (Hardoy and Satterthwaite, 1989: 9). Like most authors who write in this area, they presuppose that the discourse of development is capable of accurately representing real places.

This chapter argues that urban research in the field of development has never accurately described the world, and cannot do so. It draws substantially on evidence from Kenya, and aims to show that development academics' interpretations of non-Western cities have been shaped by understandings that are not only culturally specific, but are also political. Development is not a tangible process or even a quantifiable goal (notwithstanding the wealth of positivist literature that assumes otherwise). It exists only as a domain of knowledge or 'discourse', a particular combination of signifying practices, vocabularies, narratives, images or ideas (Barnes and Duncan, 1992: 8). And, like all discourses, it bears the cultural imprint of its creators. From the very first writings in the field to the present, researchers have been preoccupied with imaginary differences and hierarchies. The 'Third World city',[2] as described in development discourse, is not an empirical reality. It is a Western invention, and an imaginative construction that has helped to sustain a geometry of power and control that the West has exerted over its non-Western 'others' in one form or another since the first days of colonialism.[3] Consequently, this chapter concludes, development discourse is actually a barrier to meaningful communication between Western and non-Western people.

BUILDING HEGEMONIES: THE SOCIAL CONSTRUCTION OF THE 'THIRD WORLD CITY'

In November 1991 an international workshop on cities and development was held at University College London. In addition to the usual gathering of academics, the workshop was attended by representatives from the World Bank, the UN Development Program (UNDP), the German Development Agency (GTZ) and the former UK Overseas Development Agency (now DFID). This event marked something of a shift in the field of development generally, that is, the revival of the city as a development imperative. Arguably, it was also one of the first times that official donors began to define a place for non-governmental organizations (NGOs) in the arena of urban poverty alleviation, enlarging further a form of 'charitable development' that has been expanding rapidly under official patronage since the early 1980s. In the published proceedings that followed the workshop, Nigel Harris noted the significance of this new urban agenda. He drew a vivid picture of the emerging landscape in 'developing countries' and the enormity of the task ahead. After presenting the reader with a whole series of alarming statistics and predictions about population growth in 'Third World cities', he tells us:

'The most striking feature of this [rapid process of urbanization] is the vast spread of squatter settlements and shanty towns, ill supplied, if at all with basic amenities. Rapid environmental deterioration, giant traffic jams, violence and crime, urban sprawl eating into the countryside, these are some of the most striking visible features of the growth of large cities in developing countries.'

(Harris, 1992: x)

Most development academics are probably familiar with the image of disorder and crisis typified in Harris's representation of the generalized 'Third World city'. Devas and Rakodi (1993) have remarked that descriptions like this are something of a cliché in the field of urban development. But such descriptions form the standard entry point for nearly every undergraduate and postgraduate dissertation on the city in development studies. It almost seems as if the imagery itself is a mandatory learning requirement on the development curriculum. Although Devas and Rakodi recognize the hackneyed language, they still follow the convention themselves, adopting a similar style of writing and presenting all the usual statistics to emphasize their point. The researcher, they maintain, cannot escape the 'basic facts' of maldevelopment in Third World cities.

Escobar (1995) and Crush (1995), two critics of development writing from a post-structuralist position, maintain that images such as these are prevalent in development generally and can be traced throughout the history of the discourse. They offer a very particular explanation for their prevalence. Representations of disorder, they maintain, were the stock-in-trade of the European colonist in the eighteenth and nineteenth centuries. They signified not so much real disorder as difference, or the absence of an imagined order that was peculiarly white and Western. Then, as now, the purpose of such representations is to discipline as well as to describe. Historically they have provided a justification for outside intervention in the territories of other people and, ultimately, for the re-ordering of non-Western societies in the image and, it seems, in the interests of Western power.

Understandably, some people may find this argument difficult to accept. How can anyone equate an important and vibrant field of study – urban research – with racist colonial prejudices when so much effort is so clearly directed towards improving the welfare of urban populations?

This chapter proposes that urban research in the field of development is a case that illustrates particularly well both the racist foundations of development discourse and its disciplinary functions. Examination of changes in the representation of African cities in Western academia and media tells us a lot about the place of race in development discourse, primarily because most of Africa's cities were built by white Europeans and, at one time, inhabited by them.

Throughout the colonial period the disorder Europeans perceived in other peoples' territories was generally explained in terms of a hierarchy of race. Different 'races' were characterized by differing traits and capacities, and often the social hierarchy that Europeans sought to impose was expressed through the metaphor of time. At first, racial differences were seen as a given part of the natural world. 'Races' were mapped along an evolutionary timescale reflecting differing degrees of biological advancement. Later, cultural development was used as the marker, and different societies were positioned in anthropological time in accordance with the degree to which they were thought to display or to lack the characteristics of civilization – 'the general standards for which the West took to be its own values universalised' (Goldberg, 1993: 4). According to Goldberg:

> *'Those of the East were acknowledged to have civilization, language, and culture. But, generically, the East was a place of violence and lascivious sensuality, the rape of which was thus invited literally as much as it was metaphorically. Africa to the South, by contrast, was the Old World of pre-history: supposedly lacking language and culture, the Negro was increasingly taken to occupy a rung apart on the ladder of being, a rung that as the eighteenth century progressed was thought to pre-date humankind.'*
>
> *(Goldberg, 1993: 29)*

These differences and hierarchies were carried over into descriptions of Africans' and Asians' engagement with urban life. In the British colonial mentality, the presence of an indigenous urban culture in Asia was itself taken as a sign of civilization. This was one of the traits that placed the Oriental 'race' above the African, whose urban history was generally not recognized. In consequence, urbanized Asians were more easily accommodated within this colonial perspective. In colonial Nairobi Asians may have been residentially segregated from Europeans, but they were acknowledged as permanent residents of the city and afforded a certain degree of autonomy on that basis.[4] The idea of urbanized Africans, on the other hand, was perceived as an aberration of nature and culture. From a colonial standpoint, their proper place was in a rural village society. Thus for most of the colonial period, despite the fact that Africans made up the largest segment of Nairobi's population, they were designated as merely temporary residents of the city and were subject to many more controls and restrictions than Asians. According to Lord Luggard, the author of the colonial policy of indirect rule, the urbanized African was a socially 'displaced person' (Werlin, 1974: 48).

Not surprisingly, perhaps, the image British colonists had of Africa as an uncivilized and chaotic terrain was rarely applied to the African cities they built for their own purposes. If one studies representations of Nairobi in the British press and in popular magazines from the 1940s and 1950s, prior to Kenya's independence, the picture one finds is quite the opposite of the 'Third World city' as commonly perceived today. At this time Nairobi was more usually seen as a place of order and prosperity. In 1950 it was the first town in the British Empire to receive a Royal Charter designating it a city. The article that appeared in *The Times* marking the event stressed the many similarities between Nairobi and ordinary English cities. Most British people who visit Nairobi for the first time, its author claimed, 'are surprised by its size and its modernity', its 'pleasant, red-tiled, English-style homes', 'golf courses', 'green lawns and tree-shaded gardens' (Anon., 1950: 7). The article is entitled 'From swamp to city within the span of a lifetime'. In the founding of Nairobi, it celebrates the imposition of a new and distinctly English order upon a pre-existing African landscape that was represented as both chaotic and desolate.

Now, let us stop for a moment and jump forward to 1964, one year after Kenya achieved its independence. In that year Charles Abrams published his book *Man's Struggle for Shelter in an Urbanising World*, one of the seminal sources on 'Third World' urban development. After providing the reader with a whole series of statistics and dire predictions about population growth and urban–rural migration in the 'developing world', Abrams gives us the following account:

> 'With the surge of population from the rural lands to the cities, a new type of conquest is manifesting itself in the developing world. Its form is squatting. . . Little one-roomed shacks built of adobe and scrap are cropping up in Medellín, Barranquilla, and Cali, Colombia, and in fact throughout Latin America. The colonies lack paved streets, a sewage system, and a water supply. Havana has a profusion of rude huts without sanitary facilities. In Algiers, tin-can towns, or bidonvilles, stand just five minutes away from the centre of the city in almost any direction. . . Around the edges of Johannesburg, South Africa, sprawl squatter colonies that are a chaos of shacks and hovels pieced together by the homeless and destitute. In India's larger cities, squatters can be found hanging on to their precious hovels in old forts or wherever they can find a foothold.'

(Abrams, 1964: 13–14)

What we have here is an early image of the 'Third World city' as a generalized landscape. Although Abrams's description is now well over 30 years old, remarkably, it is very similar in form to the description of the 'Third World city' Nigel Harris provides today. For me, however, what is most striking about this image is how completely different it is from the picture *The Times* portrayed of Nairobi in the 1950s. Why is this? Notwithstanding Abrams's account of squatting as 'a new type of conquest', most colonial cities were not suddenly swamped with shanty towns after independence. The shanty towns were always there. The depiction of Nairobi as ordered and prosperous in the British press of the 1950s makes sense only if one accepts that the shanty towns were not part of the urban landscape, that Nairobi was not a black African city but a white European city.

So what is the point being made here? Of course, after independence Nairobi was a black African city. That said, it would be wrong to suggest that one could account for the contrary descriptions of the colonial and post-colonial city purely by pointing to the change in colour. What these examples are intended to illustrate is the disciplinary function of discourse, the way that representations of disorder are used to signify cultural difference and to justify the control of 'others'. In almost all the articles written about Nairobi in the British press during the colonial period, the greatest disorder was understood to lie not within the city, but outside it in the form of the black African masses who threatened to return this pristine urban landscape to its savage beginnings. As we saw, however, Nairobi's boundaries, who was inside and who was outside the city, were not defined in spatial terms but in terms of cultural differences. The degree to which one was a resident of Nairobi depended not on one's physical distance from the centre of the city, but on one's cultural distance from the centre of civilization, the West. For the British, Nairobi to all intents and purposes did not have a black African population because Nairobi was a Western city. The line of difference drawn was not purely black/white, it was Western/non-Western or, on a more elemental level, other/same, them/us.

So why did this image of the colonial city change so suddenly after independence? First, when we look at Abrams's description, it is important to note that Abrams himself was not British; he was a naturalized American. In fact, most of the authors writing about urban issues in the so-called developing world in the 1950s and early 1960s were American. Hoselitz (1953), Friedmann (1965) and Mangin (1967) were all Americans. Cognisant of this, it is much easier to understand why the image presented was different. Americans were not accustomed to the subtle distinctions and gradations the British had drawn between black and white, Western and non-Western, in terms of either places or categories of people. For Abrams the line between 'them' and 'us' was more simply defined: there were no white American cities in Africa or Asia. The whole of the post-colonial world was seen as a generalized field of difference. The British could not participate fully in this peculiarly American vision until they had experienced what Stewart Hall calls 'a kind of historical amnesia' (Hall, cited by Hesse, 1997: 92). This was a period that instituted the 'forgetting of Empire' and established the notion that 'race is nothing intrinsically to do with the condition of Britain' (Hesse, 1997: 92).[5]

But of course colonial cities were portrayed differently after independence, one might argue – we all recognize now that life under colonialism was highly unjust, but nobody would expect the British colonial regime to acknowledge this fact by celebrating the existence of shanty towns in the midst of Nairobi, a city they had created. Surely Abrams and others like him were merely demolishing this pretence and pointing to the reality of the situation on the ground? No, in the urban disorder they identified, Abrams and others like him were more concerned with marking imaginary differences and hierarchies than describing any reality. How do we know this? Because the discourse of development, the discourse they created, is just as blind to the possibility of any form of disorder in Western cities as was the racist colonial discourse that preceded it.

Post-structuralist theorists maintain that words and images are invariably inhabited by 'traces' or footprints of other absent images or words, that the meanings ascribed to particular objects, groups of people or places depend entirely on their relation to, or difference from, other people and places (Sarap, 1993: 38). The specialism of urban development has always relied on the assumption that the West is diametrically opposed in every feature to the so-called 'developing world'. On this basis, the generalized 'Third World city' and its inhabitants are usually described only in terms of what they are not. They are chaotic not ordered; traditional not modern; corrupt not honest; irrational not rational; lacking in all of those things the

West presumes itself to be. The Americans, in constructing development discourse, maintained an essentially arbitrary cultural distinction, Western/ non-Western, in their descriptions of the post-colonial cities they encountered. They merely changed the signifiers of difference from racial traits to economic characteristics.[6]

Once again, evidence of this is provided by the many absences in the discourse, its geographical blind spots. In the past, capitalist European countries like Ireland, Spain, Portugal and Greece, as well as communist countries like Albania, Romania and Yugoslavia, have all fallen below the income level the World Bank set for membership of the developed world. But just as Nairobi was excluded from colonial depictions of Africa as a disordered terrain, these places were rarely, if ever, included in discussions of the developing world. To their credit, Gilbert and Gugler (1992) highlight this anomaly in their book *Cities, Poverty and Development*. However, they still followed the convention themselves.

The blind spots are not simply confined to national characteristics. The unspoken assumption that underpins most representations of the 'Third World city' in development discourse, that Western cities are not like cities in Africa, Asia or Latin America, has never been true. As Trinh T Minh-ha points out, there have always been Third Worlds in the First World, just as there have always been First Worlds in the Third World (cited by Featherstone, 1995).

This was certainly the case in the decade following the war, although it is not apparent in Abrams's work. Abrams lists a whole series of former colonial cities where squatting emerged in response to housing shortages. He compares this situation with the European experience of squatting. But he locates this experience in Europe's distant past, pointing to practices of land use prior to the Acts of Enclosure in Britain in the eighteenth century. In fact, squatting was rife in Europe after World War II. In Britain in the 1940s, tens of thousands of homeless people were squatting in disused housing, in army camps, in vacant office blocks and in the empty mansions of the wealthy (Friend, 1980: 110–118). In France, population growth and rural–urban migration on a scale comparable to post-colonial countries exacerbated urban housing shortages. Several hundred thousand people were still living in makeshift shanty towns on the outskirts of Paris and other major cities as late as the mid-1950s (Power, 1993: 40).

The fact that Abrams did not see these shanty towns cannot simply be dismissed as an accidental oversight. This omission reflects the endurance of a system of representation rather than the lack of vision of a single author. When Abrams chose to locate urban disorder in the West in its distant past, he was relying on a long-established discourse. He was stretching difference out along a linear timescale, drawing on a metaphor that was similar in outline, if not in detail, to the racist metaphor of hierarchy used by the British colonial regime.

Now, if we shift our attention to the present and look once again at Harris's account of the 'Third World city', we can identify precisely the same regularities. Harris maintains that the 'most striking visible features of the growth of large cities in developing countries' are the 'spread of squatter settlements and shanty towns . . . rapid environmental deterioration, giant traffic jams, violence and crime, and urban sprawl' (Harris, 1992: x). Now, by no stretch of the imagination could one say that Africa, Asia and Latin America have a monopoly on environmental decay, traffic jams, crime or urban sprawl. To my mind, all but the first of these are equally characteristic of the growth of large cities in the West. Americans, for example, produce more refuse and more greenhouse gases than anyone else on the planet. Greater Los Angeles is the archetype of urban sprawl. It is spread out over a 60 mile wide circle and, some argue, consists not of one, but five distinct cities absorbed within a continuous urban conglomeration. As for traffic jams and crime, notwithstanding the fact that the number of vehicles on US roads has doubled since 1970, more people are killed by gunfire in Los Angeles than by traffic accidents (Anderson, 1996: 359–60; Soja, 1996: 433–38; Beder, 1997: 233).

Harris is setting up the same hierarchy we identified with Abrams. It is present in the implied polarity between Western and 'Third World' cities, the unspoken assumption that the West is free of traffic jams. Later, it is stated more explicitly when he draws a comparison between nineteenth-century attitudes to urbanization in Britain and what he claims are entrenched anti-urban attitudes among governments in 'developing countries' (Harris, 1992: x–xiii). Harris's comments in this regard are especially ironic considering the agencies he was addressing; the World Bank, in particular, spent nearly two decades bullying post-colonial governments into prioritizing agricultural development and abandoning the social welfare programmes and import-substituting industrialization strategies that largely sustained urban populations.

It would be easier to tolerate the persistence of fictional differences and hierarchies in development discourse if such wrong-headedness could simply be put down to unthinking habit. However, the image development presents of the 'Third World city' cannot be seen as purely accidental. Western representations of 'other' people and places have almost always coincided with and reinforced Western interests. In colonial Nairobi, the racist stereotyping of urban Africans as uncivilized served a definite cultural–political purpose. It enabled Nairobi's Europeans to reinforce their own identities as a 'decent', 'upstanding', urbanized gentility, while simultaneously justifying the differential treatment they apportioned to Africans. The restricted access that Africans were afforded to the basic necessities of urban life, the frequent appropriations of land and property and the arbitrary expulsions, detentions and even killings, could more easily be accepted as legitimate so long as it was believed that Africans were 'not like us'. Since the end of the colonial period, it is primarily the discourse of development that has served to legitimate this differential treatment.

This is most evident when one contrasts America's relations with Europe after the war, with its treatment of post-colonial countries. Post-Marxists refer to the arrangement that emerged between America and other Western nations after the war as 'Fordism' (Harvey, 1990; Lipietz, 1992). Theorists in international relations refer to it as the 'post-war hegemonic order' (Gill, 1992, 1993; Cox, 1993). After the war, America could have reduced Europe to the level of an underdeveloped economy by exposing its industries to relentless competition in free trade. Instead it chose to finance the reconstruction of its competitors' industries and to tolerate the protectionist bias Europe employed in international trade. According to Lipietz, the restraint America exercised in international trade allowed European governments the space to negotiate the social contract that ultimately united mass production with mass consumption. Increases in productivity in industry could be matched by higher levels of demand only when state regulation compelled the business community to pay higher wages to their workers, increase levels of employment and pay taxes at a rate sufficient to support social welfare programmes. Unbridled international competition could easily have undermined this system of regulation by encouraging industrialists to engage in continuous cost-cutting. The post-war order gave rise to what many have since called the 'golden age' of capitalism, a period of unparalleled economic growth and stability that raised living standards for millions of ordinary people throughout the Western world.

Outside the West, however, American magnanimity did not extend very far. Post-colonial nations were never fully included within these arrangements. While the American vision of 'development' appeared to offer a more inclusive path to 'progress' than had previously been the case, in fact the discourse was little more than a superficial reformulation of racist colonial prejudices. It provided a means of subverting popular aspirations for radical change in the context of anti-colonial struggles, while legitimizing the continued marginalization of non-Western peoples. After independence, development discourse worked to undermine indigenous customs of ownership as well as an expanding communist ideology, both of which threatened to obstruct the expansion of Euro-American capitalism in the former colonies. And it achieved all this while providing very little in the way of tangible benefits to non-Western people. There was no Marshall plan for Africa. The limited assistance post-colonial countries received in development aid was usually tied more directly to short-term Western interests. As a portent of things to come, Kenya began its independence in the 1960s owing a debt of £29 million, a loan arranged by the World Bank to ensure that departing British colonists would be paid for returning part of the land they had originally stolen from the indigenous population (Leys, 1975: 74).

In the decades after the war, in keeping with national Fordist arrangements, urban development was seen almost entirely in terms of state planning within a national or local context. Today, city managers compete globally to attract inward investment and the business community, rather than the state, dictates the terms under which development occurs. The explanation most often given for the emergence of this 'market-friendly'

approach to urban development is government failure. Government management failed in the 1970s, many have asserted, because state bureaucra-
cies were inherently inefficient. Post-Marxists argue that the failure was
wider than this; it involved the gradual collapse of the post-war compromise in the West, and the breakdown of the entire system of economic and
social regulation upon which it was built. The post-war order, they maintain, is currently being replaced by an even more exclusionary system of
'flexible accumulation' (Harvey, 1990: 121–89), or what in common
parlance is often referred to as the 'neo-liberal' economy.[7] How did this
happen? According to Castells (1991: 231), an important faction of the business community was, and is, willing to do whatever is necessary to rein-
state the pre-war conditions of low wages, low welfare spending, low
corporate taxes, minimal regulations and weak unions consistent with high
profit margins.[8] From the 1980s onwards, rather than resisting these
demands, Western governments chose to encourage them.

As long as America and its partners in the West sustained the post-war
social contract, one could argue that the differences established within
development discourse made some sense. Poverty in the West simply did
not occur on anything like the scale of post-colonial countries. This is no
longer the case. The collapse of the post-war order has brought about a
huge increase in levels of poverty and inequality across the entire globe.
The expression 'there are Third Worlds in the First World' is truer today than
it has ever been in the past. There are now more than 37 million people
without work in OECD countries (UNDP, 1997: 3, 1998: 27). Over 42 thousand people are officially classed as homeless in London (Shelter, 2001: 1).[9]
Recent estimates place the number of homeless in Los Angeles County at
more than 200 thousand (Wolch, 1996: 390). Nigel Harris may be right
when he implies that shanty towns are found exclusively in the 'developing
world'. However, the only reason there are no shanty towns in Los Angeles
is because any attempt by the homeless to build makeshift shelters in the
city is usually met with the kind of immediate and brutal repression
students of development more commonly associate with 'Third World'
regimes (e.g. Davis, 1992).

The support governments everywhere have shown for the work of NGOs
in recent years, and for voluntarism in public life generally, must be seen in
the context of the ascendancy of neo-liberal doctrine and the growth in
inequality worldwide. The trend towards voluntarism does not reflect a
rising interest in popular democracy as is commonly presumed, but a
deeply cynical abandonment of post-war concerns with social welfare and
social justice.

Africa's cities would not be in the deplorable condition they are today if
official development agencies had shown as much concern for the welfare
needs of urban populations in the 1980s as they did in previous decades.
Notwithstanding its failings, Kenya's state-led economy of the 1960s and
1970s did at least sustain a narrow, urban middle class and help to finance
a social infrastructure that, while not comparable to Fordist conditions in

the West, nevertheless served a wider urban population. Since the 1980s, the imposition of neo-liberal policies under structural adjustment programmes has led to chronic disinvestment, urban–industrial decline and deepening poverty, not only in Kenya's cities but throughout Africa.[10] Charitable development will not rectify this situation.

In Nairobi, those few NGOs that are active in urban areas work with hundreds of people or, at best, a few thousand, when more than half a million live in shanty towns with little or no access to adequate shelter and increasingly insufficient means to pay for basic services such as health and education.[11] However, charitable development is an inadequate response to urban poverty, not merely because the scale of assistance provided by NGOs is almost negligible.[12] It is inadequate because voluntary organizations are incapable of providing the kind of public control that is necessary to protect people from exclusionary market relationships, whether in international trade or in urban housing markets. Nor can they perform the redistributive functions the state must undertake in order to establish an equitable and effective system of social welfare. If one asks why NGOs did not figure prominently on the development scene in the 1960s and 1970s, the most likely answer is because, at the time, this fact was widely appreciated.[13]

Once again, there are many similarities between shifting attitudes in the West and in post-colonial countries. In Britain, official attitudes to charity altered considerably in the 1980s, to the extent that voluntary sector provision became accepted as a substitute for state welfare rather than merely a complement. In 1979, government grants to voluntary sector organizations as a whole totalled £93 million; by 1986 this figure had increased to £300 million (Ware, 1989: 2). By the end of the decade, charity was being used to fund large-scale provision of social housing as well as health provision, both capital costs, like the building of new hospitals, as well as the routine costs of patient care (Hanna, 1991: 23). It should be remembered that the British National Health Service was established in the 1940s to overturn the inadequate and inequitable system of care provided by hospitals dependent on charitable funding. More recently, America's new president, the staunchly neo-liberal Bush, has made the substitution of state welfare with voluntary sector provision a central plank of his social welfare strategy.

In the context of welfare retrenchment and growing inequality worldwide, development discourse often claims to seek a global solidarity. However, it continues to define the world in two opposing halves, telling each half in a different way that their problems are separate. Advocates of development transform trade, environmental and labour rights into 'Southern' or 'North–South issues' and make appeals to Western charity to provide what the 'others' lack. These narratives feed into and reinforce other discourses of Western difference and identity in popular culture, the exotic in tourist representations of the post-colonial world, and the constant media images of chaos and anarchy in Africa – the only reports that ever seem to reach Western television screens. They all say the same thing, that their places are 'other' than ours, that their problems are not our own.

CONCLUSIONS

The argument often made in support of multiculturalism, that all cultural differences should be respected equally, is naive. It does not take account of the power dynamics of culture, the way cultural differences are constructed and propagated to further narrow social interests. Real differences do exist. But they can also be transcended in specific contexts to create relations of affinity and solidarity. Where we chose to draw the line that separates 'us' from 'them' is largely a political decision. Unfortunately, researchers in the field of urban development have always been far more concerned with promoting the latest strategies for development intervention than questioning the interests on which development practice is based. If we truly are concerned with the growth of poverty in the world today, we need to ask ourselves how effective is it politically for us to perpetuate the fiction that the 'First World' and the 'Third World' are two different places?

To conclude, one cannot 'communicate for development' because, as stated earlier, development is not a tangible process or goal, but a discourse. However, more and more researchers are also beginning to recognize that one cannot communicate effectively 'with' or 'through' development because the discourse itself is ultimately concerned with power and control. It does not provide a basis for a dialogue between Western and non-Western people on equal terms. And it discourages both parties from recognizing the common problems and common interests that span the West/non-West divide, in particular, the threat neo-liberal ideology presents to social welfare and social justice at a global level. For growing numbers of development sceptics, the most significant line of difference to draw today is not the line separating the West from 'the Rest', but the line separating apologists for the prevailing doctrine of neo-liberalism from others who seek its downfall. To paraphrase Arturo Escobar, we do not need any more alternatives of development, what we need now are alternatives to development (Escobar, 1995: 215).

PART II

CASE STUDIES

Broadcast for change: a Hands On approach to the delivery of empowering information to a global audience

Janet Boston

'As I was watching BBC on my television set I came across your programme . . . I come from a village in Nepal and this project of yours is something like manna from heaven . . . this new invention will be very beneficial for our project. We are currently working in 16 village development committees.'

Veritas, Nepal

Since its foundation in 1984, the international communications agency Television Trust for the Environment (TVE) has distributed more than 50 000 films and co-produced in the region of 700 programmes. Its partners include non-governmental organizations (NGOs), governments and UN agencies, as well as a network of 54 Video Resource Centres in the South which help facilitate local distribution among broadcasters and community groups alike.

Set up by the United Nations Environment Programme (UNEP), the Worldwide Fund for Nature (WWF) and Central TV (now Carlton Television), TVE's remit is to raise awareness of global issues relating to environment and development, primarily through television but also through new media. It was in response to the opportunities offered by satellite broadcasting that TVE's director, Robert Lamb, developed *Earth Report*, a weekly strand (a strand could be a series of programmes, but in this case it is a series within a series) which goes out on BBC World TV. From *Earth Report*'s debut in 1997 TVE has produced over 150 hours of television covering all the main issues concerning environment and development.

It was during the first year of *Earth Report* that TVE identified the need for *Hands On* – it was the programmes featuring 'how to' solutions and strategies that provoked the biggest reaction from viewers who wrote in asking for details about features and how they could find out more. This demand tallied with the experience of the Intermediate Technology Development Group (ITDG), which for many years had been receiving unsolicited enquiries from people around the world anxious to obtain more information on a whole range of development projects. Recognizing the demand, TVE joined forces with ITDG to develop *Hands On*, a multimedia project designed to meet viewer demand and deliver information to assist in creating more sustainable livelihoods.

The multimedia revolution is much talked about: *Hands On* practises it. While television acts as the cornerstone of the project, the Web outputs (audio and video streaming) and printed word (back-up information leaflets to accompany each profiled topic, and two books (Judge, 2001a,c)) are all key to the project's success. With over 2000 letters and 35 000 website hits per programme, *Hands On* has achieved a greater audience response than any other programme in TVE's history, with viewers from around the world writing, faxing and e-mailing ITDG's *Hands On* enquiry service for more information after each broadcast.

However, the impact of *Hands On* extends beyond the responses it has provoked. There is now firm evidence of the project's ability to catalyse new initiatives and change government policy. Examples include a World Bank grant award to the Playpump manufacturer to disseminate the technology further; the construction of 124 biogas plants in China due to the enthusiasm of a Chinese environmentalist who, having seen the programme, made a pilot project of one of the biogas plants featured in order to raise funds from the Canadian Development Assistance Fund; and the banning of polluting diesel three-wheelers in Kathmandu and the take-up of electric models in Nepal and India.

Other recognition for the series has come via the One World Broadcasting Trust's Global Village Award, which praised the programmes for showing 'people as problem-solvers not victims'. Dario Pulgar, an independent consultant, carried out an evaluation of the project which he describes as 'The best return for such a tiny investment I have ever seen'. This chapter draws heavily on Dario Pulgar's findings, as well as those of Priyanthi Fernando, to see how *Hands On* has successfully delivered empowering information to a global audience.

ADVERTISING FOR CHANGE

'I am compelled to appreciate your efforts to make the world environment clean and pollution free through your TV programme Earth Report . . . My particular interest is Hands On *section, especially the* Hands On *'Safa Tempo' . . . to be able to cope with the situation we are facing right now we need a solution like Nepal.'*

Naesm Qayyum, Pakistan

There are over one billion TV sets in the world. Seven out of ten are located in non-OECD countries. While the majority of programmes deliver imagery that propagates a consumerist lifestyle, far less than a fraction of 1 per cent of the funds committed to development assistance are spent on 'advertising' sustainable development, despite evidence of a public appetite for empowering information.[1]

TVE and ITDG specifically designed *Hands On* to address the need for practical information. The uniting theme for the stories is replicability and affordability: can a new technology or scientific breakthrough be readily applied, and how much will it cost the farmer, the community or the would-be entrepreneur?

Appropriate 'green' technology is often regarded as a second-rate solution. *Hands On* challenges this concept by carrying a mixture of 'high'- and 'low'-tech stories from Europe, Africa, Asia and Latin America. ITDG and TVE also see the need to challenge lifestyles in the North through the promotion of more appropriate technologies which can help reduce consumption. The reaction from the UK focus group in Cornwall demonstrates the importance of this goal:

> *'I found it interesting that it was developing countries that were using these innovative ways of obtaining energy . . . and we, a sophisticated country, were not doing.'*

Subjects covered include success stories drawn from agriculture, agro-processing, enterprise, energy, building and shelter, water and sanitation. Many of the *Hands On* features reveal the resourcefulness of 'poor' people and their ability to adapt and survive, particularly those living in hazard-prone areas.

The emphasis placed by *Hands On* on showing positive images of what people are doing to improve their own lives – particularly in the South – is appreciated in Priyanthi Fernando's study (Fernando, 2001). She begins with the premise that the view that transnational communications provide for global audiences is 'at best partial and more often distorted'. In her opinion, this skewed flow of information from North to South is often caused by the discourse of global news and current affairs, which provides people with 'negative images of the South'. To Fernando these negative representations are part of a strategy of positive self-representation of the dominant in-group (the North) and negative other-representation of the dominated outgroup (the South). It is in this context that Fernando sees *Hands On* questioning 'definitions of the powerful' by profiling a range of technologies that have been developed in local situations and run by local people doing it for themselves, be they in the South or North.

If the immediate objectives of *Hands On* are to increase awareness of the potential of environmentally sound science, technology and enterprise and to catalyse new initiatives, the long-term goal is to contribute to a global understanding that the kind of projects featured can help in the alleviation of poverty. Its other aim is to redress the way information is skewed to perpetuate negative images of the South.

However, as Pulgar (2001) points out, advertising for change takes time and the need to stay on air is critical: 'Any long-term change demands constant lobbying and visibility, therefore this recommendation is perhaps the most critical for this kind of work to succeed . . . therefore TVE should place a premium on collaboration with BBC World and continue to offer it *Hands On* for exclusive first broadcast.'

THE PACKAGE

'After viewing the biogas programme I was indeed very impressed by the ideas pre-sented. ...We had made a model 8m³ biogas tank ... and The Canada Fund informed us that our project had been approved.'

Li Guangyu, Guizhou Province Research Centre, China

Output

Designed before multimedia output became a communications prerequi-site, *Hands On* is unique for the equal emphasis placed on each of the pro-ject components – video, web and printed outputs. To date, *Hands On* has recorded examples of projects and sustainable practice and enterprise in 120 locations in more than 30 countries. As Dario Pulgar underlines, this task was more complex than generally perceived as it had to take both television and development needs into account:

'The materials – video, audio output and back up information – were all produced to meet strict broadcast deadlines on BBC World . . . and the Producers managed to cover several destinations in each programme in order to create a balanced combi-nation of high and low technologies and examples from North and South.'

(Pulgar, 2001)

Key to the success of *Hands On* is the selection of projects to film. This process is underpinned by several months of painstaking research. This involves canvassing and contacting TVE's and ITDG's partner organizations in Asia, Africa, Latin America and Europe, and talking with specialist agen-cies and networks such as WWF, Department for International Develop-ment, UNEP and the Global Environment Facility (GEF), as well as with community-based NGOs and other organizations.

'We are a small organization working for women's economic and social develop-ment in northern Nigeria. Your programmes on BBC have been very enlightening and challenging.'

Dr Shehu, Sokoto, Nigeria

TV programmes

To date, 26 five-minute features and 21 26-minute thematic programmes[2] (e.g. on housing, energy, credit, water, recycling and grassroots initiatives) have been broadcast on BBC World Television direct to 170 million house-holds worldwide. Initially designed as five-minute segments which would run in parallel to TVE's *Earth Report* series (which began as a five-minute strand), the BBC eliminated the five-minute filler items and instead offered TVE a 26-minute strand. '*Hands On 1*' therefore delivered two packages: six 26-minute thematic programmes; and 26 five-minute features which were placed within the *Earth Report* strand.

For the second series of *Hands On*, the partners agreed that the 26-minute format was more effective. This response was based on the reaction to the programmes and the fact that it was easier for a viewer to follow up on a feature if there was a constant trailing of details on how to access the back-up information over a period of 26 minutes.

> *'My friend and I are interested in setting up a recycling plant in Bangalore. We need details about how we can get started.'*
>
> Mohan Devadas, Bangalore, India

Hands On technical enquiries service

Using ITDG's well-established Information Services Unit as a base for the *Hands On* response, the development agency has successfully replied to over 2000 written enquiries generated by the programmes. Indeed, ITDG created a special *Hands On* team to respond to each enquiry within a week. For viewers who made specific requests not covered by the back-up information, individual responses are provided by appropriate technical specialists.

The role of an enquiries service is crucial for any initiative of this kind, as is the input from a specialist agency such as ITDG, which has the capacity to provide extra support and expertise when necessary. The need to respond rapidly should also be highlighted, as it is important not to discourage viewers who may want to implement what they have seen.

> *'I watched your programme on paper manufacturing from waste paper. I am the Dean of the School of Forestry at Copperbelt University. This information would be very useful for teaching purposes.'*
>
> Felix Njubo Kitwe, Zambia

Back-up information

The back-up for each programme is also produced by ITDG. This provides interested viewers with the opportunity to find out more and chase further contacts in case they want to try out the technology. The information can be accessed by web, e-mail, fax or letter. All the enquiries received by Intermediate Technology's technical enquiry service are logged for evaluation purposes. The overwhelming demand for back-up information has led to the publication of two books (Judge, 2001a,c) which will act as a lasting resource for those who find web access problematic, or for teachers who want to use the materials in their classes.

> *'Having watched* Hands On *(and recording it) I'm looking forward to using it for evening classes.'*
>
> Martin Randaces, Germany

Radio

State-of-the-art technology has been used to feed sound from each of the TV programmes through One World On Line Radio News Service. This enables radio stations around the world to 'pull' down the sound and edit and re-use it in a way that is suitable for their programming and audiences.

London Radio Service also featured *Hands On* items as part of its development strand, *The Way Ahead*, which has regular outlets to radio stations in Africa and Asia (Ethiopia, Gambia, Malawi, Mozambique, Nigeria, Pakistan, the Philippines, Tanzania, Uganda and Sri Lanka). While TV is rapidly becoming the way in which most people access information, no project of this kind should neglect radio or other audio outputs. They are crucial for reaching rural audiences, particularly in Africa.

> *'Hullo people, I watched a film on BBC . . . which was educative and interesting . . . I work as a freelance consultant . . . mainly for NGOs in the developing world and am based in Uganda and I would like to get more information on solar panels.'*
>
> *David Bizimana, Uganda*

Website

The *Hands On* web pages can be accessed by subject, date and title through TVE's site on www.tve.org and, with one or two rare exceptions, the back-up information has been produced online in time to coincide with the broadcast of each programme. These information sheets have deliberately been kept simple so that people can download them with relative ease.

Since the first broadcasts of *Hands On*, visits to TVE's award-winning website have increased from 7000 per programme to 35 000 – and numbers are rising. TVE and ITDG presume that the visits to the website are the primary means by which information is downloaded. Unfortunately, the One World Site does not allow either organization to trace the names and affiliations of the users.

Outreach

> *'Hoping to see more of your very interesting and informative TV programmes soon. Thanks for all your help in showing this type of programme that is of great help to us in developing countries.'*
>
> *Abdul, Aswan, Egypt*

Initial broadcast distribution via BBC World

The audience has been estimated by the BBC to include 170 million households worldwide in 167 countries spanning Europe, South Asia and the Middle East, Japan, Latin America, East Asia and Australasia. In India, BBC World is already carried in approximately 76 per cent of cable homes. A survey in India points out that the service is number one among Indian decision-makers (73 per cent). The additional homes are calculated from secondary carriers such as M.Net for Africa and terrestrial re-broadcasters in Sri Lanka and the Berlin/Brandenburg area of Germany. Although BBC World has established a new centralized research department to commission surveys and focus group studies, and is investing in a number of audience measurement studies around the world, no data have yet been made available to TVE.

It is not possible to know exactly how many people watch all or part of a TV programme. The feedback TVE gets for *Hands On* is used by the BBC in its audience assessments. Certainly TVE has benefited from the exponential increase in viewers through sub-carriers since it started in 1998. In western Europe and the Indian sub-continent the BBC now claims a bigger viewership than CNN, its main global rival. The BBC also points to its success in achieving carriage on national services in languages other than English – these include Japanese, Greek and Chinese, and a Spanish and Portuguese service to Latin America is starting up.

> 'First of all let me congratulate you for the best environmental programme I know! We learn so much from it! So many good examples you come up with. We are "planting the seed" of environmental awareness and we would like to get more information about several subjects you focused.'
>
> Carlos Canelhas, Portugal

Onward broadcast distribution

To ensure maximum exposure it is essential to have a clear distribution strategy. To this end, TVE granted commercial television rights of *Earth Report – Hands On 1* to Southern Star (formerly Primetime Television Associates). For the first series Primetime succeeded in placing the series with Odyssee-La Chaine Documentaire of France which covers France, Andorra, Monaco, Tunisia, Morocco, Algeria, Belgium, Luxembourg and Switzerland; Carlton Entertainment LT for the UK; TV3 Television Network for Ireland; XYZ Entertainment PTY Ltd for Australia; GMBH for Germany, Switzerland and Austria; and Media Park Thematic Channels for Spain. None of these contracts affected TVE's ability to place the series with broadcasters in economically developing countries, as there was a clause ensuring that Primetime would not pitch to these markets – many of whom receive programmes for the cost of the copy.

Although it is early days, *Hands On* series two has already been acquired by a major global broadcaster – National Geographic TV. This will mean that selected *Hands On* stories will receive a second global window in 16 languages to 85 million homes in 111 countries. Other broadcasters set to acquire the latest series include the Innergy Channel (a subsidiary of the prestigious UPC network going to 35 million homes in Europe and Israel in eight languages) and Worldlink, broadcasting to 30 million homes in North

America. A far greater audience will be achieved through a new GEF/EC-financed US$2 million project for Latin America which will see *Hands On* programmes in Spanish and Portuguese going to up to 145 million TV households, with full Internet back-up in both languages.

TVE should be commended for its ability to move with the market in order to secure the most effective distribution strategy – this is less simple than it sounds in an industry which is rapidly changing due to the ongoing changes in technology.

Non-broadcast distribution

Non-broadcast and multiplier distribution for *Hands On* is based on TVE's tried-and-tested dissemination strategies. NGOs, educational institutions, and relevant government and UN agencies are among those who will be targeted now that the second series of transmissions is complete.

ITDG is already using material from the programmes as part of its Europe-wide Sustainable Technology and Environment Project (STEP) which was launched at the NEC in Birmingham in November 1999. Other uses of the programmes include screenings at conferences to specialized policy-making audiences. Those which have been particularly successful include an International Water Conference in the Hague; a Sustainable Energy Conference in Brighton; and a World Bank Rural Development Week.

THE REACTION

The audience reaction to *Hands On* can be measured in many ways. For the purposes of this chapter it has been split into an analysis of two distinct reactions: spontaneous reactions from those who wrote in having watched the programmes on BBC World; and the monitored responses from those involved in the focus group trials for the evaluation from which most of these data have been drawn (Pulgar, 2001).

> *'I watched with rapt attention a documentary on waste/recycling . . . Consequently I am spurred with keen interest to make further enquiries.'*
>
> Oscar Macaulay, Nigeria

Analysis of spontaneous audience response to TV programmes

A breakdown of the requests over the life of the project consistently reveals that over 60 per cent of these are from private individuals interested in finding out more, either out of interest in the subject, or because they are anxious to adopt the technologies featured. What the figures do not reveal is the vast cross-section of viewers – ranging from embassy and donor representatives, extension workers and teachers to farmers and academics.

Although the typical profile of a BBC World viewer is 'a university-educated 20s to mid-40s entrepreneur', the outreach of the *Hands On* programmes goes far beyond this classification.

> '*I have seen your programme on BBC news channel. The device you used in Peru for charging battery seems quite interesting. I am a Bangladeshi and I need this device for the villagers of Bangladesh.*'

> *Ahteshamul H. Bhuia, Bangladesh*

The second major category of interest comes from the industrial and small business sector. This is significant as, if the technologies – particularly those that require more investment – are to be adopted, then entrepreneurs interested in generating 'green' profits are a key target. Likewise, if a parallel aim of the programmes is to encourage the adoption of more sustainable techniques, it is important to educate and inspire actual and would-be business, industry and community entrepreneurs. This was reinforced by the focus group trial in India, when the Calcutta Chamber of Commerce thought it would be a good idea to screen the programme at their meetings as 'they can be shown as practical examples'.

> '*I want to do business in India with all waste material which can be recycled . . . so please send me information about all the items.*'

> *CPN Desai, India*

NGO/Aid agencies and social development organizations are another significant group that the programmes have successfully reached. Their interest is important, as these are the groups who will go on to use *Hands On* with particular target audiences – women's groups, farmers and small-scale entrepreneurs.

> '*Referring to waterways, Save the Children Norway in Laos PDR would like to get information on Rampump in Nepal and Roundabout in South Africa.*'

> *Souksaichai Phaiboun, Save the Children, Laos*

The numbers of requests from those in further education anxious to use the programmes to introduce students to 'sustainable development' and 'appropriate technology' show that there is a strong demand from this group which *Hands On* should work towards addressing. It should, however, be noted that an analysis of the correspondence does not always reveal the organizational accreditation of the individual writing in. For example, one apparently 'person in the street' correspondent from Copenhagen was found to be a teacher-trainer who regularly used various programmes to show to Danish students.

> '*I am a teacher of introductory technology at a secondary school . . . I will like you to send me more information. . .*'

> *Sanusi Abdullahi, Nigeria*

Analysis of controlled response carried out through trials with focus groups

Evaluating the impact of communication projects is always problematic. Both ITDG and TVE were concerned to examine the response to *Hands On* by particular target audiences – NGOs, rural and urban community organizations, private sector entrepreneurs, research and academic institutions, national, local and regional policy-makers and TV broadcasters. Dario Pulgar was appointed to oversee this work, and convened a workshop in London attended by consultants from India, Bolivia and South Africa. At the meeting it was agreed that trials should take place in each region to examine two main issues: content and format.

In an analysis of content, each consultant had to find out how relevant and valuable the technologies and models were to the audience, how applicable and what they felt the impact could be on their communities.

In India and Bangladesh, the overriding perception was that the stories featured showcased interesting ideas and, even if the technology shown was not easily transferable, ideas were certainly of great use and could spark off newer innovations at lower cost. Examples of such features included 'Play Pumps', 'Inner Tubes' and 'Cashing In'.[3] 'Play Pumps' elicited the greatest response from the audience. 'Inner Tubes' was the kind of programme which was very popular across the audience groups, as it was a simple idea and easy to transfer technology. Each audience saw benefits from 'Inner Tubes' in their own terms. For example, the municipal corporation saw it as an effective and easy recycling tool; the pollution control board as an alternative to the polluting practice of burning tyres; the NGOs as an income-generating project; and students as an example of what a creative idea can achieve.

> 'The first story about the pump caught my attention right from the beginning because it showed children ... it was undoubtedly the best story and worth exploring.'
>
> *International organization focus group, India*

While there was debate over the issue of regional content and whether it would be useful to have a series focusing purely on local stories, the view recorded by the Pollution Control Board and Environment Department focus group echoes those of the others:

> 'Even if social conditions are different it is possible to find relevance from nearly all the stories you have shown ... there will be some group or other who will gain from seeing this as it will give them things to think about and replicate and innovate upon.'

One interesting factor was that participants made suggestions about the kind of progammes they would like, for example, more programmes on innovative technologies to reduce industrial pollution; stories showing government and private partnerships; and stories on occupational health.

In South Africa the findings were similar to those in India, the programmes that had most impact being ones which were straightforward, relatively easily transferable and related to specific local problems, such as 'Inner Tube', 'Waste Busters' and 'Vacutug'⁴; 'Cashing In' was also appreciated as there was no waste disposal in some of the focus group areas.

> *"Inner Tube" could . . . provide a fashionable commodity and design challenge that would be very appropriate for African hawkers in towns and cities.'*
>
> Student Focus Group, Witbank, South Africa

A particular feature of the South African focus groups was the immediate desire to implement what they had seen. For example, the issue of pesticide-free methods for cultivating crops was interesting to several groups as there was widespread recognition of the incidence of health problems caused by pesticides; another of the focus groups discovered that they could swap food types planted from season to season and were anxious to change their methods at once. There was a sense that the less-mechanized solutions were preferred, and a desire for more regional content.

> *'African empowerment concerns were key to this group who saw the concepts introduced as a milestone in generating jobs, skills improvement and eradicating health problems in the area.'*
>
> Witbank Video Resource Centre, South Africa

The trials in Bolivia used a different approach to finding out people's views which allowed them to come up with statistics on the different questions. The response to the question of relevance achieved a 100 per cent approval rating from both the political/business group and the NGO/CBO (community-based organization) group; while from the academic/media group it scored 96 per cent. Applicability was also high, with results of 94, 95 and 93 per cent, respectively.

> *'They are helping to create an environmental awareness and helping to protect what's left. There is a clear use of these for training so that low cost solutions combining organization and simple technology can be used to create jobs. They are excellent alternatives and really could be used . . .'*

High scores were also recorded for economic and environmental potential, with respective ratings of 97, 91 and 93 per cent for economic relevance; and 94, 100 and 96 per cent for environmental applicability. In general, women were more appreciative of the programmes than men, who were more sceptical. Comments revealed that the programmes generated a sense of urgency among viewers, who felt they must act on them.

> *'Bolivia is rich in diversity . . . but there are problems for which we depend on individual initiatives. In some cities we recycle rubbish . . . but the experiences of other communities show us we should experiment more urgently.'*

CONCLUSIONS

A comprehensive list of what has made *Hands On* successful in delivering empowering information – and which programmes have had the most impact – is limitless. Drawing on the responses from the focus groups and letters from the audience, it seems that the reasons for the success of the project are that programmes:

- are innovative and command the attention of viewers
- are relevant even under different social conditions
- demonstrate that there are possibilities to tackle complex development problems
- trigger the interest of potential entrepreneurs
- may be used for other purposes, such as teaching
- can mobilize private individuals in the North for collaboration with the South
- can trigger action, which in turn brings involvement by others to make things work
- lead to adoption of new ideas that can contribute to poverty reduction.

RECOMMENDATIONS

The above conclusions led the partners to make the following recommendations for future series of *Hands On* and other projects of this nature.

Needs to work as television

While the overall goal of the project must be to improve livelihoods, reduce poverty and safeguard the environment, it is important to recognize that *Hands On* or another similar multimedia initiative needs to work within a rapidly changing, highly competitive media environment – *Hands On* has to work as television in order to maintain its ability to reach an international audience through BBC World, with audiences who are becoming more sophisticated whatever their economic status.

Needs to select programmes to create change

The 'Safa Tempo' segment of *Hands On* demonstrated that it is possible to affect policy change by encouraging citizens to be aware of the dangers of polluting vehicles and to lobby for their removal, which is what happened when the Nepalese government banned all diesel three-wheeler taxis in favour of the electric safa tempos. Clearly, not all programmes can achieve this kind of impact. However, careful selection of features with the potential to affect larger change ought to be possible.

Needs mechanisms to channel resources

Many of the viewers writing in to the programme expressed the need to find credit to help them initiate projects. Another series should give far more weight to providing information, on screen and in the back-up information, on potential sources of grants (e.g. GEF small grants programme, NGO grants facilities in donor embassies, Shell Foundation, etc.) and low-interest loans (e.g. International Finance Corporation). TVE/ITDG should also consider providing guidelines on how to prepare grant and investment proposals.

Needs to increase capacity for versioning/adaptation

In line with TVE's policy of extending all its materials to the widest number of audiences and the greatest number of multiplying agencies, each *Hands On* programme includes a UK and international version, allowing dubbing into local languages. Nevertheless, there is an expressed demand to justify additional funding to allow versioning and repackaging which ought to be accommodated in any future initiative.

Needs to develop multimedia outputs, particularly back-up information

The multimedia back-up was intended to provided subscribers with the next level of information. Referral information was provided for users who wanted to act on the information. However, it appears that most users wanted more fulsome information and not to have to gather additional details from referral contacts. In future editions, TVE and ITDG should provide a more comprehensive and seamless package.

Needs to stay on air!

Any long-term change demands constant lobbying and visibility – as the only global English language 'rival' to CNN, TVE should place a premium on collaboration with BBC World and continue to offer it *Hands On* for exclusive first broadcast.

CHAPTER TWELVE

National and regional Internet-based research networks: lessons from the UK and Central America

Harry Smith and Paul Jenkins

INTRODUCTION

The need to enhance access to research in development issues, especially in order to aid the poor, has become a topic of debate in recent years. The development of the Internet is seen by some as an opportunity to achieve increased access, allowing for the exchange of knowledge between researchers as well as between researchers, practitioners and the wider community. However, there are limitations that need to be overcome. By far the highest access to Internet technology and infrastructure is concentrated in the North, and thus is greatly dominant in terms of knowledge dissemination through this medium. There is a political issue to be addressed: the decentralization of knowledge production, management and dissemination. A way forward is through initiatives that support institutional research capacity at local level, such as building and strengthening national and regional research networks.

Technology for the creation of Internet-based mechanisms to assist such networks is available and increasingly affordable, but the appropriate choice of means of support for network management and its time frame are crucial to ensure the creation of durable and sustainable research networks. This chapter discusses some of the theoretical and practical issues related to the establishment of Internet-based research networks, and describes some of the problems encountered in practice by two of these: a national network in the North, the UK-based North–South Research Network; and a regional network in the South, the Central American initiative INVESTIGA. The chapter draws lessons from these experiences and suggests ways to facilitate the creation of similar networks in other countries and regions. It builds on the authors' personal experiences in the establishment of both networks.[1]

RESEARCH NETWORKS

Knowledge transfer through networks

It is widely acknowledged among researchers and practitioners that knowledge transfer through networks is key to successful development at all levels. This knowledge transfer ranges from horizontal, between low-income dwellers and/or researchers, to vertical, through different levels of actors in city planning and management. The latter type of transfer is useful in the generation of policies and in informing decisions on the basis of research, or in research drawing on community members' tacit knowledge. It is a rich source of knowledge in itself, as suggested in Nonaka and Takeuchi's (1995) approach to knowledge transfer.[2] Horizontal knowledge transfer is equally important, and knowledge has long been recognized as one of the valuable resources shared through social networks (Fischer, 1982).

Among researchers there is a relatively well-established tradition in horizontal knowledge transfer, which is seen as essential to advance knowledge and avoid duplication. This has traditionally taken place through correspondence, publication of research products, workshops and conferences, as well as other means. Easier and more affordable forms of travel and the recent rapid development of information and communications technology (ICT) have facilitated this kind of exchange, as well as the creation of theme-based or area-based research networks. Without these technologies, the logic of networking would be too cumbersome to implement (Castells, 1996).

One focus in the field of urban development research is the creation of networks around specific sectors or areas of interest. These can often have a geographic basis in terms of membership or in terms of primary focus. Two examples of this are the North–South Research Network, which brings together researchers based in the UK focusing on human settlements in the South, and the Network for Research on Urbanization in the South (N-AERUS), which includes European researchers with knowledge or expertise on urban issues in developing countries. In parallel, the importance of building local research capacity in the developing world is increasingly recognized, and there is growing interest in creating research networks based there, including regional research networks.

What makes a successful network?

Starkey (1998: 14) defines a network as 'any group of individuals or organizations who, on a voluntary basis, exchange information or undertake joint activities and who organize themselves in such a way that their individual autonomy remains intact'. This definition assumes that the network is created by its members, although networks can be driven by external agencies. Starkey (1998: 17) warns against the use of the term 'network' when it is 'a result of top-down planning by the international research centres, aid agencies or NGOs that fund them' – thus Starkey might well be critical of the initiatives described in this chapter, as they were respectively led by the Centre for Environment and Human Settlements (CEHS) with Department for International Development (DFID) funding in the UK, and by UN Centre for Human Settlements (UNCHS; Habitat) community development

programme (CDP) in Costa Rica. However, not all actors in knowledge production and dissemination can afford to create networks that take advantage of the new technical opportunities, and this chapter argues that
sponsoring organizations have an important role to play. However, it is also
argued here that management of such regional networks needs to be
locally based, autonomous and politically grounded. If an international aid
agency recognizes the importance of development-related networks and,
among these, of research networks, how can it best establish and/or support these in order to achieve their intended benefits while at the same
time avoiding the problems centrally sponsored networks might typically
face?

Among the network benefits listed by Starkey (1998), those most relevant
to a research network would be that they facilitate the exchange and sharing of information, skills, knowledge, experiences, materials and media;
lead to less duplication of work and effort; create a joint awareness of concerns and problems; provide a critical mass for advocacy; can help address
complex development problems; and can provide members with a source
of peer support. All these benefits appear to fit the current agendas of the
major international aid agencies (see, for example, the Foreword in this
publication) with caveats perhaps in relation to the generation of advocacy.

However, there are problems that networks can often face. Again, Starkey
(1998) provides a useful list, of which those most likely to be encountered
by aid agency-sponsored networks would probably be membership disparity; domination; centralization and bureaucracy; separate realities; and
donor interference. Lack of resources, in terms of funding, would not necessarily be a problem if a resource-rich agency is supporting the network,
but this strength is at the same time a weakness, as continuing reliance on
aid agency funding is a form of dependency that could entail lack of sustainability. It is important to establish a balance between adequate funding
support and sustainability – accepting this may take time.

Drawing on Starkey's (1998) guidelines for networks, in order to foster a
successful research network yet avoid domination, an international aid
agency or other sponsoring organization would have to ensure that the network has clear objectives that are established and accepted by the network
members/primary users. It would need to initiate concrete activities that
are interesting and beneficial to members, but avoid keeping total control
over network activities, permitting as high a degree of autonomy as possible. Significantly, Starkey (1998) points out that if institution-based networks help to facilitate independently organized activities by network
members, this will improve prospects for network sustainability in the
event of the central unit closing down. Ideally, the sponsoring
agency/agencies would establish a representative and committed core
group of active members who would take initiatives and be responsible for
coordination, management and logistics, but also rely on delegation.

It is essential that resources be provided until the network is able to
achieve a sustainable level of user support. As Starkey (1998: 38) notes: 'The

more a network can be user-supported, the stronger it will be.' User support is not only financial, but is also reliant on the levels of trust and mutual obligation and collaboration that are struck among its members (Frances et al., 1991; Powell, 1991). Strong reciprocity and a shared perception of the network's benefits will probably result in higher commitment from its members and a higher chance of these procuring alternative means of funding. These therefore ought to be aims for the sponsoring agency if it envisages setting up what will eventually become a self-sustaining network. Widespread information on the network is also an integral part of its establishment – if potential members/users do not know of the network, it cannot function adequately.

Finally, an important element in establishing a research network is the time frame. Some of the problems outlined above might pose varying levels of difficulty to consolidated networks, but could become decisive in terms of network continuity when these are still fledgling. The following case studies of research networks established with DFID and UNCHS (Habitat) support, respectively, show how even if other potential problems are addressed, an interruption of funding support at an early stage can prove fatal for network sustainability. The case studies first set out the institutional context and justification for the research networks, then describe their initial activities and analyse how these compare with the guidelines described above, finally drawing conclusions from each experience.

THE NORTH–SOUTH RESEARCH NETWORK

Background

Despite the seeming availability of research products to academics, students and professional practitioners in the UK who are involved in human settlements issues in the South, there has been no research network for them to share and access up-to-date research.[3] Perceiving this, in early 1997, CEHS, hosting the 14th Inter-Schools Conference on Development in the School of Planning and Housing in Edinburgh, took the initiative to suggest the creation of such an Internet-based network. With the endorsement of the conference, CEHS approached DFID with a proposal to develop such a network. This initial proposal was well received and, after becoming more familiar with the technological options, CEHS developed it and obtained seed funding from DFID in early 1998, allowing the preparation of the initial website in time to launch the North–South Research Network at the 15th Inter-School Conference in Cardiff in early 1998.

Objective and focus

The objective of the Network is to facilitate interaction between researchers in training and teaching institutions in the field of human settlements, based in the UK, but oriented to the South. The Network focuses on providing mechanisms for information selection and transfer by the Internet, both static – through presenting existing research via a searchable database – and dynamic – through a digital conference facility for presenting developing research and discussion/feedback.

The focus is research in human settlements – understood as a wide definition including architecture, building technology, environment, infrastructure, housing and planning. Eligible research was any form of research within these categories of relevance to the developing world or South, developed by individuals or institutions in the UK. These latter were seen as the client community, while the user community was anyone accessing and using the information worldwide via the Internet.

Why distinguish between client and user communities, and why limit this to researchers based in the UK? First, although DFID provided seed finance for the first year, from the beginning it was apparent there would be some costs associated with network sustainability. In the first instance, CEHS felt that those whose research was made available should contribute to these costs, rather than those who might want to access and use the research, as this latter would significantly reduce the possibilities of dissemination. Second, the UK became the focus for the Network because there is a strong tradition of research on human settlements in the developing world within the UK, where CEHS is based, and for reasons of manageability and politics of information it was felt that this is a sufficiently large, and relatively culturally cohesive, client group. CEHS considers, however, that the Network would ideally be one node within a worldwide network of such networks, allowing other geographic areas to disseminate their own research, information and linkages similarly and in parallel (see below).

Structure

The Network, as set up, hosts the Inter-Schools Conference website; the North–South Research database; and a digital conference facility. These represent an interconnected suite of Internet-based resources, as shown in Figure 12.1 and described below.

Inter-Schools Conference website

The Inter-Schools Conference website has information on previous conferences including a listing; information on the most recent conferences; abstracts of papers presented from 1997 onwards; and ordering information for full papers. It also provides up-to-date information on the next conference.

The objective of the digital conference is to become a dynamic link between these static annual conferences, allowing more up-to-date information flows and wider discussion.

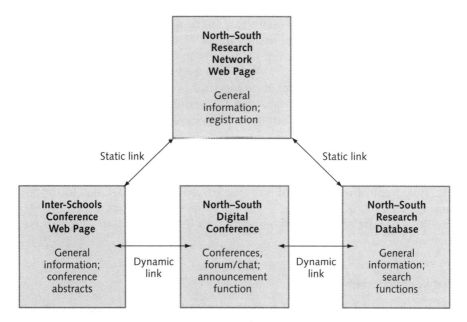

Figure 12.1   Internet-based components of the North–South Research Network

North–South research database

The Database of Current Research into Human Settlements in the South, based in the UK, includes:

- titles (and often short abstracts) on current research provided by researchers, within four main categories ranging from theses to projects
- search functions for the database, including key words
- contacts (and usually active links) to researchers and/or research institutions.

The objective of the database is to showcase research in human settlements in the South undertaken here in the UK, allowing this to be searched for specific interests, and providing direct links between interested users and researchers/institutions to further dissemination and feedback.

Digital conference

In parallel with the website and linked database, an interactive digital conference forum for registered researchers and research institutions was set up, to allow:

■ moderated conference facilities to permit posting of fuller papers on current research on an ongoing basis

■ associated discussion fora on papers and other identified issues of mutual interest

■ user-to-user e-mail, including file-sharing facilities

■ online and offline chat facilities, for multiple users

■ eventual links to other similar networks worldwide via the Internet.

The objective of this facility is to stimulate discussion between researchers, permitting some of the activities that currently take place in the annual Inter-Schools Conference to be more dynamic and constant. This hopefully will help institutions focus their research, and allow researchers to support and refine each others' work. Eventually it is planned that the conference facility – or part of it – would be opened to the worldwide user group (see below).

Network management

The websites, the database and the e-mail forum are managed by a Network Support Group within CEHS. The websites are jointly hosted by CEHS and Heriot-Watt University, whose Institute for Computer-Based Learning (ICBL) technically assisted the set-up of the Network through its Learning Technology Service. This allowed the development of a dynamic link between the database and the Internet, as well as a data-input programme specifically for the Network database. The digital conference was also set up by the Learning Technology Service, using licensed software.

User group and client body

The user group consists of anyone who dials in to the website and associated database from anywhere in the world. To make the website and database more accessible, the design was kept simple, mostly text-based and easily downloadable, thus addressing some of the problems encountered by users in the developing world, as noted by Ferretti (1999). In addition, it was planned to develop strategic web links with key institutions and search engines, and other means of advertising the website globally, using posters and postcards, commenced.

It was initially estimated that there are some 20 higher education institutions in the UK with courses and/or academic research oriented to the South in the cognate areas, and it was estimated that there were perhaps 200–250 students and staff (full- or part-time) involved in research or supporting research in this area. This represents the initial UK-based client body. There is no reason why this should be the only client body, however, although there is a question as to what other clients, such as for-profit entities, should contribute for what may amount to advertising for a product or service they sell.

Costs and sustainability

It was felt that the Network should be freely open to all worldwide, although individual researchers and institutions may decide to charge for copies of their detailed research that are requested. It was considered that the function being provided was essentially a public one, of mutual benefit to the UK-based research community and to research users worldwide. There were, naturally, costs associated with setting up and managing the Network. Financial assistance from DFID during the initial year covered most of the set-up costs, the remainder being absorbed by CEHS. However, after this initial period CEHS had to cover the full basic management costs necessary to keep the initiative dynamic and up-to-date.

Three options for covering these costs and to enable the further development of the web pages and database were considered: (i) financial contributions from the client group – this was not a likely route given the increasing financial constraints on researchers; (ii) user fees – this option seemed to go against the grain of making research more widely available in developing countries, where researchers and other users have fewer resources; or (iii) advertising – the limited and specialized client and user group made this option inappropriate, although it was considered that making the Network part of a larger initiative involving the Inter-Schools Conference and possibly a related journal would make this option more viable.

It was concluded that the Internet-based Network was providing to a great degree a public service, which justified continuing financial support from the relevant government body – in this case DFID. This is the route followed by other services providing information in the field, such as the Gateway to Information Sources on Development and the Environment (ELDIS), funded by the Scandinavian aid agencies DANIDA and SIDA, or the ID21 Development Research Reporting Service, funded by DFID. CEHS estimated follow-up running costs for an extension of the set-up period and submitted a proposal to DFID.[4]

Future expansion

CEHS envisages two forms of future expansion of the Network.

- *Internal expansion* – the Network should respond to demand in terms of the amount of material it carries (which it is hoped would grow on its own), type of material and type of service it offers. In this it was intended to respond to the demand from clients and user bodies.
- *External expansion* – CEHS deliberately decided to make the Network UK-focused in terms of the client body and showcased research. It was, however, very interested to link the Network to other, similar networks in the cognate area worldwide, and initially established links to N-AERUS and Forum: Habitat in Developing Countries. However, these are essentially linkage networks at European and global

levels, without data provision facilities. CEHS also hoped to develop interactive links with other DFID-sponsored information projects, including the British Library of Development Studies. There were many possibilities for linkages, including the institutions which are clients of the Network.

In addition, it was intended to provide a service to researchers in the South, where there may not be the institutional or technical capacity to create a research network such as this one. CEHS learnt a lot from 'doing', and subsequently sought financial assistance to respond to requests to assist in setting up something similar to the North–South Research Network in regions in the South where there are strong research links.[5]

The vision here is to mimic the Internet itself – a network of computers – through setting up a network of networks. CEHS's technical partners at ICBL considered that it was possible to create a search function which would span a series of databases, as long as these were created according to a basic protocol. This means that when a user dials on to one network, a choice of partner networks and databases would also be made available, and the user would select which of these to include in running a wide-ranging search for information.

CEHS's interest in this form of development is to assist, where appropriate, research institutions in different parts of the world to express themselves, which we consider politically and culturally essential. This assistance would include development of a common protocol for other research networks to link in with, and/or technically and managerially assist, other research entities to develop network capacities.[6]

Network continuity

After the initial work of setting up the Internet web pages to support the Network, kick-starting the database with the collation of information on current research in the UK, advertising with postcards and posters mailed to the main institutions forming the client body, and launching the Network, the Network was managed on a regular basis until DFID support ran out. It was further promoted at the 16th Inter-Schools Conference in Westminster, where its role as digital host for the Inter-Schools Conference was ratified by the participants. However, after this event the lack of resources at CEHS and the lack of funding from other sources led to network management being reduced to a minimum, at CEHS's expense.

Applying Starkey's (1998) guidelines to this initiative, it is clear some of these were adhered to. The Network has clear objectives which were accepted by researchers at the Inter-Schools Conference, and it initiated concrete activities in which registered researchers were invited to participate. On the other hand, management is centralized at CEHS, and a committed core group of active members with representation from the various research institutions was not established. In this sense, the Network displayed some of the characteristics of centralization that Starkey warns against. CEHS did not consider initially creating a management board which would advise and promote the Network, assuming that this would emerge through active participation in the Network, and ample opportunity for feedback to CEHS on management was provided. In the event, the lack of follow-up funding led to the limited consolidation of the Network across key user-group clients.

Some lessons from the UK experience

Through establishing the North–South Research Network, the core management group in CEHS became very aware of the different nature and scale of the problems in terms of technical capacity and managerial capacity. In principle, the technology is fairly simple once it is set up. CEHS's experience was that the most difficult part was to collect information to reach a stage where the database takes off – where it has enough information to attract people to use it and register more information. The main limitations in this relatively modest project were managerial, leading to the conclusion that in order to create successful research networks, it is necessary to avoid mega-projects with associated mega-managerial problems. This reinforces the appropriateness of a solution such as the 'network of networks' described above, which would rely on already developed technology and on breaking down the task into components that can be managed as local networks.

In addition to this managerial ceiling, with fast-growing Internet access worldwide, especially in institutions which undertake or use research, the boundaries are increasingly political and cultural, not technical. This is another aspect that can be addressed through the local management of networks within a wider global network, although in no way does CEHS feel this is the definitive and only solution for research and information dissemination.

Although the Network is dormant at the time of writing, the ICT infrastructure is in place. Revitalizing the Network would require only a limited amount of funding to enable its proper management and upgrading, and such revitalization could begin to address the issues of centralization and deeper client body involvement. In addition, it would be desirable that the initiative be linked to other research dissemination initiatives, which could provide added momentum and a wider advisory group for network management.

THE INVESTIGA RESEARCH NETWORK

Context: CERCA

In an assessment of how poverty is addressed in Central America, in 1993, the UN-Habitat Community Development Programme (CDP) identified the following shortcomings: (i) severe limitations of access to information on how to develop and operate local development policies; (ii) lack of training tools for facilitators and community leaders in human settlements management, those available often not being appropriate to specific needs and contexts; (iii) research and knowledge production on participatory development were rare and most often non-accessible; (iv) financial resources often failed to be directed towards primary needs and, in many cases, there was duplication of efforts and loss of efficiency; and (v) community-based organizations (CBOs) in all countries in the region were marginalized from all major decision-making, leaving development in the hands of so-called 'experts' (CERCA, 1998a).

After a three-year discussion process hosted by CDP, a project to address these problems was launched in 1996: CERCA, the Resource Facility for the Sustainable Development of Human Settlements in Central America. Its objective was 'to promote decentralized and participatory management of human settlements as a means of combating poverty in Central America' (CERCA, 1998b: 2), with a special focus on community organizations. The project was based in San José, Costa Rica, at the Ministry of Housing and Human Settlements, with an annual budget of US$400 000 and a staff of six professionals and five support staff. The project provided technical support to the Alliance for Participatory Management, which brought together Central American central governments, local governments and CBOs (the Central American Council for Housing and Human Settlements, the Central American Federation of Municipalities and the Central American Federation of Community Organizations). This technical support was provided through four components: capacity development; institutional strengthening and strategies; an information system for communities and municipalities; and an applied research programme. The latter two, known as SISCOM and INVESTIGA, respectively, are the focus of this case study.

INVESTIGA's objectives

INVESTIGA's general aim to provide support to CERCA's activities through applied research and training was addressed through several objectives, two of which directly involved researchers in the region:

'To generate spaces for reflection, exchange and collaboration among the researchers in the region and CERCA's associates (local governments, community organizations and public agencies) . . . in the field of participatory management of human settlements.'

'To provide support to the training of local researchers, as a new way of generating scientific knowledge related to ongoing social, territorial and institutional processes.'

(CERCA, 1998c: 5)

INVESTIGA thus sought to include researchers in the development process, in a supportive and informing role towards the rest of the actors involved. INVESTIGA focused its first research project – 'State of the Art in Research on Participatory Management of Human Settlements', 1997 – on identifying these researchers in order to initiate their incorporation into the development process.

The State of the Art in Research on Participatory Management of Human Settlements

Objectives and method of the research project

The objectives of this research project were twofold: to undertake a regional appraisal of research related to participatory management of human settlements in Central American countries; and to prepare a proposal for a regional exchange network involving research centres, researchers, regional and national agencies (CERCA, 1997: 4).

The project was undertaken through three types of questionnaire distributed to institutions in the seven Central American countries: research institutions; individual researchers; and research projects. These were collected and analysed, and the results were written up in a report that was presented at a conference held in San José, Costa Rica, 6 November 1997, attended by researchers from all over Central America. The project had three stages: (i) definition of criteria for the selection of target institutions and questionnaire preparation; (ii) questionnaire distribution, follow-up and collection; and (iii) questionnaire analysis and writing up. The full-time CERCA member of staff in charge of INVESTIGA at the time led the entire process. A Costa Rican consultant contributed to the first stage, targeting institutions with experience in local development and participatory management of human settlements. The next stage was undertaken solely by the project leader, who visited the institutions twice to ensure the questionnaires were completed. Analysis and writing up was undertaken by the project leader, the Costa Rican consultant and one of the authors (H.S.).

Outcomes

Questionnaires were returned from all countries, with information on 59 research institutions, 54 individual researchers and 36 research projects. The largest group of institutions that responded were NGOs (21, 35.6 per cent), followed by academic institutions. (15, 25.3 per cent). In relative terms, these were also the types of institution that showed higher participation in research, with all NGOs and 14 (93.3 per cent) of the academic institutions undertaking this type of activity. In terms of individual researchers, the most represented professional group was architects (16, 29.6 per cent), followed by sociologists (11, 20.3 per cent) and economists

(8, 14.8 per cent). The majority were involved in consultancy (37, 68.5 per cent); there were equal numbers of researchers involved in teaching and in action-research (22, 40.7 per cent); and the smallest group was that of theorists (10, 18.5 per cent).

The results from the survey showed that, at the time, community self-management and participation were issues being widely addressed by the research community in Central America. These two focal issues included a wide range of sub-topics and research methods, which suggested a great variety and richness in research experience in the region. But the survey also highlighted the lack of connection and exchange among the different research institutions and individuals in the region, particularly in relation to applied research approaches and methods. Finally, it was found that a considerable amount of research maintained strong links with primary actors (women's organizations, CBOs, housing groups, etc.), which is a key way to ensure these studies are relevant and have an impact, especially at a local level.

A Central American research network on participatory management of human settlements

Reasons for and potential of a regional research network

Forty of the 59 institutions reported belonging to national networks, and 38 to regional (supranational) networks. Among those most involved in research, 61.9 per cent of NGOs participated in national and 66.7 per cent in regional networks; and 73 per cent of academic institutions participated in national and 60 per cent in regional networks. Participation of individual researchers in networks was lower (40.7 per cent), and contacts among these were reported to be more informal. In addition, the spread of reported networks was extremely wide (27 networks); however, only four networks were reported by more than one researcher, and even those linked few of the respondents.

The survey showed there was an opportunity for a Central American network on research on participatory management of human settlements, a possibility to which the majority of respondents was favourable. Replying to an open-ended question in the survey, the respondents supplied a wealth of reasons to establish such a network.

The 'State of the Art' report finally concluded that there were three types of support for researchers that could be addressed within the framework of a Central American network: (i) the exchange of research experience addressing proposals for the solution of specific problems affecting low-income populations; (ii) the generation of debate and joint reflection around the themes of community self-management/ participation, local government decentralization and local development; and (iii) training for researchers in participatory methods and techniques.

Development of the network

The idea of a research network was floated at the conference held in San José in November 1997 as an end to the 'State of the Art' project, and was debated by the researchers who attended. Its consolidation was subsequently incorporated into INVESTIGA's programme in 1998, with a budget allocation of US$50 000 over two years.

The consolidation of the network was to be supported through related activities. These included the undertaking of specific research projects, for two of which INVESTIGA allocated funds in the first two years; building up a community library through the publication of research in various formats; forming working groups involving researchers and CERCA associates in each of the participating countries, which would run workshops, courses and conferences, and participate in CERCA-fostered or funded research projects; promoting links and agreements with research institutes, universities, NGOs and international agencies; and training local researchers. The project thus proactively attempted to consolidate the research network, adopting a supply-driven approach in response to the demand identified in the 'State of the Art' survey.

Using new technology: the Internet

Further support for the network was provided by SISCOM, the CERCA component providing Internet-based services, mainly through its website, which was used as a tool that allowed interaction between CERCA's associates. The website was managed by a network of 40 people throughout the seven Central American countries, also trained to train others in its use. Through SISCOM, INVESTIGA was able to circulate its regular newsletters which kept researchers up to date with events, and to provide online access to databases, as well as an online directory of participating institutions, with contact names and e-mails (www.siscom.or.cr/dir_inv.htm). In relation to research dissemination and access to data, SISCOM established a set of links to eight institutions with libraries, with search functions in each of them (www.siscom.or.cr/inv_enl.htm). One of these links was Fundación Acceso, a Costa Rican NGO that at the time offered what it called a 'metabase', providing access to information on the holdings of 17 institutions in Costa Rica through a single search page on the Web. This latter metabase is a network of databases, to which new databases can be linked in at any time. Indeed, by 2002 the database had extended its coverage to six Central American Countries, with funding from the World Bank (www.metabase.net). However, this metabase is not focused on human settlements, but rather is attempting to include various Central American bibliographic databases.

Network continuity

During 1998 and 1999, INVESTIGA implemented many of the actions it planned in order to support and consolidate the research network.

Researchers participated in events involving the partners in the Alliance for Participatory Management, such as the National Associates Fora held in each of the Central American countries in February 1998, which brought together researchers with policy-makers, practitioners and community members. A research project was developed into local responses to resettlement of migrants due to violence in Central America and Colombia. Research was also initiated into municipal preparation and implementation of local development plans, with a focus on coping with the effects of hurricane Mitch, as well as into land regularization in Central America. Four editions of the INVESTIGA newsletter were made available electronically on the website and circulated to the participating researchers.

In terms of the guidelines suggested by Starkey (1998) for the successful operation of networks, the research network established by INVESTIGA had clear objectives, which to a large degree were derived from the consultation undertaken as part of the 'State of the Art' project. INVESTIGA launched specific activities engaging participating researchers, in the form of research projects, conferences and training activities, although INVESTIGA retained overall control of these. In addition, core groups of active members were set up in each country, although establishing how representative these groups were would require further research.

However, funding was discontinued at the end of 1999 due to the closure of the CERCA project by UN-Habitat. This spelt the end of the network as it was then conceived. The digital infrastructure in terms of a website with accessible information and researcher directory is still available at the time of writing this, but there is no evidence that the network is functioning as intended. Some new links between specific researchers and practitioners forged during 1998–99 have continued, and this should be considered as a benefit resulting from the experience, but the achievement of a fully operating network was curtailed by the early loss of funding source and driving force.

Some lessons from the Central American experience

The 'State of the Art' study evidenced the importance of promoting meetings and exchanges among the region's institutions and researchers in order jointly to address some weaknesses or deficiencies; to promote learning at a regional level from national/local experiences; and to establish a regional academic identity that helps to underpin academic work in the region in relation to that undertaken elsewhere. In relation to the latter, possibly one of the most important results of the 'State of the Art' was to contribute to the establishment of a reference working group for INVESTIGA, including a few researchers in each country.

The undertaking of the 'State of the Art' research project highlighted the difficulty in collecting information from research institutions, as was also encountered in the UK during the development of the North–South Research Network Database. Thus, even when there is a demand for strengthening research capacity, the response from researchers in terms of driving an initiative has been found to be low, both in Central America and in the UK. These experiences suggest that to meet this demand there is a need for an initial creation of motivators and mechanisms which will drive the process, and this requires adequate funding over a sufficient period to allow the network to consolidate.[7] Careful consideration should be given to the length of time a network will require substantial funding, as well as to focusing on the right activities and approach to achieve a high level of user support as soon as possible.

CONCLUSIONS

On the basis of the experiences described in this chapter, and of the lessons learnt from these, we can draw some overall conclusions relating to the politics of information, the need to make knowledge more easily accessible in developing countries, and the myth of ICT being an easy and affordable means for dissemination and communication for all in the current world.

In terms of the politics of information, it is generally accepted that the sources of wealth have been successively based on land, labour, capital and, currently, knowledge. The trend of accumulation and exchange of knowledge, however, is once again favourable to the more industrialized countries. In order to stem this continuation in the gap between rich and poor countries, it is essential to decentralize the production, management and access to knowledge. However, there is also a need to redress imbalances in terms of creating the opportunity for this to happen, especially in regions where knowledge and research resources are limited.

In terms of access to knowledge, Internet-based or supported mechanisms such as the North–South Network or INVESTIGA may not be readily accessible to the general public in developing countries, as Ferretti (1999) rightly points out. However, this does not detract from the value of such means of communication and exchange for the research community in developing countries, whose work should, in turn, contribute to the amelioration of conditions in their countries. Again, this requires political decentralization of knowledge management which can be achieved through the creation of these suggested local research networks – if this does not happen, despite their apparent accessibility, the dominance of new technologies will lead to an even further concentration of wealth.

It is widely accepted that knowledge management and dissemination are becoming increasingly affordable through the development of ICT (Ferretti, 1999), and thus more widely accessible – this is certainly the case in terms of setting up websites and pages. However, the experience of these two case studies indicates that it is essential to motivate and manage Internet-based research networks and databases in order to keep these mechanisms alive and make them of real use to the research community and others. This relies on trained personnel which, in turn, demands appropriate levels of funding. Ideally, this funding should not be expected from the user end, as the strength of the Internet is its potential for wide dissemination and access in lower-income countries. In this, the opportunity for free availability of information at the point of use ought to be maximized, building on the concepts of the gift economy described by Barbrook (see Chapter 3).

Finally, provided funding is in place over an appropriate length of time, the kind of initiative described in this chapter *can* be replicated elsewhere, building on lessons already learnt and thus reducing costs. The technology exists not only to replicate this kind of experience on a national or regional basis, but also to link up databases as well as research networks. Thus it is possible to begin to establish international 'networks of networks' which would contribute to bridge the gaps between research in the North and in the South in politically and economically more sustainable ways. However, in the *realpolitik* of knowledge transfer, this will require specific and reasonably sustained support during the initial periods in order to overcome inherent imbalances in resources.

CHAPTER THIRTEEN

Electronic conferencing: the learning curve

Mansoor Ali and Darren Saywell

INTRODUCTION

In the recent past, 'capital' used to be perceived as the scarce factor in achieving economic growth. Increasingly, 'knowledge' assumes this role in development. The conjunction of knowledge, appropriately packaged and translatable to local circumstances, offers unprecedented opportunities for North and South to exchange information. The importance and significance of improved dissemination have been acknowledged and recognized at various international fora (Visscher, 1998; Lewando-Hundt and Al Zaroo, 1999). Explicit examples of this acknowledgement include the UN Conference on Environment and Development, which identified weaknesses in information management and sought ways to improve the sharing of experiences and dissemination of information; and chapter 40 of Agenda 21, which argued that all stakeholders are users and providers of information, thereby indirectly emphasizing the need for dissemination. The Global Report on Human Settlements (UNCHS, 2001) dedicates significant sections to the role of information and communication in a globalizing world. The report interrelates urbanization with the application of digital communication and information technologies. While access to communication and information technologies differs considerably between different groups of people, it does offer the potential for eliminating poverty and consequently reducing inequality.

Information technologies open up new opportunities to learn from each other's practices and to build capacity. With millions of computers and mobile phones worldwide, the Internet is clearly the largest global communications network. Development is closely linked with useful knowledge and the Internet can help in exchanging knowledge about experiences, successes and lessons (Ferretti, 1999). Full Internet access typically consists of e-mail, World Wide Web, file transfer and telnet. These forms of communication are increasingly applied to development contexts, spanning the health, education, environmental protection and agriculture sectors. In healthcare, for example, telemedicine through the Internet is making medical care available virtually on demand. The scientific community is gaining access to international libraries, catalogues and research material to speed and facilitate research work.

This chapter addresses the latter point, the potential for electronic information exchange – through the notion of an electronic conference – to facilitate mutual learning between geographically isolated sector professionals. In this case, lessons are drawn from the management of three electronic conferences operated under the auspices of the Global Applied Research Network (GARNET),[1] and focused on solid waste management issues in Southern countries. This chapter outlines the potential benefits which can be gained through electronic conferencing, briefly reviews the key points involved in organizing such conferences and concludes with a review of the lessons learnt from experiences of using the medium as a development tool.

BACKGROUND TO ELECTRONIC CONFERENCING

An electronic conference is a systematic and subject-focused discussion using e-mail. An e-mail list allows any number of people with e-mail addresses to communicate among one another on issues of mutual interest and concern. A mailing list is an automatic message-sending programme that stores a list of e-mail addresses of all people interested in a particular subject of discussion. Participants subscribe to a list. Each discussion group has its own e-mail address, and every time a message is posted to the list address, all subscribing members receive that message. An electronic conference will typically use a mailing list as the platform for a directed, time-limited discussion on a particular topic or theme. The proceedings could be simultaneously stored and available at an Internet site. Electronic mail is among the simplest and most widely understood of the new information technologies. Because e-mail correspondence is analogous to the postal system, even those with limited experience of the medium can learn its fundamentals relatively quickly. To some extent, this may explain the reason why electronic discussion groups have become popular as an aid to pursuing work and leisure goals.

Adapted from Ali and Saywell (1999) and the experience of J. Woodfield (Water, Engineering and Development Centre, Loughborough University, UK, personal communication, 2001), the following are some of the key points involved in running an electronic discussion.

- Selection and clarification of the conference topic is extremely important. The conference topics and key concepts should be interesting, widely understood and well explained, as the conference participants may come from wider geographical locations and backgrounds. Links with the known key issues and current literature could enhance further interest of participants.
- Conference objectives should be clear from the outset. Planning and design of the conference will be largely determined by the question: 'what are we trying to achieve in the end?' This will also help in the selection of the core group and targeting the key audience.

- Ideally, the conference should run on a written background paper. The background paper must be concise and clearly written, with a system of numbering. In planning a conference, it is useful to decide about sub-themes and the time to be allocated for the discussion of each theme. Themes and sub-theses must be linked with the background paper.
- The conference team must be selected and well briefed prior to the start of the conference. The team should include a conference facilitator (chairperson), a listserver operator and a core group of topic experts. It is the responsibility of the conference team to facilitate and stimulate discussion.
- A simultaneous mechanism is required to archive conference messages. It should be properly arranged and easy to search, as participants may join the conference at different times and may access archives after the conference.
- The conference must be announced well in advance, at least one month. This gives time for participants to join the conference and to read the background paper.
- The conference team must maintain a presence during the conference. The team must take the responsibility of summarizing the messages into intermediate and final summaries.
- Evaluation must be done immediately after the conference.
- Participants must get enough out of the conference. The conference output could be a useful resource, but other incentives, such as further networking, certificates of attendance, etc., should be considered.
- Timing and timetabling are important aspects of conference planning. Holidays and festive seasons may not attract sufficient participants. Participants also appreciate a clear conference timetable.

BENEFITS OF ELECTRONIC CONFERENCING

The principal benefits of electronic conferencing, as indicated by those who participated in GARNET's conferences, are:

- immediacy (rapid information exchange takes place in a short period)
- wider access to specialists and participants internationally than may normally be achieved at face-to-face conferences
- relatively low costs compared to normal conferences
- automatic archiving (where possible) makes production of post-conference synthesis documents simple
- flexibility for participants with regard to contributing to debate.

Some of the benefits from the conference organizers' point of view are:

- ease of focusing the issues

- participation of a large number of people from different geographical areas and backgrounds
- rapid exchange of ideas
- flexibility of conference management and inputs from organizers.

CASES: THE THREE CONFERENCES

GARNET's solid waste management network has organized three electronic conferences to date on issues pertaining to solid waste management. The conferences were facilitated through the Mailbase[2] initiative. Each conference provided important lessons which were incorporated into the next event. Participation increased as subsequent conferences were organized. The following section outlines some basic details relating to the three conferences.

The first conferencing event was organized in July–August 1998, and focused on the topic of source separation in solid waste management. The conference was co-organized with a Netherlands-based non-governmental organization, WASTE Advisers.[3] The background paper to the conference was made available on the conference website 10 days before the conference, and a discussion schedule was announced. The schedule for discussion during the conference was loosely organized, allocating a certain number of days to a broad topic. The conference was attended by 100 participants and messages were sent by 25 participants. A total of 100 messages were exchanged during the two-week duration of the conference, all of which were made available as archives on the conference website. Although no summaries of conference themes were attempted, final conference messages acted as an ad hoc Conclusions and Recommendations section. The key lessons that emerged from the first conference included the following.

- The background paper used for the conference was not modified for the purpose of the conference. The substantive issues were not prioritized, some poorly defined terms were used and comprehensive sectioning of the paper (which could have helped with referencing during the conference) was absent. The length of the paper and range of issues it was trying to cover was a major cause of distraction.
- The conference mailing list was not moderated, which meant that any message sent to the conference list was automatically distributed to all members. This led to a number of irrelevant messages being posted, which in some cases led to complaints about additional costs being incurred by Southern countries participants who were paying high charges for Internet access. In some cases the cross-communication between participants was beyond the control of conference organizers.

■ A core group of experts was not formed or consulted, although some participants sent more messages than others. The presence of a core group of experts on the subject could attract more participation and better quality of messages.

■ The conference moderator (chairman) had no experience of running such conferences.

■ Summaries were not distributed at the end of each section, nor at the end of the conference.

■ The total duration of the conference was limited to two weeks, with the length of discussion for each section restricted to three to five days. This was very short for some participants because of global time differences and restricted access to e-mail and the Internet.

The second conference was organized in December 1997, and focused on micro-enterprise development for the primary collection of solid waste. The conference lasted 21 days. The background paper was placed on the conference website 15 days before the start of the event. The conference was attended by 150 participants, with a total number of 40 messages sent during the conference by 15 authors. The following changes were made to the conference organization, based on the lessons learned from the first conference.

■ The total conference duration and the length for each conference thematic discussion was increased.

■ A core group of experts was contacted to facilitate active participation during the conference.

■ The background paper for the conference was concise and included substantive issues, properly sectioned to facilitate the discussion.

■ The conference list was moderated so that only messages relevant to the conference theme were sent directly to the list members.

■ A synthesis paper based on the conference's key points was prepared and distributed.

As a result, the second conference was more purposeful and comparatively more successful. However, the following areas were identified which needed further improvement.

■ The roles of the conference organizer and any chairperson need to be divided, as they involve different and demanding roles.

■ The core group of experts needs be proactive in facilitating discussion.

■ There was a need to prepare and send summaries of each thematic section and the final outcome of the conference.

The third conference was organized in May 1998, on the topic of gender and waste management. The conference ran for a duration of 21 days. As with the first event, this conference was also organized jointly with WASTE Advisers. The background paper was made available on the conference website 15 days prior to its start. The conference was attended by 200 participants with a total of 85 messages exchanged during the conference. The conference proceedings and intermediate summaries were prepared and sent to the list by the conference chairperson.

The following changes were made in the conference organization.

- The roles of conference organizer and the chairperson were taken up by two different people.
- The messages sent were moderated by the chairperson and the conference organizer before posting.
- Summaries of each discussion session and the final outcome were distributed.

Table 13.1 compares the key components of the three conferences.

Table 13.1 Key components of the three conferences

	Conference 1	Conference 2	Conference 3
Theme	Source separation	Primary collection	Gender and waste
Co-sponsors	WASTE Advisers	None	WASTE Advisers
Messages sent	100	40	85
Core group	None	Yes	Yes
Background paper	Prepared and circulated	Prepared and circulated	Prepared and circulated
Intermediate summaries	Not sent	Few sent	All sent
Final summary	Not prepared	Prepared	Prepared
Conference evaluation	Yes	Yes	Yes
Active participants	25	15	25
Passive participants	100	150	200
Messages sent/active participants	4	2.5	3.5
Relevance of messages	Moderate	High	High

LESSONS LEARNED

GARNET has learned particular lessons from the planning, staging and evaluation of these electronic conferences.

- It is important to plan ways of managing and using the information obtained during the conference before it begins. Clear guidelines should be provided to participants which outline the specific format in which contributions during set phases should be made (this greatly reduces the time spent in editing outputs from the conference, such as synthesis documents after the conference ends).
- The role of a facilitator (chairperson) is critical in any conference. This person needs to encourage discussion and maintain its focus while keeping the objectives of the event in mind.

- The presence of a core group of experts is important to moderate the conference at a minimum standard and to attract participants.
- Ideally, electronic conferences should strike a balance between information exchange (such as the provision of descriptive case-study material) and discussion of key themes (which requires more analytical input). There may be a tendency for information exchange to dominate as it is relatively straightforward to provide. Hence adequate time and encouragement must be given to abstracting lessons during the conference.
- There may be problems associated with unsubstantiated claims, where participants make statements without adequate referencing or justification. This should in part be dealt with through peer review during the conference itself, and can also be reduced through guidance provided in a protocol document. In moderated conferences, the chairperson may screen out such messages.
- There may be time delays associated with conferencing among participants across the globe. GARNET has found that it may take up to 48 hours for a message sent to be received in some parts of the world. E-mail connections in some countries are few and frequently interrupted. This has implications for the length of conference sessions, and may lead to messages being posted which are not relevant to a particular session.
- Participants should be convinced that there is a clear incentive for them to participate in the event. Given the growing problem associated with information overload, it is important to demonstrate that tangible benefits (for example, a quality output document) will be produced from the conference.
- Core group experts and chairperson need an incentive to participate. Reliance on goodwill is, in the long term, unsustainable. Remuneration for core group experts might be a consideration.
- Production and dissemination of the synthesis report from the conference may be neglected, or difficult to achieve after the conference has ended. The proper allocation of time, budget and personnel resources to its production during the planning of the conference needs to be emphasized.
- Use of e-mail may be expensive in some countries with poor telecommunications infrastructure. It should be remembered that some participants will not enjoy institutional support for these costs, and may pay on a personal basis for incoming mail. Local nodal points may be set up to relay the conferences.

CONCLUSIONS

Claims about the radical nature of the Internet and its revolutionary effect on society are commonplace. Distinguishing hype from reality is a much more difficult task. GARNET's experience indicates that significant value can be gained through using electronic mail in directed, time-limited conferences. For the research community, this approach offers a genuinely innovative means by which sector professionals from North and South can discuss in detail specific development-related issues. At the same time, technological constraints continue to restrict wider access, and a thorough understanding is needed of the social and human dimensions of the Internet.

CHAPTER FOURTEEN

Putting over the message: a programme in Pakistan to build capacity among industrialists for pollution abatement[1]

Rizwan Hameed and Jeremy Raemaekers

INTRODUCTION

Lahore is the ancient capital of the Punjab, and Pakistan's second city. It is typical of fast-growing cities in developing countries at an early stage of industrialization, in which polluting and bad neighbour industries inter-mingle with residential areas during imperfectly regulated urban expansion (Hameed and Raemaekers, 1999).

Industry accounts for a quarter of Pakistan's output, about the same as farming, and half as much as services. Pakistan's per capita GNP is US$470 (World Bank, 2000a). This places it below the level of wealth at which we can expect to see pollution intensity fall as income rises (Wheeler, 2000, figure 9; World Bank, 2000b, figure 1.5). Lahore is a city of some 5 million people growing at around 3 per cent a year. It lies on the Indian border, on the River Ravi (Figure 14.1). A quarter of its output is from manufacturing, particularly textiles, metal parts and food processing. In 1997 the city region held about 850 large-scale factories (large-scale is a euphemism, being a census class which covers all units employing 20 or more people; most lie at the bottom end of the scale). Between them these factories employed 120 000 workers (BS, 1998).

Industrial nuisances in Lahore are mainly:

- discharge of untreated effluents into drains (often open and unlined) and sewers, which in turn fall into the river
- fly-tipping of noxious wastes
- no control of gaseous emissions
- unabated noise and vibration
- bulk on-site storage of hazardous materials.

These are aggravated by the juxtaposition of industry with sensitive land uses.

The reasons why these problems arise have been analysed in terms of a three-actor model of state, industry and residential community (Hameed and Raemaekers, 2001). Here the focus is on one actor, industry, asking factory managers how they perceive the issues of nuisance, and how the

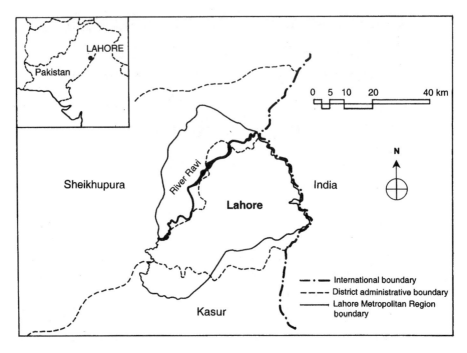

Figure 14.1   Location of Lahore

message that a change of attitude is desirable can be disseminated among them. This chapter concentrates on a national programme led by industry.

METHODS

Field information was collected during 1997 and 1998. Surveys of the distribution of industry in Lahore Metropolitan Region identified 15 clusters (Figure 14.2). These were defined as geographical concentrations of primarily large-scale industrial units. In 13 of the clusters, factories exist side by side with other land uses in a haphazard manner, whereas the other two clusters are planned industrial estates. The degree of intermingling of industry with housing varies within the 13 non-estate clusters, although it tends to be greater in those lying within the densely developed parts of the city than in those on its periphery. Further factories also exist throughout the city outside the clusters identified.

The clusters were used to select firms and communities for guided interviews. Representatives (usually factory-owners or managers) of 23 firms from across the 15 clusters were interviewed. The firms were chosen to cover different ages, types of ownership and waste streams, but all were situated close to housing. Tables 14.1 and 14.2 demonstrate that the sample

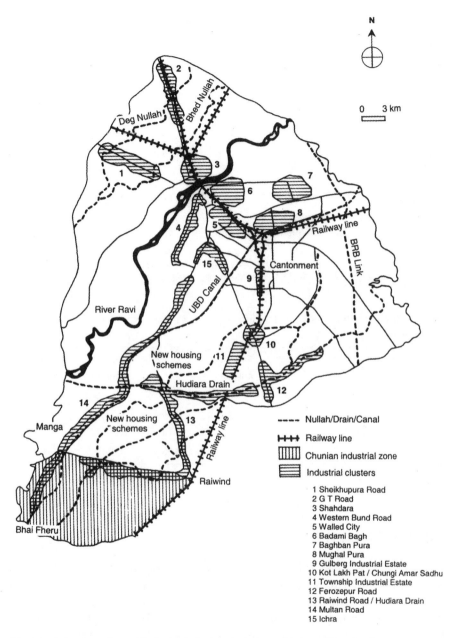

Figure 14.2   Location of industrial clusters in Lahore Metropolitan Region

of firms interviewed is a reasonable representation of large-scale industry in the region by industrial activity and ownership. Officials of regulatory regimes were also interviewed to gain access to data, to identify cases, to clarify institutional and legislative issues, and to seek explanations of operational weaknesses (Hameed and Raemaekers, 2001).

Table 14.1 Industrial classification of factories – survey sample compared with Lahore Metropolitan Region

Sector	Sample number	Percentage	Region number	Percentage
Food processing	4	17	85	10
Textiles	3	13	177	21
Footwear	1	4	45	5
Leather and leather products	1	4	31	4
Printing and publishing	1	4	26	3
Chemicals and chemical products	4	17	76	9
Basic metal	3	13	110	13
Fabricated metal products and machinery	3	13	111	13
Manufacture of transport equipment	3	13	46	5
Total	**23**	**100**	**707**	**83**

Sources: survey sample, 1997–8 (R.H.); Lahore Metropolitan Region (BS, 1998).

Table 14.2 Ownership of sample factories – survey sample compared with Lahore Metropolitan Region

Ownership	Sample number	Percentage	Region number	Percentage
Private	18	78	802	95
Public	2	9	34	4
Joint foreign enterprise	3	13	11	1
Total	**23**	**100**	**847**	**100**

Sources: survey sample, 1997–8 (R.H.); Lahore Metropolitan Region (BS, 1998).

INDUSTRIALISTS' ATTITUDES

Firms were asked why they did not abate some or all of their pollution. The most common reasons given were the lack of finance and of technical know-how. However, a good number of firms did not recognize their wastes as significant enough to require any abatement. We were not in a position scientifically to assess such claims; but we did find a couple of cases in which there was little doubt that the claim was fair. Some firms, in industrial estates or in clusters of plant away from sensitive land uses, appeared to consider that this exempted them from the need to mitigate noise or discharges.

Firms were next asked whether they think it is fair that industry should pay the whole cost of pollution abatement, or whether the government should give some form of subsidy. The majority of firms were of the view that industrial pollution can be controlled only through collaboration between industry and government, and that government should provide some incentives in the form of grants, soft loans, duty-free import of pollution control equipment, etc. Industrialists felt their case was strengthened by the economic recession which had eroded profits.

When asked specifically about willingness to invest in pollution abatement, most firms were willing to do so only with some form of subsidy. There was a general view that adoption of pollution-control measures would cost them money which they said they did not have to spend on this. The only firm willing to invest without subsidy was a joint foreign enterprise. One-third of firms saw no need to invest in abatement.

When asked whether they had a general idea about the cost of measures to control what they thought of as their main waste stream, nearly one-third of the firms replied that this question was not applicable to them. A further half could offer no estimate of cost. More than half the firms confessed that they had never heard of the National Environmental Quality Standards; joint foreign enterprises were more aware of the standards than were others. Of the seven firms who said they knew about the standards, five (including the three joint foreign enterprises) commented that the standards are fair and should be enforced properly. However, all seven showed concern about the transparency with which they are likely to be enforced. One even remarked that 'unless corruption is eliminated, it is difficult to imagine that the national standards would be able to achieve the desired result'.

Local communities can pressure firms to abate once they start realizing the impact of pollution on their health and the environment. Nearly one-third of the firms had received complaints from local individuals and citizens' groups. In one case, a group of local people had legally registered a nuisance case against the firm. Nevertheless, this was not enough to force firms to undertake significant abatement measures. Four of the firms said that nuisances suffered by local residents were not their fault, because housing developed close to their plants after the latter opened. Similarly, one firm laid the blame on faulty public sewers.

Lastly, firms were asked for their opinion about the attitudes of officials of the pollution regulator, the Environmental Protection Department Punjab (EPDP). Almost all firms were sceptical about the positive role of EPDP, and feared it would become just another government agency harassing them. They urged that EPDP should try to understand their problems and adopt a motivating attitude towards them (by teaching, instructing and demonstrating how to curb pollution) rather than a policing and punitive attitude.

To sum up, the survey reveals that many industrialists perceive no nuisance problem. If they do recognize a problem, they do not necessarily know how to tackle it and what it might cost them to do so. Nevertheless, there are also signs of awareness, and even of willingness to act if aided by the state.

HOW CAN THESE ATTITUDES BE CHANGED?

In developed countries, the public expects that, by and large, the law will be clear and known to firms, that firms will comply with it, that the state will monitor their compliance and that the state will enforce the law if firms do not comply. In a developing country in the early stages of industrialization, such assumptions cannot be made. How then do you persuade firms to abate nuisances?

In terms of external pressures on industry, the answer lies first in improved regulation. The pollution controllers must have a clear legislative foundation and remit, the resources to implement it, cooperation from other state agencies, credibility and the backing of a system of justice able to deliver prompt enforcement (Hameed and Raemaekers, 1999). Second, communities can bring pressure to bear on polluters directly, or indirectly via regulators (World Bank, 2000b), but this avenue has limited potential in Lahore, where the most affected public is the least able to apply such pressure (Hameed and Raemaekers, 2001). Third, there is commercial pressure. Investors and markets may both require better environmental performance, and firms seeking to export to World Trade Organization countries are increasingly bound to comply with environmental performance standards. However, only a small proportion of the factories scattered through the mixed-use areas of Lahore will be subject to such pressures.

That leaves pressure from within industry. Joint foreign enterprises are likely to be required to meet a minimum standard of environmental performance required globally by the transnational partner (contrary to popular belief and the infamous case of Union Carbide in Bhopal, transnational corporations generally require higher standards than do local owners). However, only 1 per cent of firms in Lahore are joint foreign enterprises (Table 14.1). No doubt over time, a new generation of factory-owners and managers will arise who bring a different outlook as a result of their education. But for the present:

> '*Most of the industrialists in Pakistan belong to the community of small entrepreneurs of the 1950s and 1960s. . . [Their] plants were imported during the regime of no environmental controls. . . The management style of these entrepreneurs remains conventional. . . [They] think that the new international conditionalities for quality production are a threat and conspiracy of the developed world against their enterprises.*'

> *(Khan, undated)*

Thus, in order to be proactive now, the best hope lies with a programme of awareness-raising, technical education, demonstration and information, led by those elements within industry itself who are in a position to take a longer view. Some industry sector associations, such as those of the tanners and the sugar millers, have mounted their own sectoral programmes, just as they have in developed countries (Khan, undated). Most promising is a multi-sectoral programme mounted nationally at the highest level, which the following section describes.

A VOLUNTARY APPROACH: THE ENVIRONMENTAL TECHNOLOGY PROGRAMME FOR INDUSTRY

The Federation of Pakistan Chambers of Commerce and Industries (FPCCI) is the body representing all the business, trade and industry organizations of the country. It operates through a large network of industry and trade associations and individual industrialists, providing a forum for dialogue between business, government and other agencies. From the early 1990s, the FPCCI started feeling pressure to control pollution from both government and many non-governmental organizations (NGOs), as well as realizing that competing in international markets would require a certain standard of environmental performance. However, the FPCCI was also aware of the problems faced by industry in developing and implementing environmental solutions: pollution-control technologies either are not available in the country, or lack the organized support and service structure required for their commercial application. By the mid-1990s, FPCCI further realized that the environmental protection agencies lacked, and would continue to lack for some time, the capacity to lead the way forward.

The FPCCI therefore conceived the idea of developing an environmental programme to be implemented in collaboration with industry associations. It obtained the cooperation of the Netherlands Government in supplying technical expertise and financial aid, and launched the Environmental Technology Programme for Industry (ETPI) in mid-1996, as a five-year programme to be implemented in two phases. The ETPI is a non-profit joint programme of the FPCCI and the Netherlands Government, the FPCCI being the lead partner. A steering committee comprises 26 members from industrial associations, local chambers, government environmental monitoring institutions, two leading NGOs and the Netherlands Embassy. An implementation core team has been formed of experts with diverse experience drawn from a consortium of Pakistani and Dutch consultants.

The objective of the ETPI is:

'. . . to promote the use of environmentally safe technologies for the production of environmentally safe products by Pakistan's manufacturing/industrial sector. This objective will be achieved by adopting measures of pollution abatement, waste management and recycling, chemical recovery, more efficient utilization of natural and/or economic resources, production and installation of instrumentation and control systems for utilizing the more efficient and environmentally safe production technologies.'

(National Environmental Consulting (Pvt) Ltd and Haskoning Consulting Engineers and Architects, 1996)

Table 14.3 sets out the components of the programme. The demonstration projects are in those industrial sectors identified in the Pakistan National Conservation Strategy as priority ones for environmental action (GoP/JRC/IUCN, 1992). Project costs are shared equally between the FPCCI, the Netherlands Government and the selected industrial unit. The latter's share includes costs of laboratory testing and analyses, preparation of detailed working drawings of the proposed environmental solutions, purchase and installation of pollution abatement equipment, etc. Other costs (consultancy fees, logistical support, and research and development) are met by the FPCCI and the Netherlands Government.

Entry to the programme of demonstration projects is competitive. The three winning factories in each industry sector are subjected to environmental audit, and one of the three is then chosen for the demonstration project. A substantial technical report is also prepared for each sector, informed by general knowledge of the sector and the results of the three factory audits for that sector, in order to generalize and disseminate the findings. As of May 2001, reports had been issued on seven sectors within the ETPI, along with one that is not in the programme, but which was considered to merit it. These reports review and prioritize the environmental issues facing the sector, give typical pollutant outputs at plant level compared with National Environmental Quality Standards, appraise technical options for abatement, and recommend choices of options. The reports are also made available in summary form, still with a useful level of information for first-level inquiry by the factory operator and other interested parties.

Since February 1998, the ETPI has sent a monthly journal to 5000–8000 major firms, industry associations, chambers of commerce, research and development institutions, education institutions and trade consulates. It acts both to spread the message of environmental responsibility and to proclaim the achievements of the programme to various political audiences. It contains a range of review and technical articles. An update bulletin on the programme is also disseminated twice yearly. All these documents, along with news and events pages, are mounted on the ETPI's website. Finally, ETPI runs, is represented at and disseminates notice of seminars on relevant topics, oriented towards solutions to practical challenges faced by industrialists.

PRELIMINARY ASSESSMENT OF THE ETPI

The ETPI started in 1996 and was due to end in May 2002. Interviews in 1998 with officials of the Lahore Chamber of Commerce and Industries, and information supplied by a member of the ETPI core team, suggest that the programme and the demonstration projects within it have been well received by industry associations and industrialists. A formal programme impact assessment was carried out in June–July 2000 (ETPI, 2000). This surveyed, mainly by interview, representatives in the nation's five major

Table 14.3 Components of the Environmental Technology Programme for Industry, Pakistan

Component	Purpose	Outcomes
Database development	To provide relevant information on priority industrial sectors, concerned institutions and environmental technology suppliers	Status reports on: 20 industrial sectors with emphasis on key environmental issues, possible solutions for major problems and recommended technologies Public, private and non-governmental institutions with relevant functions and fields of activity Environmental technologies available at the national and international levels, and a list of more than 60 vendors worldwide
Institutional networking	To create an institutional base owned by public and private sectors to ensure implementation of environmental solutions in the industries of Pakistan on a sustainable basis	Coordinated operational networks of all the partners related to the industrial sector Enhanced institutional set-up for the implementation of environmental technologies
Dissemination and communication	To promote viable environmental technology solutions and enhance understanding of national and international environmental legislation and mechanisms of financing the environmental investments	Well-informed constituencies of private and government institutions, NGOs, industrialists, etc., about environmental technology solutions, legislation and financing Effective communication tools with proper outreach in the industrial sectors of Pakistan
Institutional support and training	To create environmental cells and train professionals in the most relevant private sectors which will facilitate the implementation of ETPI over a longer period of time	In-house capability of the chambers of commerce and industrial associations to facilitate environmental projects all over Pakistan More than 100 trained professionals and 1000 trained workers for replication and multiplication of environmental projects all over Pakistan
Demonstration projects	To demonstrate in-house improvements and end of pipe treatment technologies	Identification of technologies for 20 selected industrial sectors 20 demonstration projects all over Pakistan to demonstrate the benefits of using environmentally friendly technologies

Source: adapted from FPCCI/Government of the Netherlands (undated).

cities of selected industries, industry associations and chambers of commerce, the demonstration project factories, NGOs, government agencies, donors, research and development institutions, and universities. Sixty-five responses were obtained.

Almost half the respondents rated the programme as a success, one-third as average and the rest as a failure. Respondents considered that the programme had raised awareness in industry and had been successful in setting up cells in industry associations and chambers of commerce. However, they criticized it for inadequately advertising what it can do for others, and for failing to involve research and development institutions and universities or to work with international agencies promoting environmental projects. The majority of firms involved in the demonstration projects rated positively the technical, financial, human resource, commercial and environmental outcomes of ETPI intervention in their businesses. They claimed that they had acquired know-how and made savings, and felt the projects had also helped to improve the environmental images of their respective sectors (ETPI, 2000).

Three pertinent questions may be asked about the programme's design:

- Is it targeted at identified obstacles to improved environmental performance?
- Are the demonstration projects replicable – can their results be read across to other firms, and are other firms likely to take them up?
- In a broader sense, is the ETPI sustainable – is it creating institutions that will perpetuate its function?

With respect to the first question, the programme's overall design (Table 14.3) appears well targeted to tackle constraints identified in our survey: a need for awareness-raising and for information on technical possibilities and their cost, and an attitude that the state must help industry to tackle the pollution issue. Ironically, the environmental protection agencies themselves do not explicitly feature in the programme outline. This tendency to go it alone is echoed in the findings of the programme impact assessment summarized above.

With respect to the second question, the approach is welcomed of giving participating firms free technical assistance and supervision in the implementation of environmental solutions, but requiring them to pay for capital equipment. Firms undertaking abatement measures will have to pay capital costs, whereas the type of assistance that is free to demonstration factories will, up to a point, also be available free to other firms after the demonstration programme expires.

- The sector reports drawing on the findings of the environmental audits of the three demonstration factories are available to the rest of the sector.
- Participating firms are bound contractually to open their doors to other firms to examine the environmental solutions applied to their factories.

■ Participating firms are also bound to give presentations on the solutions implemented and their performances at workshops organised by the ETPI.

The ETPI core team member who was interviewed provided an example of such replication in the pulp and paper sector, in which a mill has taken the initiative on its own to adopt the solutions recommended in the technical report on its sector.

With respect to the third question, the second, third and fourth components of the programme in Table 14.3 are clearly directed to ensuring that its functions outlive it, by engaging the superstructure of industry in the initiative. The creation of environmental cells within industry associations and chambers is one of the successes specifically cited in the impact assessment commissioned by the ETPI.

CONCLUSIONS

The ETPI has been intelligently designed to foster awareness at firm level. First, the database component will, among other things, ensure that local resources and expertise are not overlooked. Second, the demonstration programme will produce visible results such as might convince hard-nosed plant managers, yet which do not depend on capital subsidies to the participating firms. This should reduce the tendency of other firms to dismiss the projects' achievements as simply beyond their financial means. Third, three of the five components of the programme are directed towards sustaining its momentum beyond the lifespan of the programme itself. This latter aspect is absolutely crucial, as right across the spectrum of development efforts, history is littered with the carcasses of projects and programmes that failed to lay the foundations of their continuation beyond the expiry of the initial funding. One of the most encouraging signs in this respect is that a tour of the ETPI website's contents indicates almost exclusively Pakistani authorship of reports and papers, rather than dependence on the programme's Dutch partners.

It would be naive to become starry-eyed about the ETPI, which remains a drop of effort in the ocean of need. Concern is also noted that the programme, being a business-side initiative, seems almost to exclude the regulators, which could be damaging to the development of a positive relationship of mutual respect and trust. It would be particularly damaging in the case of small single-plant firms scattered through residential areas, which will be the last to be reached by a voluntary industry-side initiative and which, although they may contribute minor proportions to sectoral pollution arisings, contribute disproportionately to the nuisance suffered by residential communities. Nevertheless, the ETPI does demonstrate one important approach towards communicating for environmentally more benign industrial development.

CHAPTER FIFTEEN

Keeping ideas alive: communicating building for safety in Bangladesh

Iftekhar Ahmed and Matthew Carter

INTRODUCTION

Despite current rapid urbanization trends, the majority of the world's population remains rural. Among the many pressing needs of rural inhabitants in the developing world is the need for secure, affordable and lasting housing. Increasing population, combined with economic pressures, puts ever more demand on the already scarce supply of natural building materials with which the majority of rural housing is built. Tropical climates and insect attacks cause rapid decay of these materials, making the housing made from them vulnerable to natural hazards.

Bangladesh is the eighth most populous country in the world, and also one of the poorest. Eighty per cent of the population live in rural areas (BBS, 1996: ix) in *kutcha* housing constructed from bamboo and mud. The price of bamboo almost tripled in the decade 1980–90, outstripping the general price index by a long way (Ahmed, 1998: 356–8). Consequently, many people cannot afford to maintain their houses properly, and allow them to fall into a state of disrepair. Flooding, storms and cyclones annually wreak havoc on these houses. In the aftermath of the 1998 flood, hasty repairs were made but field observations indicated that, beneath a veneer of quick recovery, a vast stock of vulnerable housing remains which might be damaged or destroyed during the annual floods and storms in following years (Ahmed, 2000).

However, there are affordable and appropriate building technologies with potential for reducing the vulnerability of *kutcha* housing. As early as the 1970s, Chisholm (1979) identified a range of simple building technologies which could strengthen Bangladeshi bamboo housing. To date there has been little widespread communication of these ideas. Organizations have often sought to provide improved housing systems quickly in the aftermath of disaster. Several studies have pointed out the shortcomings of such an approach. To successfully bridge the gap between post-disaster rehabilitation and long-term development, there should be a shift of focus away from aid and innovative new designs towards a new agenda which embodies participation on all levels. A fundamental message of the Building For Safety initiative of the UK Department for International Development (DFID) was that:

'The only form of building improvement programme which has the potential to result in widespread improvements is one which changes the building decisions made by the poor in their own construction projects, designed and paid for by themselves.'

(Dudley and Haaland, 1993: 1)

The Housing & Hazards Group (H&H) was established in 1994 with the aim of making secure housing available and affordable in rural areas. H&H is working on two fronts to establish this new agenda in Bangladesh. Through village-level fieldwork, H&H is researching and implementing participatory communication projects. At a more national level, the Group has established partnership links with the Bangladesh University of Engineering and Technology and the Grameen Trust's Programme for Research on Poverty Alleviation to develop a framework for broadening the outreach of this work.

TOWARDS A NEW AGENDA

Since the evolution of the non-governmental organization (NGO) movement during the past two decades or so, much has been accomplished. New approaches to delivering development to the poor have been devised; new approaches to relationships between development agencies and communities have been forged; and a plethora of literature on innovative concepts such as appropriate technology, participatory development, action planning, safe building for hazards, micro-credit, human resource development, environmental sustainability, etc. has been published and applied. Yet quite often the poorest households remain outside these achievements. Additionally, a mismatch between agency intentions and household needs typically persists.

To address these problems, H&H is promoting changes in the thinking of those involved in the study and practice of low-income housing in Bangladesh. Some of the concepts promoted are established ones in current development discourse, but have not been applied so far in this field. New techniques of doing and making have to be embraced. And, perhaps most importantly, new professional habits and behaviour must develop, allowing formation of a relationship of mutual trust and responsiveness between agency and community. Only then can professional assistance be extended and effective communication established, allowing for a multi-level partnership to evolve between the community, NGOs and professional teams in a truly participatory community development mode.

This is a new agenda in this field, pointing to the potential for communication between different parties. The following points summarize some of the main aspects of this agenda for rural housing in Bangladesh.

Participation at all stages

Despite generally widespread endorsement of the participatory mode, most agencies in Bangladesh lack an understanding of how it may be applied in the field of housing. Many projects that incorporate community or household participation do so in a minimal sense. It is important to consider ways of involving the community from the beginning and in policy decisions, not only as a device for economizing on labour cost during construction, as is often done.

A basic 'don't' for agencies is applying preconceived ideas without consulting the community. Notwithstanding that participation can sometimes prove onerous for vulnerable households, for the majority of households, especially if involved from the earliest stage of the project, it can be a means to avoid becoming victims of corruption, especially in contractor-built projects. Indeed, the employment of formal contractors, especially from outside the project locality, can be questioned, primarily on grounds of the corruption typically evidenced. Only if unfamiliar and locally non-replicable building technologies are chosen are the services of a contractor needed. The use of such technologies should generally be discouraged because of a variety of associated problems; local building skills could be used instead, benefiting the local economy. Small technical improvements could be incorporated, providing the opportunity to impart training to local builders (and also to learn from them), thereby accomplishing communication effectively.

Integrating long-term development with post-disaster rehabilitation

The importance of an 'emergency–development continuum' needs to be recognized; in a disaster-prone context such as Bangladesh, the distinctions between the two are usually blurred. A disaster can present the occasion to introduce and promote safer building techniques. However, these need to be sustained, and local NGOs are often in a position to do so. In order to introduce simple, affordable and sustainable improvements during project implementation, it is not sufficient for an outside agency simply to impart training to local builders and then leave. Rather, training members of local NGOs to become trainers of local builders – a 'training of trainers' programme – might prove more fruitful over the long term. There is a great deal of literature on such programmes in other fields of community development with which many NGOs are already familiar; lessons from this can be employed in the field of housing. Participatory training workshops, drawing together households, local builders, agency staff and trainers-to-be of NGOs, among other relevant individuals, should comprise an essential component of project implementation. The primary intention of such an approach is to build local capacity for community self-reliance, hence it would be important throughout the workshops not to impart false hope and to dispel the impression that 'free' housing and handouts will be forthcoming. Because of past experiences, the 'relief culture' might have become endemic in some areas, and it is necessary for agencies to find ways to overcome it by not raising expectations that might retard community self-initiatives.

Expanding the sphere of community participation

Regardless of the hype in development discourse about promoting the involvement of women, there is virtually no programme in Bangladesh addressing their role in housing. Yet women play an important part, especially in house maintenance, and also increasingly in household decision-making during construction. Thus for agencies to be faithful to their agenda and also to enhance the effectiveness of their housing interventions, women have to be involved at all stages in the participatory process – before, during and after implementation. Once again, there is no lack of community development manuals and guidelines on women's participation; these need to be adapted for the field of housing. It is important to note the limited involvement of women staff also in agency-based housing programmes and in the building profession in general, especially at the grassroots level. There has, nevertheless, been a recent emergence of NGO-based grassroots women fieldworkers in healthcare, education, family planning and other areas of community development, notwithstanding their lack of involvement in housing programmes. This is encouraging progress, and women from such ranks can begin to be enlisted and trained to contribute to the wider realm of women's participation in housing programmes. Fieldwork of H&H volunteers has involved investigating ways of integrating women's participation in rural housing (Magne, 1999).

A method of implementation attempting to involve members of the local community is support of small-scale rural building materials producers or entrepreneurs. A leader in this field is Proshika, a national Bangladeshi NGO, although its choice of some building components for promotion has serious drawbacks. This initiative could prove worthwhile for other agencies involved in rural housing. In addition to local employment generation, the benefit to agencies would be reduction of overhead costs in operating their own building component production units. These costs could be utilized better in promoting quality control and the accountability of small entrepreneurs through supervision by agency staff. Local producers could also serve as construction specialists for in situ production of building components, expanding communication within the community. This mode is as yet at a rudimentary stage, and a great deal of research and improvement is necessary before proclaiming it as a viable option. Despite this, it might be worthwhile to explore prospects for what appears a potentially valuable implementation method.

VILLAGE-LEVEL FIELDWORK: AN EXAMPLE OF THE NEW AGENDA

Although this chapter is restricted to housing, it should be borne in mind that low-income rural housing cannot be effectively implemented as an isolated programme. It has to be part of a larger community development programme, well integrated with other components of the programme. In its first fieldwork projects, H&H did this through its connection with the Tiverton–Sundarban Link (Ahmed and Hodgson, 1997), a small-scale community development programme in northern Bangladesh.

In 1996–7 H&H carried out a 9-month programme working in partnership with a well-established grassroots NGO called Chetonar Dak, the Bangladeshi partner of the Tiverton–Sundarban Link. A volunteer from the UK (M.C.) spent time living in Sundarban village, establishing mutual trust and learning from people building and maintaining their houses. The main purpose was for the volunteer to live within the community for an extended period to study local housing and aspects of its vulnerability to hazards. This was expected to lead to an understanding of problems from an insider's point of view which might then assist in proposing appropriate solutions through communication with local feedback.

The H&H fieldwork programme attempts to overcome problems experienced in the past relating to the mismatch between agency and community aspirations. By living in the village for an extended period, it is believed that a thorough understanding has been gained of local socio-economic–cultural conditions and traditional building practices. Participant observation was used to learn about specific local issues, to collect information and to explore possibilities for improvement. This is typically embodied as participatory rural appraisal or participatory learning and action (Theis and Grady, 1991; Pretty et al., 1995); methods which have been extensively employed by anthropologists and used in rural societies to learn about and improve agriculture. However, these methods have had limited application in the field of housing, especially in Bangladesh. Adoption of these methods arises from the conviction that improvement should not introduce costly, alien or unproven construction technology; rather, it should relate to locally acceptable and affordable techniques, based on identification of time-proven building practice in the village. The volunteer's role was to facilitate participation of the villagers in analysing important issues themselves, resulting in their own proposals, achievable by them in their local context.

The participatory programme took time to unfold, but eventually led to the conception of appropriate methods of communicating the 'big ideas' of building for safety, and a process by which members of the community could learn about and consider specific issues relating to these ideas. A project was developed to communicate these ideas and implement this process. The project was carried out by Chetonar Dak and funded by both the Grameen Trust and the DFID Aid Management Office, Dhaka.

PARTICIPATORY WORKSHOPS

The core activity of this pilot project was a course of workshops using participatory methods described by Theis and Grady (1991) and others. The themes of the workshops aimed to develop a critical view by first discussing aspects of the current vernacular building practice, in particular considering household aspirations and vulnerability. This set the stage for assessing low-cost innovation through practical workshops, where householders could try out technologies for themselves and then debate the practicality, cost and likely effectiveness. Financial and institutional aspects were then brought to light by looking at long-term budgeting, credit and maintenance through group exercises, role-play and brainstorming. The themes and the main activities of the workshops are listed in Table 15.1.

The workshops took place on one morning each week, allowing time for the participants to think about and discuss the various themes. This was believed to lead to participants bringing more ideas to the workshops and remembering more afterwards than if the workshops had been in an intensive daily course. It was also more practical for villagers and trainers alike to spare one morning a week from their ongoing work activities. A completion party was held shortly after the workshop courses were over, including a formal presentation of certificates of attendance.

The workshops acted as a two-way communication tool. Although the purpose had been to catalyse discussion between villagers and to serve as a method for communicating and assessing low-cost building innovations, the results of the workshops are as instructive to any outside agency as to the participants themselves. For example, group discussions by householders of what they considered the good and bad points of their housing show the complex range of issues involved, and also the modest level of their aspirations (Table 15.2).

Local training staff from Chetonar Dak led the workshops. Using local trainers, known to the participants all their lives, was probably integral to the success of the workshops. Chetonar Dak has been working in the village since 1990 and is an important part of the community. The staff are all

Table 15.1 Workshop themes and activities

Theme	Main activities
Welcome	Registration, expectations/objectives, discussion of housing needs
Hazards	Discussion of vulnerability and disaster response
Building with mud	Practical exercise: building mud walls
Building with bamboo	Practical exercises: treating and framing bamboo
Roof construction	Practical exercise: building a roof, discussion of long-term budgets
Credit and maintenance	Credit role-play and discussion, planning maintenance routines
Conclusions	Assessment of demonstration building, costing exercises

Table 15.2 Aspects of local housing types

House type	Good points	Bad points	What do we want?
Thatched and mud walls	Cold in hot weather, hot in cold weather Low cost to build Mud is available nearby for free	Sometimes rats and termites burrow into the walls Floods destroy the house	We want *sapra* (mono-pitched) corrugated iron (CI) sheet roof or hipped CI sheet roof if there is more money It's better to have a side veranda (*bao chal*) to protect the walls from rain Make the base of the wall brick to protect from floods, rats and termites
Sapra CI sheet and mud walls	Needs less CI sheet than hipped roof Less expensive to build	Needs a lot of bamboo Strong wind blows away CI sheet Cold in cold weather and hot in hot weather	A mud ceiling is good for insulation Hipped CI sheet is better It is better with a veranda
Hipped CI sheet and mud walls	Long-lasting Protects from cold in winter Protects from cyclones and rain You feel the wind less Everyone sees it as a good status symbol	Rats and termites easily destroy the house Flood easily destroys the house If there is no ceiling it is hot Rafters and battens are easily broken	Make the base of the walls brick Rafters and battens could be painted We want to protect our house from rats and floods

Table 15.2 (Continued)

House type	Good points	Bad points	What do we want?
Thatched and bamboo frame	Comfortable in cold weather Even though cyclones and rain can destroy the house it is not so dangerous because it will not kill people Even though the bamboo posts rot quickly they can easily be changed	After 1 year the house is already damaged and old Bamboo mat walls are easily damaged Bamboo posts rot quickly	Paint bitumen on posts so that they last a long time; protect posts with plastic Make the bamboo fence a diagonal weave (*dhara*) using very thin bamboo sticks (*pati*) and paint with bitumen so that they will last a long time
Sapra CI sheet and bamboo frame	Protects from rain	It is difficult to stay inside during sunny weather In winter you get condensation under the CI sheet It needs extra *bao chal* around the house CI sheet gets blown away in strong wind	Instead of bamboo posts we can use concrete pillars If we make a hipped CI sheet roof with a wooden frame then it will be good An internal ceiling is good

Sundarban villagers, and the workshops became an extension of the natural process of learning embedded in casual conversations that take place in the market place, in the fields and at home. If a programme of workshops were to be embarked upon on a wider scale, there would be much value in any outside trainers planning and conducting the workshops together with local people, be they workers from a grassroots NGO or respected and articulate members of the community.

The workshops were well attended, and the enthusiasm of the participants developed during the course. The participants gradually took more control of the group discussions and the role of the training staff shifted from teacher to facilitator. As participants shared their knowledge and ideas of innovation with each other, it became clear that the catalytic function of the workshops in developing existing internal knowledge is as important as their function in communicating new external knowledge.

SUPPORTING ACTIVITIES

The workshops were supported by a demonstration building and a traditional song team. Although the workshops comprised the core activity for the exchange of ideas and the practical assessment of innovations, they might be quickly forgotten without ongoing activities to keep the ideas learnt alive. A model of how the supporting activities integrate with the workshops is given in Figure 15.1

Demonstration buildings have long been recognized as an important tool for communicating new building concepts. There is no substitute for the real thing when visualizing a technology, and a building serves as a lasting and visible reminder. A sewing training centre was built in a style very common locally, but a range of the innovations discussed in the workshops were also used, increasing costs by only 8 per cent over a similarly sized local building of similar form (Carter, 1997: 35). Construction took place in parallel with the workshops, allowing the participants to evaluate the nearly complete building during the final workshop. It was a valuable exercise to consider the innovations in the context of a full-scale building and to have information on actual costs.

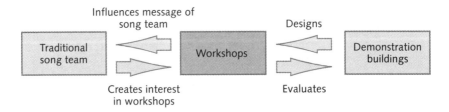

Figure 15.1   Model showing integration of the activities with the workshops

Although the demonstration building proved effective at the time, evaluation a few years later showed that the long-term value of the building was limited because it was not a private house (Magne, 1999). Although the idea of a community-owned building was laudable, it was not maintained as carefully as somebody's home might have been, so that after a few years it looked shabby despite being structurally sound. Moreover, the building had to be larger than a typical house for practical reasons. While at the time of the workshops the percentage increase in cost may have been understood, this concept was forgotten over time, and people now view the demonstration building as 'a rich man's house', simply because of its size.

Finding suitable media for further dissemination of information poses serious difficulties. In a society with a low literacy rate, communication of messages by workers from outside the community can encounter barriers. In the past, it was often assumed that presentation of information in pictorial form would be able to overcome barriers to communication. For example, in the late 1970s the Swedish Free Church Association prepared a set of drawings to promote improvement of rural housing in Bangladesh (Chisholm, 1979). However, the messages of these drawings do not appear to have been adopted, at least on a widely observable scale. The misunderstanding that can arise from differing cultural interpretations of visual messages has been well documented (Dudley and Haaland, 1993). To avoid these problems, local popular media might be employed as a vehicle for communication.

In the context of Bangladesh, song teams which play at weddings, markets and festivals provide an excellent opportunity for raising awareness of development issues. A local poet (*baul*) wrote a building-for-safety song that generated interest in the workshops when it was performed around the village. His team continues to use the song during their performances around the area. This should retain interest in the process and provoke discussions between participants and their friends and neighbours who, though unable to attend the workshops, know about them and may be interested in what was learnt.

EVALUATION

Two years after the workshops took place, their impact was evaluated (Magne, 1999). A seminar was held with the original trainers to discuss their understanding of the workshops' purpose, their experience of the process as trainers, and their opinions of the successes and failures of the workshops. Following the seminar and an informal survey of the impact, the participants were interviewed to see how much they remembered about the content of the workshops and whether they had used any of the ideas in their own building projects.

Although there had been some spontaneous adoption of the ideas discussed in the workshops, poverty remained a barrier to the poorer households, despite the low incremental cost of the ideas. This is illustrated by the plight of one of the workshop trainers:

> '*The living house of his homestead had fallen down. Being a day labourer, he was building the new home bit by bit as money came in. Meanwhile, he and his wife were sleeping outside and winter was advancing. On days when he had enough money he would stretch it to use H&H ideas such as painting bamboo pillars with tar to ward off insects and rot. When money was short he put in pillars without treatment. The need to complete the house, so that he and his wife could sleep in warmth and security, was a greater force than any thoughts of waiting a few days to accumulate the funds to make the house more durable.*'

> (Magne, 1999: 9)

To counter this, the evaluation recommended that very specific material assistance be made available, for example in the above case the provision of tar and brushes. Such assistance would only target the incremental cost of the improvement, and not seek to subsidize the house-building itself. Material distribution programmes in the past have provided graphic examples of the problems of a dependency culture, and such assistance appears to contradict the self-help ethos which H&H is trying to promote. However, linked in with the workshop process, such assistance might be appropriate.

It was also clear that the community would have benefited greatly from better follow-up support than was available at the time of the project. This underlines the necessity to establish a framework within the country which could provide that continuity, and could draw together experiences from projects within different villages.

REPLICATION PROJECT

Observations from the results of the initial project and the subsequent evaluation led to a framework for further projects in Manikganj and Gopalganj districts during 2000–1. The key points that these projects, particularly the one in Gopalganj, sought to address were as follows.

- Exploring how effective participatory workshops would be if facilitated primarily by a Bangladeshi villager, not an urban/educated or non-Bangladeshi person (as done in the Dinajpur project).
- Building private houses incorporating building-for-safety options with the homeowner's participation, instead of using a community building with the problems described above.
- Replicating the main aspects of the first H&H project in other parts of Bangladesh with different socio-environmental conditions. This would allow adding new insights to existing knowledge, as well as gaining new lessons from the experience.

■ The initial H&H projects were undertaken in Dinajpur, a somewhat different environment from the more seriously flood-prone areas that make up most of Bangladesh. Carrying out an H&H project in a flood-prone area might present scope for developing more widely applicable concepts.

The facilitator for these projects was a charismatic villager who had been a trainer and research assistant during the pilot project. After receiving further training for the Gopalganj project, he spent time there within the target community, supported by periodic visits from the researcher (I.A.) and two research investigators, both graduate architects with an interest in this field.

As these were action research projects, most activities were carried out in the field and an agenda for action for the community was developed. Although some work was done in Dhaka, such as compiling reports and accounts, three main stages of the project were principally field-based: reconnaissance, workshops and demonstration/dissemination. The details of these stages are described in Table 15.3 for the Gopalganj project.

Table 15.3 Action research project stages

Stage	Action
1 Reconnaissance	Visiting and spending time in Gopalganj for the research team to become familiar with the area
	Local housing patterns and building methods were studied, documented and mapped, and building materials inventories were prepared
	Initiatives were taken for arranging village workshops
2 Workshops	Workshops were held in the village to discuss and 'brainstorm' ideas for improving rural houses and to develop a range of 'building-for-safety' options that were relevant locally
	Separate workshops for women and men were held because that was more effective in the Bangladeshi traditional rural context
	Women research team members played an important role in facilitating the women's workshop as well as developing rapport with village women
3 Demonstration and dissemination	Two self- and/or peer group-selected households in different nearby villages volunteered to implement some of the building-for-safety options developed at the workshops, during reconstruction of their houses
	These houses were built as demonstrations to disseminate the research results; two houses were built in separate villages for broader impact
	A children's song team was trained to sing and disseminate the lessons gained in this project
	A documentary film about the work has been produced to serve as a dissemination tool

The Gopalganj project represents a more sustainable version of the pilot project. Being action-oriented, it is more focused and more efficient than the initial pilot project, which allowed a great deal of time for the Western 'outsider' and the village 'insiders' to become accustomed to one another. It has also been implemented using human resources from entirely within Bangladesh, so is building a usable capacity for future projects. It is hoped that other workshop projects will follow using the same facilitator, and other facilitators who may be discovered and trained in the process.

CONCLUSIONS

In the hierarchical social structure of Bangladesh, formidable impediments arise in re-orienting institutional values and behaviour to improve communication between different groups. Therefore the basic step towards this agenda of participatory and non-hierarchical inclusiveness would be to promote and develop a thorough understanding of it (currently lacking) which H&H aims to achieve through its links at various levels and spheres – international, national, educational and grassroots. It must be recognized that, in recent years, the NGO sector has been able to demonstrate to some extent effective participatory practice for communication in fields other than rural housing. Therefore this sector is a prime target for the framework to implement training-of-trainers workshops and programmes.

In 1979, Chisholm observed the absence of trained personnel working in rural areas in the building sector. He called for the equivalent of a paramedic, an extension worker within the building industry – a 'para-architect'. The organic growth of the H&H workshop process, through a trainer from one project receiving training him/herself to become a facilitator in future projects, should be encouraged in order to better understand what constitutes an effective building extension worker and to develop people to fulfil that role.

The volunteer programme signals the beginning of a gradually unfolding, long-term process of improving rural housing in Bangladesh, through participatory communication between diverse individuals and groups pooling different experiences to achieve common goals. Signs of this process are the continuity of songs created by the song team, and the spontaneous adoption of improved building techniques by some villagers. It can thus be expected that through sustained commitment, the H&H initiative will, over time, be fuelled by rural communities themselves, fulfilling a genuine participatory communication process.

CHAPTER SIXTEEN

Communication in HIV/AIDS prevention: a case study from Vietnam

Toyoko Kodama and Le Thi Minh Chau

INTRODUCTION

In the 21 years since the first patients were diagnosed in 1981, AIDS (acquired immunodeficiency syndrome) has become pandemic. Despite the efforts of governments and local non-governmental organizations (NGOs), the virus has spread at a terrifying rate and taken many lives from generations of young people, their parents and their children. HIV (human immunodeficiency virus), first identified in 1983, is a virus that attacks the immune system of the human body, eventually developing into AIDS. It is now recognized that HIV/AIDS already existed among geographically isolated people in 1950s. Although it was to beginning to spread rapidly during the 1970s, because of its lengthy incubation period, the effects of the virus only became evident in the 1980s. Now, cases are found in virtually every country in the world. In the countries most affected, families who have lost members through AIDS – usually children and the elderly – suffer, in general, from poverty and lack of social support. In view of the social and economic impact that the disease has brought in these countries, well-targeted HIV/AIDS awareness-raising programmes aimed at reducing the transmission of the virus are urgently needed.

This chapter discusses the HIV/AIDS programme from a communications point of view, focusing on the situation in developing countries where HIV/AIDS is most prevalent. It begins with an overview of HIV/AIDS and communication programmes. It argues that an analysis of social and cultural perspectives is an essential contribution to programmes designed to influence the norms and behaviour of target groups. This is followed by a case study based on the work of the Save the Children Fund UK (SC/UK) in Vietnam. The case study illustrates how alternative means of communication and active learning approaches have enabled a deeper understanding of attitudes and risks, minimized discrimination, and promoted supportive attitudes and practical action for prevention, as well as support for people living with HIV/AIDS.

HIV/AIDS IN THE CONTEXT OF DEVELOPING COUNTRIES

According to the recent report from the World Health Organization (WHO) and the Joint United Nations Programme on HIV/AIDS (UNAIDS), there are 36.1 million people worldwide living with HIV. In the year 2000 alone, 3 million AIDS patients lost their lives, 500 000 of them children under 15. Their causes of death include pneumonia, tuberculosis, diarrhoea disorders and tumours. The virus has spread at different speeds in different parts of the world, depending on the availability of medical treatment and resources. Over the past two decades, the concentration of HIV/AIDS cases has shifted from developed to developing countries. In the year 2000, developing countries hosted 95 per cent of the total people affected by HIV/AIDS, and the number is growing at a faster rate than WHO and UNAIDS predicted (WHO, 2000; UN/WHO, 2000).

HIV infections are indiscriminately found among all people in society: homosexual and heterosexual people, men and women, adults and children. When first discovered among homosexual people in the USA, HIV/AIDS was diagnosed as a disease associated with lung infections and skin cancers. Soon after, in 1983, a heterosexual AIDS case was reported in Africa. It is now known that HIV is transmitted through bodily fluids such as blood, semen or mothers' milk. HIV/AIDS has been contracted by haemophiliac patients who received untreated blood through transfusions, and by drug-users who unwittingly shared needles with people who were HIV-positive. HIV/AIDS can also be transmitted between heterosexual men and women who have unprotected sex. Naturally, people who have sex with multiple partners are more exposed to the danger of the infection than others. Babies born to women with HIV are also infected either in the womb or through breast-feeding. Statistically, more men than women are infected by HIV/AIDS, except in sub-Saharan Africa. WHO expects that in the near future, women will outnumber men in other regions, which suggests that the number of children with HIV/AIDS will also increase.

Despite extensive research and investigations since it was first reported, HIV/AIDS remains incurable. However, it is now possible to delay the development of the virus through anti-retroviral therapy. One popular treatment is a so-called 'cocktail treatment', in which doctors prescribe several kinds of drugs, such as AZT (azidothymidine) and DDI (dideoxyinosine). This treatment was first approved for use in the USA in 1987. Ten years later, Brazil became the first developing country to make the therapy available through the public health system. In addition to medical support, patients also require a balanced nutritional intake to generally strengthen their bodily resistance to the virus. As a result of such treatments, statistics from UNAIDS and WHO show that in Latin America and the Caribbean, many HIV sufferers benefit from longer and healthier lives.

Unfortunately, in most developing countries the appropriate medication and environmental conditions for HIV/AIDS treatment is rarely available to sufferers of the epidemic. There are often insufficient doctors to provide even basic medical care for people in need, and fewer with specialist knowledge related to HIV/AIDS treatment. Lack of medical staff and facilities denies patients the regular check-ups and support they require. The cost of drugs required for treatment is another obstacle, as HIV/AIDS is often associated with poverty in these areas. In Malaysia, for example, the medication for HIV treatment costs about US$400–800 per month, which virtually exceeds the GDP per capita (US$3400). Many AIDS sufferers never receive the medical attention they require, and their inability to fight infection eventually leads to death from associated causes. In developing countries, the idea of maintaining safe sex and good health to delay or avoid the development of HIV into AIDS requires an entirely different perspective from that found in developed countries.

Prevention programmes and therapy are, without doubt, effective tools in the fight against the HIV/AIDS epidemic; campaigns and workshops help make people aware of the problems. People need to know two basic facts: that nobody is totally free from the danger of the virus infection; and that the best form of protection is to avoid risky behaviour. The ultimate aim of prevention campaigns should be to change people's behaviour and ways of thinking. Such ambitious goals are, however, difficult to achieve in developing countries because of the deeply rooted social and cultural backgrounds of target groups. Different regions indicate different transmission patterns of the virus infection: some have a high level of infection due to drug-users sharing needles; others through heterosexual intercourse. HIV/AIDS project planners need to take social and cultural perspectives into account to understand the behavioural differences and norms of target groups.

METHODS USED IN HIV/AIDS COMMUNICATION

Several methods are used in HIV/AIDS communication. Theatre plays, mass media and music may be used to deliver a message to large groups of people. Of these, the most powerful are mass media campaigns through TV, radio and newspapers. The main objective of media campaigns is to deliver the same message to a large audience in a relatively short period of time. In relation to recipients, such campaigns are unable to discriminate in terms of gender, age and ethnic group. In developing countries, not everyone has access to TV at home. So the people who have access to media campaigns are not necessarily the intended targets of HIV/AIDS programmes. Also, TV images can create an over-reaction to people infected by HIV/AIDS in a society. Political or social repression or censorship in many societies often hinders the presenting of explicit messages on TV or in public places. Even if the message reaches the target groups, behavioural changes cannot be forced or observed. Hence, large-scale media campaigns raise a number of questions concerning their effectiveness.

Other methods of communication, including role-playing educational programmes with audio-visual tools and workshops, are aimed at smaller groups of people. The difference between large-scale campaigns and these smaller types is that the latter are aimed at more specific audiences or individuals. Role-plays are easy to understand and influential for students of school age and adolescents. Non-governmental organizations often organize and present educational programmes and workshops in target communities. Sometimes, they invite community members to participate. Participation enables people to become more involved in such events than passive observers, and enjoyment of a programme is more likely to lead to a deeper understanding of the issues. Programme planners can gain feedback by examining the response of an audience through follow-up surveys.

SOCIAL AND CULTURAL PERSPECTIVES

In implementing health education or communication programmes for AIDS, there are some common obstacles. Among those, one basic problem is that HIV/AIDS education models are usually designed in developed countries, such as the USA, and later adapted to suit developing countries. Obviously, these models and the messages delivered in communicating AIDS prevention will not be understood by communities and tribal societies from developing countries with different cultures, values and beliefs, and different perspectives in relation to health education. The differences in lifestyles, values and beliefs between developed and developing countries often make it difficult to apply effective health education introduced from outside these societies. Furthermore, community leaders may offer strong resistance to the public discussion of sexual behaviour and AIDS prevention, for cultural or religious reasons.

Misinterpretation or partial understanding of the HIV/AIDS problem can create a bias against people infected with HIV. AIDS health education focuses on individuals, rather than social conditions, and it could appear to be placing the blame on HIV-infected people, rather than the social environment that causes the virus to spread. Even in developed countries such as the USA, some homosexuals suffer stigmatization, which makes it difficult for young people to 'come out' (WHO/UNAIDS). In developing countries, people in higher-risk groups, such as prostitutes and drug-users, are often targets of discrimination. Therefore people with different cultures, values, beliefs and education may have different moral claims and value judgements in relation to HIV/AIDS education, which may create obstacles for campaigns aimed at AIDS prevention communication.

In order to remove such obstacles, people need to acquire the correct information on preventative HIV/AIDS methods, and disseminate it widely in societies. Communication planners need to make it clear where people can gain access to accurate information and voluntary testing services for HIV. Once they know how the virus spreads (what the risk behaviour is), the next step will be to learn how to live with and deal with people suffering from HIV/AIDS. Segregation and name-calling certainly does not halt the spread of the virus: prevention programmes require community involvement. People, especially younger generations, need to be made more aware of the dangers of the epidemic and address it through family or school. While HIV/AIDS is a sensitive issue and requires strict privacy protection, peer communications to fellow patients are quite helpful, and talks by people with HIV/AIDS are known to have a strong impact on target groups. This also proves that sufferers can also contribute to the HIV/AIDS programme (see the case study below). Such efforts will help to eradicate discrimination against patients.

CASE STUDY: THE HIV/AIDS PROGRAMME OF THE UK SAVE THE CHILDREN FUND IN HO CHI MINH CITY, VIETNAM

Vietnam is located in the eastern part of the Indochina Peninsular. It has a population of 75 million (2000). After the 1964–75 Vietnam war, North and South Vietnam became unified as the Socialist Republic of Vietnam. Vietnam initiated its reform policy, *doi moi*, in 1986; a major shift in foreign policy and economic strategy has led to remarkable achievements on the economic, social and political fronts. The country's wealth of natural resources has increasingly faced multiple challenges, including population growth, natural disasters and environmental degradation, and Vietnam remains one of the poorest countries in the world. Over 70 per cent of the Vietnamese workforce is still employed in farming, although there has been an expansion in industrial production and the service sector. It has been acknowledged that the HIV/AIDS epidemic poses a major challenge to the development of Vietnam, particularly as HIV affects Vietnam's greatest resource – its literate and energetic population.

Since 1992, SC/UK has been involved in a wide range of intervention initiatives to help slow down the spread of HIV/AIDS in Vietnam. Working with Vietnamese partner organizations, SC/UK has promoted and supported safe practices in the general population and with groups engaged in high-risk behaviour. Through communication and capacity-building, SC/UK aims to promote supportive and non-judgemental approaches to HIV/AIDS work. With funding from SC/UK, Oxfam Hong Kong and the European Commission, the programme started its first interventions in Ho Chi Minh City under close collaboration with the National AIDS Committee and the Provincial AIDS Committee of Ho Chi Minh City. Such collaboration between national and provincial level has been expanding to other provinces in Vietnam over the past few years. This case study addresses mainly the experiences SC/UK had gained through its involvement with different groups in Ho Chi Minh City during the period from 1992 to 1998. These experiences cover the critical issues and major approaches to HIV/AIDS communication attempted by the programme. Some conclusions are also drawn from the analysis.

HIV/AIDS communication – issues, approaches and activities

Issues

Given the evolution of the epidemic, HIV/AIDS has, more often than not, become associated with homosexual men, commercial sex industry workers and drug-users. Such a belief has left the majority of the population with a false sense of security that they are very unlikely to contract HIV/AIDS.

At the time the SC/UK Programme started in 1992 in Ho Chi Minh City, the only response by the Vietnamese government to the HIV/AIDS crisis was an institutional one-way propaganda approach. The messages targeted mainly sex workers and drug-users; both groups were considered to be 'social evils' and believed to be the root cause of the HIV/AIDS epidemic. Such interventions involved placing sex workers and drug users in institutions in order to keep HIV/AIDS under control. As this hard-line propaganda became established, so equally hard-line public judgemental attitudes developed in relation to the so-called 'risk groups'. This reality presented SC/UK with a major challenge to reverse the message.

High-profile information campaigns (usually one-off events) were the main approach to HIV/AIDS communication in Vietnam, apart from mass media communication. Although such activities provided some information, they did not enable people to internalize the messages and to take practical measures to prevent transmission. Communication should be designed to equip people with the knowledge and skills required for the practice of safer sex.

HIV/AIDS-related language obviously needs careful consideration. Those who are infected should preferably be referred to as people with HIV/AIDS, as opposed to HIV/AIDS victims. In its education messages, the SC/UK Programme addressed *risk behaviour*, rather than *risk groups*. The way the message is communicated also has an effect on its reception. For example, telling someone 'Don't do that, you will get HIV!' without a giving accurate and sufficient information will result in confusion and a reluctance to follow certain instructions.

In its activities, the SC/UK Programme tried out and used terminology such as *cac chi* (sisters) to refer to sex workers or prostitutes; drugs users were known as *cac anh* (brothers). This has proven to be more acceptable, friendly and culturally appropriate. It has reduced the emphasis on the social identity of such groups, to which they have become very sensitive, and which is generally the cause of stigma and prejudice.

The 'wh' questions: Who? What? With Whom? When? and How? are of crucial importance in HIV/AIDS communication. They are used in the selection and training of HIV communicators, in the choice and design of appropriate messages for use with certain targeted population groups at a particular time, as well as in the adoption of appropriate methods and materials. The realization that HIV/AIDS is more than just a medical issue also determines the approaches and information necessary for effective HIV/AIDS communication.

Communication approaches and activities

- *Outreach communication.* Reaching out to people in their community, on the street, café shops . . . getting to know them, adopting non-judgemental attitudes towards them, exploring their understanding of HIV/AIDS and building on such knowledge. Experience shows that sex workers and drug-users often shy away from people who they believe may stigmatize them, as their identity/behaviour is often viewed as socially unacceptable. This has made it difficult for such groups to acquire relevant HIV/AIDS information. Persistent efforts through outreach work with individuals and small groups have significantly raised their awareness of HIV/AIDS.
- *Peer communication.* This was a major attempt by SC/UK to pilot a peer-support approach to HIV/AIDS education, learning from experience gained in Australia and Thailand. Recognizing the strength of both sex workers and drug-users in relation to their knowledge and experience of their community, the SC/UK Programme worked with them to train a number of peer communicators. Training included HIV/AIDS messages, use of certain materials, facilitation and communication skills. With the advantage of easily reaching their peers, trained peer communicators have contributed significantly to the dissemination of HIV/AIDS information. Messages discussed include information on HIV and other sexually transmitted diseases; how HIV is and is not transmitted; what the practical ways of prevention are and why; who and what is involved (e.g. condom availability, clean needles and syringes, negotiation with sexual partners, peer support and pressure). Many peer communicators talked about their self-esteem being built and confidence re-established through this involvement. They were happy with their role and their ability to contribute to HIV/AIDS communication. They also provide a pool of invaluable input for HIV/AIDS communication: many drug-users have composed HIV/AIDS songs that carry their messages in a very powerful manner. The SC/UK Programme, however, believed that peer education did not just apply to those two groups, and is attempting to develop the peer approach in other groups such as students, street children and workers.
- *Community-based communication.* SC/UK activities have been targeted at the wider community through a partnership project to build a district's capacity in implementing HIV/AIDS prevention. This approach stresses that all groups in the population need to take precautions, as well as being prepared for the epidemic.
- *Active learning approach.* HIV/AIDS is both a very public and a private issue. Public because of its widespread effect and response. Private because it affects the personal lives of people in ways never experienced before. HIV/AIDS communication needs to take account of this, and the work should be designed accordingly. The creative use

of educational games, dynamic individual/group exercises, role-plays, dialogue, puppets, cartoons, films, cassette tapes and problem-solving activities facilitate the participation of learners. The process has been referred to as 'learning-by-doing': reflecting upon daily attitudes and behaviour as well as analysing the risk factors using the information provided. When people are able to relate to an issue and appreciate that it affects them personally, they will have the incentive to do something about it, such as practising new behaviour. Such methods enable people to internalize or personally interpret messages, and also have fun in the process of learning, which is the basis of popular community communication/education. People are generally preoccupied by the many other concerns in their lives other than HIV/AIDS, and only become interested when the issues are communicated in practical and appealing ways.

This active learning environment encourages the practice of new skills: negotiation of safer and protected sex, improvement of communication and analytical skills in general, and problem identification to enable people to make the right choices for their own safety. Of course, for these new skills to be sustained they need a lot of follow-up support. Such approaches allow communication to take place not just between individual learners and the communicator, but more importantly, among the learners themselves. The design of messages and tools (such as pictures) has also been carefully considered by SC/UK to ensure that HIV/AIDS communication is neither threatening nor likely to result in negative behaviour, such as alienating people with HIV/AIDS or discriminating against them. (It is essential to understand how HIV is transmitted, but it is also critically important to know how it is *not* transmitted.)

CONCLUSIONS

The magnitude of the impact of HIV/AIDS on developing countries cannot be overstated. As Dr Peter Piot, Executive Director of UNAIDS, says: 'HIV needs to be the centre of development policy'. Issues that HIV/AIDS project planners should bear in mind include: identifying target groups; determining appropriate communication methods to reach the target groups; and securing adequate resources. In designing programmes, the first step should be the identification of HIV/AIDS sufferers and how they are affected by HIV/AIDS. Aspects such as gender, ethnicity, age, income and the characteristics of target people should also be recorded. Focus groups and participatory need assessment are the most common ways to gather information for baseline surveys prior to project planning (Buchanan and Cernada, 1998). Quantitative and qualitative information gained from surveys will allow planners to understand behavioural differences and norms, and enable them to design a programme that will best suit the cultural context. Different communities require different approaches, and programmes should be adjusted to suit individual target groups.

Behavioural changes in human beings present a challenge in HIV/AIDS prevention programmes, and also make projects more difficult to monitor and evaluate. As has been mentioned, 'knowledge is not sufficient to change the behaviour of individuals' (Freimuth, 1992). Even if behaviour has changed, maintaining the change requires a different set of activities. HIV/AIDS communication entails sensitivity towards the social, economic and cultural aspects of society. To avoid stigmatization and unnecessary confusion in society, language and methods of communication need to be carefully selected and used. Ultimately, practitioners need to develop alternative approaches to complement mass media communication.

Securing financial as well as human resources is essential to the success of HIV/AIDS programmes, as is the case in other developmental projects. Medical projects are necessarily costly in terms of drugs, expertise and long-term intervention needed to monitor the level of success of projects. However, it is increasingly recognized that HIV/AIDS is not purely a medical issue. The social and economic dimensions of HIV/AIDS have received growing attention in HIV/AIDS policy and programming. Prevention and responding to the impact of HIV/AIDS have been identified as programmatic priorities. Multi-faceted interventions are needed to address the social, economic, cultural and political aspects of HIV/AIDS besides the medical aspect. Hence, sustainability of projects depends on strategic resource mobilization and management, and appropriate technical capacity in research, planning, implementation and monitoring.

This case study demonstrates how alternative approaches to HIV/AIDS communication have helped shape the development perspective towards HIV/AIDS communication. It is about mobilizing and optimizing resources, building capacity and empowering people. Such efforts can promote changes in attitudes and beliefs towards HIV/AIDS: a more friendly response of the community to the so-called 'social evils' and a less discriminatory perspective towards people with HIV/AIDS and others involved in risk behaviour.

In a world with HIV/AIDS, information from communication and prevention programmes is very critical as it gives people the power and capacity to live safely as well as to cope effectively: protecting themselves from the virus or minimizing social prejudice as a result of infection, as well as having a supportive and empathetic attitude towards people with HIV/AIDS. Well-targeted and well-designed communication programmes can contribute greatly to constructing the right awareness about HIV. They go further than that in enabling people to change their attitudes and behaviour. The success of HIV/AIDS prevention depends tremendously on communication: its messages, languages, styles, approaches, communicators and audience.

CHAPTER SEVENTEEN

Knowledge transfer in a democratic context

Pachampet Sundaram

INTRODUCTION

This chapter raises a number of questions on the subject of knowledge transfer in a large democratic country such as India. What traditional and modern means of communication and knowledge transfer strategies are needed to ensure that research is relevant and practical solutions are a feasible outcome? Are we looking at more advanced techniques of communication, or are we considering the use of prevalent forms of information dissemination and media in developing countries, in innovative ways, in order to transfer research knowledge? Have we learnt enough about indigenous knowledge from developing countries as a basis for solving problems of local communities? What of the politics of communication in emerging democracies and the resistance of those with a vested interest in secrecy and withholding information? Consequently, should we study how the collection and transmission of information fits into more participatory forms of urban government? What are the skills and strategies that the government and different stakeholders require in order for effective capacity to be built for transmitting information and knowledge? How, given the concerns of bilateral donor agencies such as the UK Department for International Development (DFID), should we link the entire process of development communication to ongoing efforts for good governance and citizen-centred administration in different countries?

This chapter cannot answer all these questions, but attempts to describe the ingrained attitudes of government and other organizations to the transfer of knowledge and information; the constraints limiting the population when obtaining access to research; and the perceptions of the urban poor in relation to obtaining knowledge for improving their daily lives.

THE INDIAN CONTEXT

India is the largest democracy in Asia and, according to the latest census, has a population of just over 1 billion. The urban population forms about 26 per cent of the total population. The country has over 30 metropolitan cities, including mega-cities such as Mumbai, Calcutta and Delhi. India is a country of tremendous diversity in language, culture, resource endowments, geography and climate. There are 3700 towns, 627 000 villages and at least six states that have a population exceeding 80 million people. The country is governed by a federal constitution with 28 states and seven union territories, and there is a constitutional division of powers and resources. Recent amendments to the Constitution have ensured a statutory base for the elected local bodies below the states.

Despite years of planned development and the successes scored by recent policies of liberalization, the challenges are daunting for this country of sub-continental proportions and diversity. India has a large and growing population divided by religion, caste, language and ethnic tensions. While levels of poverty have been declining, it is estimated that 27 per cent of the country's population live below the poverty line (Planning Commission, 1997). The poverty levels are aggravated by widespread inequalities: between regions, between rural and urban areas, within parts of the same city, within communities and, most significantly, between men and women. Despite impressive schemes for education and healthcare, levels of illiteracy and lack of healthcare are still high. The pursuit of determined efforts to reduce poverty and expand social opportunities is hampered by a number of factors, such as lack of resources, administrative bottlenecks, inadequate citizen orientation and lack of transparency in administration, the politics of patronage and rent-seeking in an era of coalition governments, and insufficient popular pressure for reform.

It is possible, however, to note a number of developments since the early 1990s. First, there is political consensus for honest, open and participatory governance, for women's empowerment and for poverty reduction. Striking efforts have been made to implement strategies for good governance in a number of states (some of which are supported by DFID).

Second, there is pressure for genuine decentralization and devolution of resources to elected local bodies (the rural bodies described as *Panchayati Raj* institutions in the Constitution), which is driven by the voice of over a million elected representatives. From these, one-third of the representatives and chairpersons of local bodies are women and people from disadvantaged groups.

Third, government programmes or donor agencies support the growing movement of civil society and citizen groups in cities and rural areas. Non-governmental organizations (NGOs) and their networks are engaged in raising the awareness and capacities of community groups and elected representatives. They engage in advocacy on behalf of neglected groups such as slum-dwellers, street children and women in difficult circumstances.

Campaigns on public issues such as the right to information and shelter for the homeless are being scaled up from one region or city, then linked with mainstream issues of legal and regulatory reform. An active judiciary and media bolster efforts to increase the accountability and responsiveness of the administration. The explosion of communication and ideas is fuelled by the entire media, the Internet, a free press in different languages and the widespread use of information technology.

PRESENT SYSTEMS OF KNOWLEDGE TRANSFER IN INDIA

In this context, it is useful to look at a number of problems that hinder the transfer of knowledge in India. These often stem from political and financial issues. The lack of access local institutes and practitioners have to the results of research is due to either the high cost of publications, the non-availability of funds in institutes, or ignorance about the availability of the publications in different research and academic institutions. The readers' inadequate understanding of English, or any other language foreign to them, aggravates this position. The low level of access of many institutions to computers, and their problems in using the Internet, make it difficult for scholars to track and use existing publications even when they are listed on the disseminator's home page on the Internet. The above factor also explains the failure of training schools and academic institutions to assimilate research findings and incorporate them in their curricula for training and instruction, or to follow up on the findings. Thus the smaller Indian institutions face problems in establishing two-way relationships with researchers in India and abroad.

A related problem is that of validating research findings, as uncritical dissemination can often undermine the scaling-up of good programmes and send wrong signals to researchers and citizens alike. Often, the premature publication of research findings on a technique or process, or the hasty implementation of what was considered to be an otherwise good idea, may lead to contrary results.

Government officials are confronted with different obstacles in relation to research programmes in the urban and housing sectors of developing countries, which are supported by multilateral and bilateral donor agencies and private foundations, either as part of an ongoing credit or as a part of an independent programme. Elaborate internal rules of access and confidentiality govern the publications of donor agencies and, until recently, not enough effort has been made by them to disseminate reports. Even the research reports of regional institutions, such as the Urban Management Program (supported by the UN Development Program), are not readily available to most training institutions. Officials from developing countries often vent their frustration on this subject at international conferences. Such instances of inadequate access are mentioned in part to balance the popular impression in developed countries that developing countries do not act on the sound advice of experts funded by external donors.

EXPERIENCES IN COMMUNICATION

In partial appreciation of the problems of dissemination of available knowledge, the Central Ministry of Urban Affairs in India and the National Institute of Urban Affairs, New Delhi, made efforts during the 1990s to bring together researchers and practitioners in cities to share their innovative experiences, project findings and survey reports for a wider audience. This effort covered:

- workshops under the Financial Institutions Reform and Expansion (FIRE) project, assisted by the US Agency for International Development (USAID), to bring together senior officials and experts to talk about issues such as property tax reform, commercialization of urban infrastructure, partnerships with private sector and municipal accounting
- a series of seminars which brought together the members of State Finance Commissions to share information and perceptions on local government finance, and helped disseminate the findings of research institutes among elected representatives and the people
- seminars on urban land policy experiences and future strategies
- national and regional discussions of good models of urban basic services and community management of poverty alleviation programmes
- research studies to evolve training modules for officials and elected representatives, based on field studies.

In terms of local dissemination in English and regional languages, a number of research institutions and NGOs circulate newsletters and periodicals to a wide audience (and place them on the Internet). The institutions include the National Institute of Urban Affairs (since the early 1980s); the Human Settlement Management Institute (since the mid-1980s); the Public Affairs Centre, Bangalore (since the mid-1990s); a number of state-level training institutes; and a number of sector-based NGOs in fields including environment, health, women's development and disadvantaged groups.

In the area of local governance, a number of government-sponsored institutions and voluntary agencies undertake dissemination of information through newsletters and periodicals, and the publication of case studies and papers on field experiences and research findings. There have been many efforts to produce and distribute video cassettes and audio-visual material for the purpose of training elected local representatives and for informing citizens. All India Radio collaborated with a number of national and state agencies to produce information capsules in local languages, and secured audience interest by delivering messages through the medium of soap opera.

Some city agencies such as the Guntur City Corporation disseminate information to a wider audience through the Internet and information centres. Other instances are the use of ward- and village-level publications and posters as in the state of Tamil Nadu. Donor agencies and research institutions have organized workshops on city development plans or strategies for slum upgrading (as in the DFID-assisted slum improvement projects or the Ahmedbad city slum upgrading project). The city of Bangalore started newsletters in English and Kannada language to disseminate field experiences in slum improvement in a project assisted by the Netherlands Habitat foundation. The state of Kerala has been using similar methods in its mass literacy and poverty alleviation projects. Information, education and communication are essential components of urban and rural projects for health, nutrition and education of the general population and women's development, which are administered by central and state government agencies, sometimes with the assistance of donor agencies.

There have been efforts for a similar sharing of experience and local problems in the participatory learning method workshops organized in the DFID-assisted projects in India for slum improvement and primary education in a number of states (DFID, 2000a). UNICEF has been advocating case study and piloting approaches and assistance for scaling up good initiatives. Following the examples of awards for city- and state-level innovation in the USA and the Citizens' Charter Awards in the UK, central government is involved in piloting innovations under a Citizens' Charter in a number of sectors and disseminating good practices (DARPG, 1997). The Human Settlements Management Institute, New Delhi, has already started rewarding successful efforts by agencies for affordable housing and urban improvement.

DEVELOPMENT COMMUNICATION AND THE UNSERVED GROUPS

Despite these efforts, there is a nagging concern among a growing number of administrators and voluntary groups in India that government agencies, donor agencies or national research institutions devote insufficient effort and resources to disseminating knowledge in terms that are intelligible to the majority of the population. Development communication has to deal equally with the problem of the transfer of knowledge and information to less-informed groups among the literate population. The problems of communication to less-literate groups are complex in a country such as India, which is spread over huge distances and is characterized by information barriers.

Further, in a democratic country such as India the question is not just one of disseminating research findings, but also of explaining the broader governance issue of the obligation of a democratic government to promote proactive dissemination of information to enable the active participation of all sections of the population in decisions affecting them. Many citizens' groups are no longer content with the present system of top-down communication by government agencies. They demand institutionalized avenues for government to consider and respond to the views of citizens.

The campaign for freedom of information in India illustrates forcefully this view of development communication. A striking instance of the campaign is the struggle for information in the state of Rajasthan, led by a local voluntary agency called *Mazdur Kisan Shakti Sanghatan* (MKSS; struggle for empowering workers and farmers). MKSS has campaigned successfully for the opening of records of local agencies to poor people; for public hearings on development projects; and for removing the shroud of secrecy surrounding government activities (Goetz and Jenkins, 1999). The importance of the work of organizations such as the MKSS lies in informing other civil society organizations in India about the criticality of access to information for whatever activity is pursued by them.

NGOs in India perceive transparency in administration and the right of citizens to information as part of the struggle for the right to livelihood (in terms of information on minimum wages, laws and access to basic services for the vast majority of citizens). The NGOs also urge that information needs related to basic survival and functional literacy be met before undertaking the task of communicating research knowledge to people less blessed with services and literacy.

Effective communication undoubtedly rests on strengthening the system of public records in Indian government offices, to enable easy retrieval and dissemination. Both sensitive officials and citizens' groups are concerned about the extremely inadequate and fragile databases in cities. They undermine rational planning, and defeat efforts for consistent monitoring and oversight of the programmes of different agencies. The imperfect access to information of most citizens in urban areas explains the exploitation of residents by builders and brokers; the inability of the poor to make informed decisions on shelter and location; and the power of politicians over communities through patronage on land titles and housing subsidies.

Secrecy in administration also explains the unholy nexus of officials and political leaders, as well as middlemen, who profit from monopoly over information and the lack of well-enforced rules for the disclosure of reasons for decisions. This nexus flourishes despite many crises born of rumour, sensational reporting, and failure to gain the people's confidence and disseminate correct information, as seen in a scare over an alleged plague in the city of Surat (in the western state of Gujarat) in the early 1990s, or in many incidents of communal violence. Ultimately, secrecy and poor communications undermine the credibility of government and the trust that people have in administration.

A resolution of a Conference of Chief Ministers in India in May 1997 (DARPG, 1997) on effective and responsive administration led to decisions by a number of state governments and central government to enact laws for freedom of information. This was accompanied by the issue of instructions in a number of states for obligatory publication of all information on development works and village budgets; for the proactive release to the public of all non-classified information; and for public hearings on major projects affecting Indian people. The government proposes to accomplish this objective through procedural changes including delegation of powers and one-stop information systems, as well as the use of information technology and Web resources. The central government also proposes to enact a law on fiscal transparency.

A number of voluntary agencies, such as the Development Initiative for Social and Human Action, state of Gujarat; *Vidhayak Sansad*, Maharashtra; Consumer Unity and Trust Society, Rajasthan; and the Centre for Budget Planning and Studies, Karnataka, have been equipped by the Ford Foundation since the late 1990s to make public budgets easy to understand, thus enlightening the public about the use of public funds for schemes intended to benefit poor and marginal groups (Ford Foundation, 1999).

PROCESS OF KNOWLEDGE TRANSFER

The principles for more effective transfer of knowledge may be transferable across different levels of administration, including urban government, but the delivery and content must vary according to the target group and its receptive capacity. Development communication in different projects has been achieved through different media tools such as radio, television and theatre. A number of state agencies encourage and develop the use of traditional and interpersonal methods in development projects. A number of campaigns have successfully used street theatre and folk songs in service delivery projects in urban slums and social sectors.

Official documents such as the Indian Five-Year Plans (the latest being the Ninth Five-Year Plan for the period 1997–2002) recognize that participation and the empowerment of women and marginal groups, as well as public accountability, depend on access to information from different formal and voluntary agencies. As seen from a number of field studies on rural decentralization and the urban poor, peer-to-peer exchanges and training are very productive in transferring information and heightening consciousness (SEARCH, 1999).

NGOs in the state of Karnataka have used a variety of innovative communication tools to promote capacity-building of elected local representatives. One voluntary agency found games and songs to be more useful and popular than written material, considering the level of literacy of elected representatives. The games helped to boost self-confidence, enhance communication skills and build team spirit. The use of radio for disseminating information on participatory governance in Mysore district in Karnataka provided a non-intrusive way of reaching people in their homes (SEARCH, 1999; Kripa and Prasad, 2000).

The outstanding examples of participatory planning and management are to be found in the Vijayawada city slum improvement project in the state of Andhra Pradesh, and the community-managed urban poverty eradication project in Alleppey and other cities in the state of Kerala. These projects rested on concurrent evaluation of project experience, technologies for sewerage and drainage, methods of delivery, savings-and-loan systems, economic activities, involvement of local business, etc., and the transfer of this knowledge to the people. Sustained dissemination was achieved by convergent information systems and community-level monitoring systems of the type developed for urban basic devices projects in cities such as Nashik, Maharashtra. Dissemination was effected through community development workers, local newsletters and one-day orientation sessions with local resource persons, and participatory workshops for neighbourhood leaders and government personnel from different sectors.

By looking at information on all the activities of city development together, instead of taking a narrow, sector-based view, it was possible in participatory infrastructure projects to discover sector linkages and optimize investment outcomes. This comprehensive exercise also helped broaden the outlook of technical experts in different sectors. The transfer of information in the slum-upgrading projects on different standards of infrastructure and their costs, for instance, permitted the ranking and prioritization of cost and service options by the community in the cities of Cuttack, Kochi and Baroda. The exercise further led to community decisions to make a financial contribution, where the residents expressed a need to install an option that was more expensive than the project cost ceiling. The project design was built for sanitation and sewage treatment in locally manageable technology, and thus saves on effort and resources for the municipality.

The Indore city project, assisted by DFID in the early 1990s, relied on the simplification of technology for sewerage, drainage and road-laying, networking of slum works with city services and interactive communication with community associations. The project idea was capable of being transferred not only to professionals in the country, but could be transmitted to neighbourhood associations through city-level civil society organizations. An effort was undertaken in the transformation (*parivartan*) project of the city of Ahmedabad (western India) through the partnership of the municipal corporation, business and NGOs in the late 1990s.

It is often forgotten that the Municipal Corporation, as constituted on the British model of late 1940s, is in itself an excellent medium of knowledge transfer to different stakeholders within municipal limits through elected representatives and local administration. The city of Surat proved how it is possible to move from an abysmal level of environmental sanitation and health status to high levels of sanitation and health indicators by a combination of political support, administrative leadership, enforced employee compliance and citizen support.

KNOWLEDGE TRANSFER THROUGH INTERMEDIARIES

The report card, which is a tool for eliciting people's responses on the performance of different public agencies or similar agencies in different cities, is used for checking people's feedback for a systematic assessment of public services. The card is a scientific, Gallup poll-type survey of citizens applied in one or more cities. Responses are ranked by giving scores for different agencies in terms of defined criteria, such as response time and corruption. This is an instance of knowledge transfer within and across cities undertaken by a committed NGO research agency.

Agency performance scores are recorded on report cards. The card has become the basis for citizens' awareness of concrete measures for assessing agencies and for mounting campaigns for improving services. Report cards are referred to in World Bank literature (World Bank, 1997). The Public Affairs Centre, Bangalore (Public Affairs Centre, 1995), used report cards to highlight citizens' perceptions of services provided by different public agencies and to increase their accountability to citizens. The findings were widely publicized by the media and by resident welfare associations, and formed the basis for further mobilization of citizens around civil issues. Thanks to this, NGOs and research organizations in other cities started experimenting with the techniques underlying the report card. The use of the card was also extended to specific sectors such as public distribution systems, industry, municipal budgeting and comparative rating of services by units within organizations.

Knowledge transfer from the Citizens' Voluntary Initiative for the City of Bangalore (CIVIC) and local research institutions such as the Public Affairs Centre sustain the *Swabhimana* (self-reliance) city network of resident groups in Bangalore city. The Public Affairs Centre has built partnerships with NGOs in other cities and neighbouring countries to help them undertake exercises for public feedback and ranking of services of different public agencies.

The Baroda Citizens' Council has been functioning for about 20 years in the city of Baroda (western India) as a local partnership of businesses, the Municipal Corporation and voluntary agencies. The Council has a core professional group and an information unit to collect and continuously collate research findings and relevant information, and uses this to identify and support areas for intervention to upgrade services with community participation. The Council not only funds NGO requests in different city services, but builds their capacity through training, skills-building, transfer of technical knowledge and deputation of personnel from the corporate sector for short periods to install the project. A similar effort to build the capacities of local NGOs underlies the activities of a number of national NGOs in the field of decentralized rural governance, such as the Society for Participatory Research in Asia and the Association of Voluntary Agencies in Rural Development in New Delhi.

An initiative in the city of Chennai (south India) called EXNORA (Excellent, Novel and Radical) is an instance of a city-wide effort in waste management through a network of neighbourhood-level societies. The effort was improved by the transfer of knowledge from EXNORA on effective techniques such as community-driven waste collection, storage and recycling, rehabilitation of informal waste handlers and the generation of resources from waste. The same approach guides the waste management initiative and community composting in the cities of Ahmedabad, Mumbai and Pune. This activity is often integrated with the rehabilitation of street children, as seen in the waste management initiative in Bangalore.

Asian cities present many such examples of transfer of research knowledge in the field of sanitation, waste management and treatment of sewage, such as India's Sulabh International, the Manila city waste dump project, the pisciculture project in the wetlands of Calcutta and so on. In these projects, knowledge transfer is mediated effectively by city-wide networks of NGOs rather than by official agencies. Some of these networks, such as those for waste management – or street children, ActionAid, women's development or the savings groups – extend over many cities.

There is a considerable element of networking and mutual support to citizens' groups involved in some cities. The Society for the Promotion of Area Resource Centres (SPARC) in Mumbai has provided professional support and information back-up for women living on the pavements of Mumbai, and has sustained their dialogue with city authorities for permanent shelter and means of livelihood. The transfer of knowledge and replication of the experience have been achieved through networks with other NGOs. More significantly, knowledge transfer has occurred directly from the collectives of pavement women (*Mahila Milans*) and the Slum-dwellers Federation in Mumbai to similar groups in other cities (and even to peer groups in South Africa) via discussions and newsletters. SPARC has transferred the techniques of participatory survey of socio-economic conditions, community-managed savings and shelter construction to cities in India and abroad. SPARC has built partnerships with city and state agencies in a number of cities' projects for the relocation of slum families on railway tracks and community sanitation. The SPARC example also illustrates ways in which the urban poor are able to utilize information on financial institutions, land availability and planning systems to devise affordable collective solutions for shelter and survival.

At the national level, the savings groups of the poor in different cities have come together for the transfer of knowledge on successful local systems of resource mobilization, links to formal institutions and effective lending. The Self-Employed Women's Association (SEWA) in the city of Ahmedabad organized groups of women in the informal sector to form banks to provide flexible credit for their shelter and economic activities. SEWA is now extending this approach to a number of other cities.

The intermediary NGOs enjoy superior access to knowledge from both research reports and internal documentation, because of their ability to employ professional staff and attract competent volunteers. This advantage enhances the benefits from knowledge transfer, which is mediated by these NGOs. A number of government departments and local agencies seek to benefit from the NGO networks. This government/formal sector–NGO–community networking in India is driving many social sector projects in the cities and national programmes in, for example, women's development, family welfare, AIDS control, children in difficult circumstances.

The model of community-driven participatory planning has replaced the partnership model. The people's campaign for planning has been in operation in the state of Kerala for over five years (ISS, 1996). The plan has the unique feature of utilizing resource people from the society on a voluntary basis for transmitting knowledge on resource mapping and planning to the people at neighbourhood and city levels. The approach helps to match priorities to resources. The volunteer resource people are trained by the state government to obtain the basic information and planning tools to assist the people in preparing plans and later to help in the decentralized execution of projects.

PARTNERSHIP WITH THE MEDIA

The metropolitan city of Pune in western India is an example of a decentralized, community-centred city government which is characterized by ward- or district-level consultation. It is also the home for an initiative by a national newspaper for continuous dissemination of the consultation process and response by city authorities. Recognition of this consultation exercise in the media provided incentives to municipal staff to be more responsive, and helped sustain the enthusiasm of citizens' groups. There are similar instances, for example of the media projecting the activities of the Campaign for Right to Information in the state of Rajasthan and other places, and generating demands from the people for similar positive responses from the government. The media have also helped in disseminating the findings of important research in issues such as the disposal of hospital wastes, environmental impact of harmful occupations, beneficial uses of fly ash and the benefits from flexible use of development rules in Mumbai.

Efforts are being made in India to communicate messages through media and films on issues such as the drug menace, family welfare, AIDS control, immunization of children, violence against women and so on; but even sustained campaigns often do not have the desired impact. In this context, and without effective institutions to back the effort, it is difficult to see how episodic reporting of research findings can lead to action. The problem is also one of high levels of illiteracy and the low order of reporting of development research by regional newspapers. In the context of scarce resources for communication, a number of voluntary agencies and some state agencies are tapping into existing infrastructure such as radio, which has extensive coverage, and devising imaginative ways of holding listeners' interest. There is a problem relating to the multitude of languages spoken in India and the identification of resource persons to package messages for media use (Kripa and Prasad, 2000).

The National Foundation of India, New Delhi, and a number of similar organizations are promoting investigative journalism and popular reporting of social and development issues by regional newspapers. Donor agencies such as the Ford Foundation assist voluntary agencies in the innovative use of media for broadcasting episodes on elected rural local government (*Panchayati Raj*) and local issues.

DRAWING ON INDIGENOUS KNOWLEDGE

There is considerable interest, even among donor agencies such as the Ford Foundation, in the development of indigenous knowledge systems and learning from local traditions and practices (Ford Foundation, 1999). State and voluntary sectors recognize the need to be sensitive to the plurality of India's languages, religions and cultures. Indigenous knowledge and folklore, which are unique to specific regions, generate local knowledge related to construction projects and the use of natural resources. Grassroots community organizations and folklore institutions have begun to assist local communities to draw on their cultural heritage and traditional techniques as a resource, as for example with the crafts cooperatives which emerged in the 1980s in western India to link rural crafts with urban buyers. Puppetry has been revived as a powerful medium of grassroots communication in south India.

Folk music and theatre employ local idioms that emerge from community contexts, and serve as effective, low-cost tools of communication. Folk arts frequently comment on contemporary issues and problems close to the poor, and have served as a catalyst for dialogue and change.

TRANSFER OF APPROPRIATE TECHNOLOGY

The transfer of knowledge on appropriate technology and building materials for housing falls into a different category. Policy-makers were perplexed by the failure to translate laboratory research into field applications, and by the limited application of the techniques and use of the low-cost materials in public and private housing. The fact was that the existing planning and building standards did not recognize the incremental construction process followed by poor people and the use of recycled, often semi-durable materials and components. The prevalent construction standards were more suited to the lifestyles of 20 per cent of the population, and did not respect the need for shared services in conditions of high density and low affordability. The situation has now changed, with the adoption of a national code for housing the economically weaker sections.

The solution began with breaking down the mental barriers of engineers and architects, who had for years been trained to work with durable materials and structures. The next problem was to formulate new standards for the low-cost technologies and materials, systems of cluster planning, repairs and reconstruction, and slum renovation, and to persuade city authorities to adopt these new standards.

The subsequent step was to get the standards into tender and contract documents and to motivate private builders to bid for public projects. Then came the important part – validating the techniques and materials in small projects to establish their comparative advantage in terms of cost, utility and maintenance costs. This brought out the need to devise dissemination mechanisms for public and private building organizations and professionals on the one hand, and for the general public in the formal and informal sectors on the other. An institution with the representation of all leading departments and professional bodies was set up to achieve the validation of techniques and materials, introduce standards, provide fiscal concessions and knowledge to manufacturers for assured supplies, and to educate the public through exhibitions, posters, newsletters, TV documentaries and so on.

At the field level, a network of autonomous building centres was set up throughout the country to train artisans in techniques, provide information to local people and undertake on a trial basis the manufacture of the recommended materials, as well as the construction of houses. The selection of the right manager for the building centre and the provision of the right advice for using the suggested technique and materials was crucial, as the entire credibility of the transfer process could be undermined by the failure of the technique.

The rehabilitation of houses by a number of NGOs following the earthquakes in the states of Uttar Pradesh and Gujarat sought to promote improvements in traditional systems of construction, rather than importing energy-intensive modern systems. This led to more sustainable and popularly accepted shelter systems.

A STRATEGY FOR THE DONOR AGENCIES

The donors could look at a simple organizing framework to guide the strategy for knowledge transfer. This strategy should be based on: (i) what we know and do not know; (ii) how to find knowledge; (iii) how to learn to learn; and (iv) how to learn and share. This could translate itself initially in knowledge-sharing and facilitating initiatives such as online databases sharing best practices on thematic areas and publications. It could also include help in developing local area networks for the sharing of local knowledge by clients and communities and for gaining access to global knowledge, supporting client feedback surveys, and a venture capital fund to try out research findings and new ideas. In terms of what has been admitted by international aid agencies about gaps in internal transfer of knowledge among various divisions, some indicators could be worked out to assess whether the knowledge transfer process is making a difference and bringing value.

The indicators could consist of measures to check the use of knowledge by the personnel in the aid agency or knowledge transfer agency; lead indicators of client and staff satisfaction (for example, Service Charters) with knowledge-related services; and evidence on sharing knowledge with colleagues and with clients. The real issue is one of narrowing the knowledge adaptation gap in the organization, which is a measure of the ability of the agency's staff to adapt the available knowledge to a specific local setting. In other words, the incentive systems and processes for project staff in aid agencies should stress the knowledge transfer objective as much as aid disbursement.

CONCLUSIONS

In response to the questions raised in the Introduction, there is a strong case for contextualizing the question of knowledge transfer within the larger concerns of governments and donor agencies about good governance, transparency, accountability, human rights, participation and equity. The requirements of building capacity for development communication and transparency should include not just the intermediate agencies and training institutions, but the personnel in different public agencies and local bodies. The new orientation proposed would also help to address the issue of what is likely to happen after research findings are transmitted to the urban poor. This broader approach would redefine the role of researchers, training institutions, public agencies and donor agencies in mainstreaming into good governance and expanding social opportunities for the people. These agencies have a role in using a common language which will be understood by all, and in devising ways to widen access by eliminating secrecy. They also have a role in the use of indigenous knowledge as a base for interpreting problems of local communities.

In terms of dissemination, it is necessary to veer away from overemphasis on techniques of communication which are beyond the reach of majority groups and researchers in small towns. Successful examples advocate the use of prevalent channels of information dissemination, such as the messages used in Indian mass literacy campaigns; neighbourhood information centres; and media such as radio which reach a wide audience. The parallel route is to operate through democratic channels of local government down to the neighbourhood groups and user committees, and allow for peer exchange and networking of NGOs across cities and sectors. Responsive initiatives would provide for the installation of special facilities for disadvantaged groups, and stress the imaginative use of television, radio and news media. The strategy would support development writers and journalists who can package the findings and information into easily readable messages.

Research institutions in the North (developed) and South (less-developed) have a special responsibility to devise relevant training materials, disseminate validated research results, assist in training and orienting officials at all levels for knowledge transfer, and help in recasting the conventional wisdom in tune with the needs and circumstances of the people. There is scope and opportunity for much greater interaction between development workers and business groups of the North and South. While it is important to debate the tools and technology of knowledge transfer and their widespread use, the task will not be complete unless the institutional culture of researchers and donor agencies changes:

- from an emphasis on *what* we learn to *how* we learn
- from asking what knowledge transfer can do for an individual, to asking what one can do to share, and in sharing, to learn and gain from the experience.

CHAPTER EIGHTEEN

Conclusions

Catalina Gandelsonas

The contributors to this book have each explored different aspects of communicating knowledge for development, including various communication models, networks, intermediaries and media. Communication problems resulting from cultural and educational differences are fully explored and applied in a number of case studies. Finally, interesting and controversial approaches to development and communication offer new and challenging perspectives in relation to this field.

COMMUNICATION MODELS AND MODELLING

The theoretical discussion on communication processes and modelling highlights the importance of new communication models and the strategic importance of social networks, intermediaries, key informants and media. As knowledge delivered by international agencies has to date been supplied rather than demand-driven, and often provided in unsuitable formats, new communication models are proposed to counteract such problems. Key conclusions arising in relation to these themes are as follows.

- The communication process is a complex participatory process that requires more than one- or two-way information flow models. Thus a 'many-way' or circular exchange of information with the urban poor and various intermediaries should be used to apply research knowledge to development practices (Chapter 1).
- Models proposed in Chapter 2 encourage empowering people in poverty through access to knowledge and information, as lack of choice and an unbalanced distribution of information and knowledge lock the urban poor in an inescapable and unavoidable poverty trap.
- The good or best practice communication model is most effective when backed by direct experience of good practices and face-to-face communication (Chapter 1).
- Knowledge transfer should form part of a more general research communication and networking strategy based on the idea of partnership and knowledge exchange (Chapter 1).
- The possibilities and limitations of modelling and how they facilitate the communication of knowledge are highlighted in Chapter 1. Modelling allows the mapping of types of information flows, channels,

media and institutions, which provides communities with access to new knowledge and information. Information models resulting from this process are difficult to transfer and adapt to new circumstances (Chapter 2).

VEHICLES FOR COMMUNICATING DEVELOPMENT: NETWORKS, INTERMEDIARIES AND MEDIA

Social networks are vital and strategic as a medium for communicating knowledge. They can be found within poor communities, and are important resources for the poor to gain advice, information, and emotional and practical support from network members. They are also a principal asset in relation to the livelihoods of poor communities.

- Networks can be an effective means for communities to exchange information, share work, and disseminate knowledge and information.
- The social capital of networks should be strengthened for development purposes.
- Word of mouth (easily achievable through networks) appears to be an important vehicle for the transmission of information (Chapter 2).
- Urban poor communities and their social networks may suffer greatly as a result of the spatial characteristics and psycho-social environment of slums and squatter settlements. Social interchanges will not be facilitated in such conditions, which may generate communication barriers (Chapter 4).
- Communicative processes based on street theatre should be fostered between inhabitants of the same locality (Chapters 4 and 15).
- In communicating knowledge, intermediaries, key informants and community leaders are crucial in bridging the gap between researchers and communities (Chapter 1). A possible problem is that transmitted information is sometimes distorted by 'corrupting agents' (Chapter 2).
- The use of digital media is not widespread in developing countries, and this may widen the communication gap between North and South (Chapters 5 and 12). Information and communication technologies may play an important role in informing the urban poor and helping them to educate themselves (Chapter 5).
- Giving and receiving knowledge and information – without payment – is seldom questioned in the North. The Internet can be seen as part of a gift economy. This is achieved by Internet users who contribute to the collective knowledge accessible to those already online. In return, each individual has access to information made available by others on the Internet. In contrast, communities in the South often lack even the basic resources necessary to access the gift economy of the North (Chapter 3).

DEVELOPMENT AND COMMUNICATION

Development and communication are fully discussed in a controversial style in Chapter 10, introducing new ideas which challenge everyone involved in so-called 'development'. It is asserted that development theorists have perpetuated a fiction that the 'first world' and 'third world' are two different places. It is also concluded that researchers in development have been more concerned with discussing and adopting the latest strategies for development intervention than questioning the interests of communities on whom development practices are applied.

Chapter 9, which discusses communication practices in Amazonia, describes what happens when communities reject the ready-made recipes devised by development theorists. This chapter concludes that development practitioners should ensure that indigenous groups are allowed to express development in their own terms. They should be freed from the influence of the latest fashionable development agendas. Chapter 9 addresses the theme of communication in development by examining bad communication practices and draws a number of conclusions which, again, challenge the validity of the concept of 'communicating for development'.

BARRIERS IN COMMUNICATION

Barriers in communication may be caused by cultural differences and lack of consideration of communities' language, values, beliefs, frames of reference and needs.

The use of social networks, intermediaries, key informants and media are proposed as mechanisms to overcome the problems of transferring development knowledge to different cultures. Lack of media accessibility or legibility in communicating for development is fully discussed in Chapter 6. Various ideas for more legible media are described, and a number of recommendations and questions are raised which highlight further research required in this area. In relation to this, the nature of media is challenged in relation to its appropriateness. Questions about the adaptability of media to a variety of situations and contexts, together with their cost-effectiveness, are raised. Also the clarity, purpose and target audience of media, together with their content, are important in relation to achieving a degree of success. It is concluded that the media used should be made sensitive to differences in age, gender, class, income, geography and ethnicity. Some key points that emerge under these themes are as follows.

- When the background and education of people involved in a communication process differs widely, sharing the same language may not be sufficient to overcome differences in the way people perceive an environment or give meanings and values to specific messages received.

In view of the above, it becomes clear why, in communicating between different cultures, languages and frames of reference are so problematic (Chapters 7 and 8).

■ Information and knowledge communicated by researchers must relate to the day-to-day needs of urban poor communities. In order to understand such needs, an ongoing dialogue is required which can only be achieved through contact with key informants, gatekeepers or existing local leaders related to the social networks of the community (Chapters 2, 4 and 5).

■ Although a large number of organizations generate information on development issues, such information is often not available because it is either located in the wrong place or only available in an inappropriate format. Hence, knowledge may become blocked (intentionally or unintentionally) before reaching the beneficiaries (Chapter 2).

■ The use of indigenous knowledge would help in the understanding and interpretation of problems and needs relating to local communities (Chapter 16).

LESSONS FROM THE CASE STUDIES

The case studies included in Part 2 of the book provide various practical and useful ways of communicating development.

Vehicles for communicating

■ Although the mass media have generally achieved little in improving the communication of information and knowledge in relation to development, the *Hands On* media series has been very successful for development communication (Chapter 11).

■ Chapter 13 provides hints and useful advice relating to the organization of electronic conferences. Such vehicles for communicating knowledge and information could have an impact on development communications, as they offer innovative ideas which may be related to development issues. The problem is that technological constraints in the South restrict the wider access of Southern professionals, which limits the value of electronic conferencing in development communications in the South.

■ A discussion on regional and national Internet-based research networks describes the positive and negative aspects of these in relation to communicating knowledge worldwide and on a regional scale. Although Internet-based mechanisms (such as the North–South Network or INVESTIGA) may not be readily accessible to the general public in developing countries, this does not diminish the desirability of this type of vehicle for communicating and exchanging information for the research community in developing countries (Chapter 12).

Barriers in communication caused by lack of transparency and bureaucracy

▪ Lack of transparency and infrastructure to access information is mentioned in Chapter 17. In some cases, bureaucracy and lack of transparency make it difficult for communities to obtain information. A case study related to communicating in India describes such problems in detail and concludes that building capacities to improve communication should include intermediate agencies, training institutions, and the personnel and civil servants of public agencies and local bodies.

▪ To improve access to knowledge and avoid lack of transparency, a common language should be used aimed at avoiding secrecy (Chapter 17).

Communicating or transferring knowledge

▪ Chapters 14–16 provide a clear explanation of the communication of specific knowledge in relation to the different cultures of Pakistan, Bangladesh and Vietnam. These chapters show that knowledge cannot be imposed from outside in a top-down approach, and that new ways of communicating knowledge must be devised which take into account the different cultural characteristics of each country.

▪ Chapter 14 demonstrates an important approach towards communicating ideas for achieving a more environmentally benign industrial development in Pakistan. Perhaps the process undertaken and experience gained in this case can be replicated in other parts of Pakistan. Pollution is one of the serious problems affecting developing countries, so this particular and valuable experience could be of great value for similar situations in other parts of the world.

▪ The conclusions of Chapter 15 are based on optimizing the value of participatory communication between diverse individuals and groups to improve rural housing in Bangladesh. Succeeding with this particular experience was based on communicating knowledge through a song team of community members and the spontaneous adoption of improved building techniques by some villagers. Apparently, the success of this experience resulted from a genuine participatory communication process that happened through horizontal exchanges and face-to-face contacts between villagers and expert engineers who lived in the village for some time. The fact that the tacit knowledge of the community was blended with the explicit knowledge of the professionals involved in the improvement programme is a reason for the success of the project.

▪ AIDS prevention in Vietnam was greatly improved thanks to a communication programme that took into account the cultural characteristics of the Vietnamese (Chapter 16).

RECOMMENDATIONS

The above overview shows that no single factor can explain why communicating knowledge is difficult even when the same language is used. When cultures and languages differ, communicating knowledge clearly requires an understanding of people's culture, frame of reference, background, needs and interests.

The need to send messages that are compatible with the culture of the receivers has been recognized since World War I, when linguists realized that communication should be accomplished 'in a language people accept. . .'.[1] The communication of any message requires that, once a message has been sent, it has to be understood or decoded by the receiver or it has no meaning. Successful communication requires a clear understanding of the mechanics of the process (Chapter 8).

Participation is the key in communicating for development, and real participation of all groups should be ensured. This should be achieved by improving groups' means of communication with other stakeholders in the development process. Participation of groups should take place in meeting places designed to encourage horizontal, face-to-face contact. This is necessary for the exchange of both tacit community knowledge and explicit knowledge, which it is believed is the only way for new knowledge to be generated and therefore transferred. New knowledge should combine the 'tacit knowledge' of communities with the 'explicit' skills of researchers.

New knowledge can be generated only if people discuss ideas that are compatible with what they need and understand. Good examples of the application of this idea are given by the Shack International case study in Chapter 8, and by the Bangladesh house construction technology case study in Chapter 15.

Barriers and gaps in the communication process may be avoided through the generation of trust, acknowledging the real needs and interests of communities and respecting their vernacular tacit knowledge and culture. Adequate time is required and must be allowed to ensure that new knowledge is generated, codified and transferred.

Further research

It is suggested that further research on the following aspects would greatly improve the communication process.

- Communication barriers and gaps must be identified right from the beginning of a research process. Specific guidelines should be drawn up for this purpose.
- The role of horizontal and vertical networks is a relatively new subject in development discourse, and substantial research is required to assess their impact.
- Social networks and their value as social capital should be identified

and used as vehicles for transferring knowledge. The real value of social networks as social capital should be assessed and monitored.

- Intermediaries, key informants and local leaders should be approached to identify existing social networks, which can explain the specific needs and interests of particular communities.
- Legible media, which are compatible with the values, beliefs and frames of reference of communities, should be studied for each specific case. Questions relating to the adaptability of media to a variety of situations and contexts, the clarity of its purpose and target audience, together with its contents, should be further investigated.
- The transfer of good and best practices should be tailored to accommodate differences in cultures and geographic settings. This transfer should use knowledge management methods to generate new knowledge through appropriate conversion processes. Specific research should be promoted on this topic.
- Communication models relating to specific community needs should be devised to encompass all the above aspects.
- Communication processes, rather than outputs, could be useful to other communities and could be transferred and repeated in similar circumstances. It is more important to communicate knowledge or good practice processes than to provide communities with ready-made products.

Last words

Nearly 30 years ago, the Dag Hammarskjold Report (Hammarskjold, 1975) devoted one of its main conclusions to the need for improved public information and cross-cultural understanding. The points it made then are equally relevant today:

'Citizens have a right to inform and be informed about the facts of development, its inherent conflicts and changes it will bring about, locally and internationally.

Under present conditions, information and education are only too often monopolized by the power structure, which manipulates public opinion to its own ends.

A global effort should be made to give the new international relations their human dimension and to promote the establishment of genuine co-operation between peoples on the basis of equality and recognition of their cultural, political, social and economic diversity.

Such an effort should be concerned both with information and with education in the broadest sense of the word; it should be directed towards "conscientization" of citizens to ensure their full participation in the decision-making process.'

While we recognize that new developments in information technology since the 1970s have radically changed the ways information is shared and updated, can we confidently say that all this innovation has improved the situation of the poor and disadvantaged in this world?

Contributors

Dr Iftekhar Ahmed grew up in Bangladesh and studied architecture at the Indian Institute of Technology, Kharagpur. He has a master's degree from the Massachusetts Institute of Technology, USA, and a doctorate from Oxford Brookes University, UK. He now teaches at the Department of Architecture at the Bangladesh University of Engineering and Technology. His main area of interest is low-income rural housing in the developing context, especially in Bangladesh, and in recent years he has carried out a number of action-research projects in this field.

Dr Mansoor Ali is a Project/Programme Manager at the Water, Engineering and Development Centre (WEDC), Loughborough University. He specializes in urban infrastructure and services for the poor. He initiated a number of activities in knowledge management at WEDC, including electronic discussions, CDs and synthesis notes. He has also coordinated electronic discussions for international participants. His current research interests include the linkages of knowledge and information with sustainable livelihoods, good governance and urban poverty.

Dr Richard Barbrook was educated at Cambridge, Essex and Kent universities. During the early 1980s he was involved in pirate and community radio broadcasting. He helped to set up Spectrum Radio, a multilingual station operating in London, and has published extensively on radio issues. In the late 1980s and early 1990s, Richard worked for a research institute at the University of Westminster on media regulation within the EU. Some of this research was later published in *Media Freedom: The Contradictions of Communications in the Age of Modernity* (Pluto Press, London, 1995). For the past few years Richard has been coordinator of the Hypermedia Research Centre at the University of Westminster, and he was the first course leader of its MA in Hypermedia Studies. In collaboration with Andy Cameron he wrote 'The Californian Ideology' (*Science as Culture*, 26(6): 44–72, 1996), a pioneering critique of the neoliberal politics of *Wired* magazine. At present, Richard is preparing *The Cyber-Communist Manifesto* for publication as a book.

Janet Boston is a Director and Series Producer with Television Trust for the Environment (TVE). She developed and produced the One World Media award-winning multimedia series *Hands On* for TVE's *Earth Report* on BBC World TV. As a freelance she has directed various films examining the impact of pesticides in Asia, and a series on land tenure and shelter, with the UK Department for International Development (DFID), for Istanbul plus 5 in 2001. Although she specializes in broadcast media, she has worked on campaigns and press strategies for NGOs such as the Intermediate Technology Development Group and has carried out consultancies for DFID. She has over 10 years' experience of international media and a commitment to covering development issues while working with local crews.

Robert Brown is a Senior Lecturer in Architecture at the Universities of East London and Plymouth, and is a researcher at the Max Lock Centre at the University of Westminster currently contributing to DFID-funded research on community development in Africa in which he is investigating architectural interpretation and communication and its place within architectural education. He has over 15 years' experience in the UK, the USA and India in community-based housing and regeneration, and has published and lectured on community participation in design and on architectural education.

Matthew Carter is a civil engineer working for Ove Arup & Partners. After graduating from Cambridge in 1996, he spent nine months living and working in a remote community in northern Bangladesh. Since joining Ove Arup in 1997, he has been seconded to manage a bicultural volunteer workforce building a village school in Tanzania, and later to work for Medecins Sans Frontieres in Albania and Kosovo during the summer of 1999. The latter secondment was through the Register of Engineers for Disaster Relief (RedR), of which he remains a member.

Catalina Gandelsonas is a Senior Research Coordinator at Max Lock Centre and teaches BA and MA urban design courses at the School of the Built Environment, University of Westminster. As a professional architect– planner and urban designer she has worked as a consultant for a variety of local authorities in the USA and Spain. She has also taught, undertaken research and participated in juries at various universities, including Berkeley and Princeton in the USA, and Buenos Aires, Chile and Mexico in South America. For the past 10 years she has been based in London, teaching at University College London and at the University of Westminster, combining teaching with research relating to Pakistan, India, Kenya, Brazil and northern Cyprus.

Dr Nick Hall is a Senior Research Fellow at South Bank University (SBU) specializing in urban management, primarily in developing countries. Recent work includes a review of Oxfam's urban programme, and the management of DFID's C3 city challenge fund pilot programme in Zambia (in conjunction with CARE). He coordinated a Kenyan Government Task Force which recently revised that country's building and planning regulations,

and was author of the global NGO statement to the UN Habitat II conference in 1996. Before joining SBU, his work with an international NGO
(ITDG) involved diverse technical and project management work, mostly
with an urban focus. He was a roof thatcher in Devon in the 1970s and then
wrote a PhD thesis on the technical and economic history of thatching in
Europe. He has written several books and papers about thatching, a book
about the work of international NGOs tackling urban poverty, and a number
of papers about community-based approaches to urban management and
vulnerability reduction in the context of natural disasters. Dr Hall is a
trustee of Africa Now and is active as a volunteer in urban regeneration
work in London.

Professor Nabeel Hamdi is a Professor of Housing and Urban Development
at Oxford Brookes University and Director of the Centre for Development
and Emergency Planning. He taught for nine years at the Massachusetts
Institute of Technology where he was Associate Professor of Housing. He
has published four books and numerous papers and articles in journals
worldwide. He has worked as a consultant for a variety of government and
international development agencies including UNCHS, UNDP, UNHCR,
UNICEF, UNRWA, DFID, SDC, USAID, the EU and the World Bank, among
others. His project work, training programmes and research extend to
some 15 countries.

Dr Rizwan Hameed is a faculty member of the City and Regional Planning
Department, University of Engineering and Technology, Lahore, Pakistan.
He took his doctorate from Heriot-Watt University, UK, in the field of
Environmental Planning and Management. In addition to teaching at the
university, he also works as part-time independent consultant on planning and environment-related issues. He worked on the World Bank-
administered Shelter for Low Income Communities Project, one of the
biggest nationwide studies on the housing sector.

Dr Paul Jenkins is Director of the Centre for Environment and Human
Settlements in the School of Planning & Housing, Edinburgh. An archi-
tect/planner by training, he has worked during the past 30 years in, and
with, a wide range of central and local government, NGO, private sector,
international aid and community-based organizations. This has been in
urban development, housing, architecture and construction – in policy,
practice, training and research – with some 20 years in southern Africa. His
areas of special interest are policy advocacy and professional practice
development in housing and planning, with a focus on low-income groups,
community empowerment, action research and widening access to
knowledge-based services.

Toyoko Kodama was born in Japan and completed an MSc in Social Policy
and Planning in Developing Countries at the London School of Economics

in 1999. Prior to the master's programme, she worked in the project planning division of the Toyonaka International Centre, a non-profit organization in Osaka, Japan. Her current activities involve HIV/AIDS project work
in Malaysia, while working as an information technology communication
specialist for a private company.

Le Thi Minh Chau was born in Vietnam and completed an MSc in Social
Policy and Planning in Developing Countries at the London School of
Economics in 1999. She worked for Save the Children Fund UK in Ho Chi
Minh City, Vietnam, for a number of years, and was actively involved in
many leading projects including community development and HIV/AIDS
communication. She is currently working at UNICEF in Hanoi, Vietnam,
coordinating a project involving children and teenagers who are in an out
of school called: 'The Life Skills Education Project'.

Tony Lloyd-Jones is Senior Lecturer in Urban Design and Development at
the School of the Built Environment, University of Westminster, and
research manager at the Max Lock Centre. He has conducted a number of
urban development-related research projects and has published papers
and articles in journals and books worldwide. He is a consulting Urban
and Physical Planning Adviser for the UK Department for International
Development and represents the UK government on human settlements
matters at the United Nations.

Lucky Lowe trained as a professional in the UK construction sector, becoming involved in appropriate technologies in Nepal while working as a Low
Income Housing Adviser with the Agricultural Development Bank. After
postgraduate studies in infrastructure engineering, she joined ITDG as a
Technology Policy Officer and later applied her interest in communications
issues, drawing on knowledge gained as a marketing professional in the
UK, to become ITDG's Knowledge and Information Services Unit Manager.

Norma V. Madrid is currently a researcher for The John Hopkins Sector
Project at the Institute for Advanced Studies in Administration, Caracas,
Venezuela. She has an MSc from the London School of Economics. Having
a special interest in urban management and NGOs, she worked for seven
years in NGOs in various jobs relating to strategic planning, capacity-
building, volunteer management, project management and funding. She is
also the Director of *Projecta Consultants,* an organization which provides
professional support to NGOs and local governments.

Michael Mutter is a consulting Urban and Physical Planning Adviser for the
UK Department for International Development.

Dr Carl O'Coill is a consultant in participatory urban regeneration, and a
lecturer. He teaches on the master's course in Post-Development Studies at

the Hull School of Architecture, as well as within the general architecture programme. Carl recently completed a doctorate at the University of York in which he explored the racist foundations of development discourse, looking in particular at how the discourse has shaped the practices of British NGOs working in urban areas in Kenya. His current preoccupation is the adaptation of participatory planning methodologies developed outside the West for use in community-led, urban regeneration initiatives in the British context.

Dr Jeremy Raemaekers leads the undergraduate planning course in the School of Planning and Housing, and the undergraduate combined studies course in the Faculty of Environmental Studies, Edinburgh College of Art/Heriot-Watt University. His research and teaching interests centre on British rural policy, sustainable development, and the interface between the planning and other environmental regimes in developed and developing countries. Before his present post he led the environment and mapping unit of Grampian Regional Council, Scotland. Prior to that, he researched and taught primate ecology and behaviour in South-East Asia for 10 years.

Kathleen Richardson studied Anthropology and Linguistics at UCL, followed by an MSc in Development Administration and Planning. She is now studying social anthropology at the University of Cambridge, and writing a thesis on the relationship between anthropology, development and environmental narratives in Amazonia.

Otto Ruskulis worked for Intermediate Technology Development Group (ITDG) for about 11 years, after undertaking research in civil engineering and building in a number of UK-based universities. Initially his work centred on developing activities of the Building Advisory Service and Information Network (BASIN). Later his work broadened to include a number of ITDG information and communication-based projects, including the Technical Enquiry Service, Poor Women, Information and Communication Technologies, and Strengthening Poor People's Knowledge and Information Systems. He is currently a freelance writer and researcher.

Dr Darren Saywell has been working with the Water, Engineering and Development Centre (WEDC), Loughborough University, since 1994. He has worked and published extensively in the areas of low-cost sanitation and knowledge dissemination. He edited the DFID research newsletter *Urbanization* and coordinated the Global Applied Research Network (GARNET). In addition to his research activities, he also taught on postgraduate programmes at Loughborough. Currently he is working on a leave in absence with Water Supply and Sanitation Collaborative Council with the World Health Programme.

Dr Harry Smith is a Postdoctoral Research Fellow at the Centre for Environment and Human Settlements (CEHS), Edinburgh. Trained in architecture in Spain and in planning in the UK, where he has engaged in professional practice, his recent activities include research on housing in Costa Rica; teaching planning and housing at CEHS; and the management of community self-build projects in Scotland. His main research interests currently include planning for sustainable urban development, housing policy, participation and bottom-up processes in urban development, with a focus on low-income groups, particularly in developing countries.

Dr Pachampet Sundaram has over 32 years' extensive practical experience as a senior Indian civil servant in public economics and administration, urban management, infrastructure and service delivery, urban poverty, housing policy and partnerships with various stakeholders. This experience has been interspersed over the years with academic work, field research, consultancy and training in India and other countries. He was closely involved in formulating national policies for housing, urban services, municipal government, decentralization and private-sector partnerships in India. On retirement, he became a Visiting Scholar at the Department of Policy, Planning and Development, University of Southern California, and a consultant in public administration and urban affairs. His most recent book (together with S. Schiavo-Campo) is *Public Administration in a Competitive World,* published by the Asian Development Bank.

Notes

INTRODUCTION

1. The *Collins Dictionary* gives several interpretations of the term community including:
   'A group of people living in close proximity' (the current popular use);
   'having cultural, ethnic and religious or other characteristics in common';
   'common ownership or participation';
   'a group of nations having common interests';
   see also the discussion in Chapter 4.

CHAPTER 1

1. This chapter is based on sections of the final report of the DFID-funded R6168 Knowledge Technical Transfer research project (Max Lock Centre, 2001a). I am indebted to the work of the Max Lock Centre research team in informing this text, as well as to the many researchers worldwide who contributed to this study.
2. The knowledge transfer research undertaken by the Max Lock Centre sets out a broad framework for addressing these issues. This framework is embodied in the *Improving Knowledge Transfer* guides which offer guidance for, and are intended to be used by, a range of stakeholders in urban development, including donors and a variety of intermediaries (Max Lock Centre, 2001b).
3. This includes DFID-funded urban development and infrastructure-related research projects R7234, Community Learning (www.lboro.ac.uk/garnet/UrbanKaR/DFID-KAR-URBAN.html) and Information Centres, and the Intermediate Technology Development Group's C9 Knowledge Information Services.
4. In line with its policy of untying aid, DFID recently opened up its research programme to projects led by researchers in developing countries.
5. See the *Improving Knowledge Transfer* Guides No. 1: *Identifying the Users of Development Knowledge* and No. 2: *Targeting Research Knowledge to Create Partnerships in Urban Development* (Max Lock Centre, 2001b). The latter includes a table setting out the interests, roles, responsibilities, knowledge and communications of the different types of stakeholder in general terms.
6. This section and the following one draw on *Improving Knowledge Transfer* Guide No. 5: *Identifying the Appropriate Media for Communication* (Max Lock Centre, 2001b).
7. This section draws on Gandelsonas and Lloyd-Jones (2001).
8. See www.bestpractices.org. The other main approach adopted by the Habitat centre to promote the implementation of the Habitat Agenda is the use of urban observatories and urban indicators – see www.unchs.org.

9. The implications for how models of good or best practice are framed are the subject of research being undertaken by Max Lock Centre together with WEDC and research partners from Kenya, India, Brazil and Spain in the DFID-funded research project R7963, Localizing the Habitat Agenda for Urban Poverty Reduction (see www.citypoverty.net).
10. See, for example, The CityNet and Technical Cooperation among Developing Countries Transfer Process of Best Practices (www2.itjit.ne.jp).

CHAPTER 4

1. See, for example, Davis (1991) and Castells (1997) for an in-depth range of interests in which local communities *do* act.

CHAPTER 6

1. This chapter is based on a paper prepared for the UK Department for International Development, September 1998, entitled 'Learning and Dissemination'.

CHAPTER 8

1. See also a paper written by Gandelsonas and Lloyd Jones, presented at the conference 'Urbanizing World and UN Human Habitat II', organized by IRFD, Columbia University New York, 4–6 June 2001.
2. Coding is a term created by communication theory. It means that the message is organized or arranged in a code.
3. Decoding refers to the translation of the code in which the message was written.
4. Information derives from data and knowledge derives from information (Polanyi 1966). Good or best practices have been defined as practices that have a visible impact on improving people's quality of life and living environment and are proven to be sustainable. They have also been defined by O'Dell and Grayson (1998) as 'knowledge in action'.
5. As knowledge management theories have generated ideal strategies for 'getting the right knowledge to the right people at the right time' (O'Dell and Grayson, 1998), their methods and principles could equally be applied to improve the communication of knowledge for development (Gandelsonas and Lloyd-Jones, 2001).
6. The term 'knowledge management' refers to the practical framework that enables the generation and building of new knowledge. It is a practical approach that explains ways to generate, exchange, transfer or share knowledge through the use of horizontal exchanges and or technology as a facilitator (knowledge-enabled intranet sites, etc.). Thus knowledge management as a theory attempts to explain how valuable the knowledge contained within organizations is, and how this type of knowledge can be transferred to improve the organization's performance.
7. A clear definition of knowledge based on Polanyi (1966) states that knowledge derives from information, which in turn derives from data. These concepts are non-interchangeable (O'Dell and Grayson, 1998).
8. Explicit knowledge is the type of knowledge that can be verbally explained, codified or written down in specific documents.

9. Tacit knowledge is knowledge embedded in communities' traditions and is defined as personal knowledge rooted in individual experience. Thus, it is not written and is only transferable face to face. (Polanyi, 1966). This type of knowledge is not easily translated into formal language because people who have got it are seldom able to adequately convey to others the knowledge that they inherently possess (Nonaka and Takeguchi, 1995).
10. Best practice (any practice, experience, know-how or knowledge) is knowledge in action proven to be valuable or effective in a specific situation and may be applied in a different situation through adaptation or transformation (O'Dell and Grayson, 1998).
11. O'Dell and Grayson (1998); Davenport and Prusak (1998); Brooking (1999); Scarbrough and Swan (1999); and Ahmed et al. (2002) have all developed different approaches to the subject of knowledge management.
12. Maslow (1987) described a hierarchy of human needs that starts from basic physiological needs (survival) and develops into more complex psychological needs of affiliation, esteem, cognitive, actualization and aesthetic needs. As most physiological needs have a psychological component, this theory was questioned by Lang in 1994.
13. The Shack Dwellers International case study, a clear example of communicating knowledge or good practices through the generation of new knowledge, was included in a paper written by Gandelsonas and Lloyd Jones, presented at the conference 'Urbanizing World and UN Human Habitat II', organized by IRFD, Columbia University New York, 4–6 June 2001.

CHAPTER 9

1. Brazil was the first Latin American state to pioneer constitutional change, in 1988. It made amendments to respect the rights of indigenous peoples. Bolivia, Ecuador, Peru and Venezuela have all followed suit throughout the 1990s, recognizing the rights of indigenous peoples. This was a historic precedent for Latin American societies. One example is the Ecuadorian Constitution of August 1998 which established the collective rights of the indigenous people, and that they would be 'consulted about plans and programs for exploration of non-renewable resources on their territories and which can affect their environment or culture' (Malo, 1999).
2. The rainforests have, for example, been described as the 'lungs of the earth', implying that they support life on the planet by producing oxygen. While the forests certainly produce oxygen, as do forests of all types, the implication that they make a significant net contribution to the global oxygen supply has been questioned (see *New American Magazine*, www.newamerican.com).
3. By 1500, when Brazil was 'discovered', the indigenous population was estimated at 3 500 000. Data from 1997 suggest that there were 325 652 indigenous people from 206 nations remaining in Brazil. Officially there are 556 indigenous lands in Brazil alone, of which 383 are located within the Amazon region (Greenpeace Briefing, August 2001).
4. In India, protected areas have already displaced some 600 000 tribal people and forest-dwellers, and have affected many more. According to Colchester (2000) and some social activists in India, the Ministry of Environment and Forests plans to establish a further 650 wildlife sanctuaries and 150 national parks in the next few years, displacing many more people. Many developing world environmentalists in countries such as Ecuador, Venezuela, Indonesia and the Philippines believe that national parks are often purposely established as a means of denying local peoples' rights and reserving the areas for future

exploitation. In India, conservation groups have realized that protected areas from which tribal peoples have been expelled are unusually vulnerable, deprived as they are of their first line of defence.

CHAPTER 10

1. This quotation is from Swift's *On Poetry: A Rhapsody* (1733) and is cited by Anne McClintock (1994, p. 27).
2. The term 'Third World' was not simply a Western construction, but was part of the vocabulary of the non-aligned movement. However, as Harris (1986, p. 7) points out, the expression no longer signifies the non-aligned countries it was originally intended to describe, but has gradually come to stand for all 'developing countries'. The term is used here in a wider sense to refer to a discourse about non-Western cities with its origins in Western modernity.
3. 'The West' here is not meant to denote an area defined by lines of latitude and longitude on a map. As Stewart Hall points out, '"the West" is a historical not a geographical construct' (Hall, 1994, p. 277). Michael Keith and Steve Pile refer to the term as a 'linguistic condensation of the globally powerful' (Keith and Pile, 1993, p. 22). It delineates a cultural space occupied by a particular form of rationality or modernity, a collection of principles for organizing people in time and space rather than an area on a geographical map. And it is defined as much by how it represents its 'others', the non-West or, as Hall puts it, 'the Rest', as by how it sees itself. In this sense of the word, Japan, although east of Europe, could be understood as similarly 'Western'.
4. For example, while Asians were allowed some direct representation on Nairobi's Municipal Council, Africans were not.
5. It is interesting to note that John Turner, one of the early and more celebrated British authors writing about cities in 'developing countries', lived in Peru in the 1950s and spent the 1960s in North America working at the same research institute as Abrams and Friedmann.
6. The position I am taking here, some will say, is nothing new. In the mid-1980s Nigel Harris himself was arguing that the 'Third World' had come to an end (Harris, 1986). The distinction traditionally drawn between developed and developing regions, the 'First' and the 'Third World', he claimed, was no longer valid. 'Newly industrializing countries' like Korea, Malaysia and Singapore had grown so much economically in recent decades, he maintained, that they now have more in common with the West than they do with most other developing countries. My argument, however, is that the distinction has always been arbitrary, that the economic changes Harris identifies are not nearly so significant as he thinks because development discourse has always been far more concerned with marking cultural difference than charting economic statistics.
7. The term neo-liberalism is most widely used in Latin America. It is a term more often applied in criticism than in praise, having been adopted to describe the economic policies imposed in the region after the international banking crisis of the early 1980s, or the so called 'third world debt crisis'. Broadly speaking, neo-liberal doctrine is distinguished by the primacy it affords the role of 'the market' in human affairs and the *laissez faire* approach to government it advocates. It is so-called because it is generally seen as a revival or variant of the economic liberalism that prevailed in the nineteenth and early twentieth centuries. As an ideology, it stands in opposition to Keynesianism and the post-war consensus of the welfare state, the system that supplanted the nineteenth-century liberal order. Its declared aim is 'efficiency', welfare maximization through market competition. State intervention in the market place is conceived

as stifling of competition, by definition inefficient. Thus the liberalism espoused is always an economic liberalism, the freeing of business from state control. Although neo-liberalism is generally associated with the right-wing governments of Margaret Thatcher and Ronald Reagan, neo-liberal policies were implemented before this in the 1970s, by the Pinochet regime in Chile, and by the Labour governments of Wilson and Callaghan in Britain. The policies neo-liberalism encompasses include the privatization of public enterprises, reductions in government spending, deregulation of domestic markets, removal of barriers to international trade and investment, the promotion of 'export-led growth' and monetarist policies directed toward the control of inflation. Today, the neo-liberal outlook is taken for granted in countries all over the world and is embraced as much by traditionally left-of-centre, social democratic governments as by the right.

8. The neo-liberal agenda is extremely short-sighted. As Harvey (1990) and Lipietz (1992) point out, in the long run the business community must employ sufficient numbers of people and increase wages sufficiently to allow workers to become consumers of the goods they produce. Cutting wage costs while pushing for greater levels of productivity makes no sense. The overproduction that inevitably results creates deflationary pressures that can eventually lead to recession or even depression. In other words, the neo-liberal agenda is not even in the long-term interests of capitalists themselves.

9. It is notoriously difficult to arrive at an accurate estimate of the number of people sleeping rough in London on any given night. The figure given here for the number of homeless in the city was compiled by the British voluntary organization Shelter from statistics of local authorities and the Department for the Environment, Transport and the Regions. It includes people in temporary accommodation as well as people living on the streets. However, as Shelter points out, these statistics show only the number of households who approach local authorities for help and are found to be homeless. Under the Housing Act 1996, councils have a duty to house 'priority need' homeless households in temporary accommodation for a period of two years. Thus the figure of 42 thousand homeless does not include people for whom local authorities have no responsibility to provide accommodation and who do seek or receive help from their council. The majority of single people or childless couples are included in this category.

10. By insisting on the elimination of trade barriers, official development agencies removed one of the few bargaining chips that post-colonial governments held in the competition for inward investment. Once these trade barriers had been removed, multinational corporations no longer needed locally based production centres to supply Africa's domestic markets with goods. The African market could be supplied from America, Britain, Mexico or China, or wherever investors were offered the best deal in terms of low production costs, minimal regulation and high-value incentives. Encumbered by debt, African governments could not and still cannot compete with the scale of business inducements offered by countries in the West and in South-East Asia. Between 1989 and 1994, the number of British manufacturing companies with equity holdings in Anglophone Africa dropped by one-third. In the five years between 1988 and 1993, an annual investment from France of US$1 billion turned into a net outflow of US$800 million (Ayittey, 1998). Total inflows of foreign direct investment in Kenya amounted to US$39 million between 1986 and 1990. These inflows dropped to a total of just US$8.9 million in the four years from 1990 to 1994 (Ikara, 1996).

11. Rising costs of living have seriously eroded peoples' incomes in Kenya's urban areas. Real wages in Nairobi fell by 45 per cent between 1982 and 1994, and by 55 per cent in urban areas as a whole (Ikara and Ndung'u, 1999, p. 99).

12. In fact, the scale of assistance provided by NGOs in general is negligible. If we add up all the money Western NGOs spent in 'developing countries' in 1995, US$6.7 billion, it amounts to less than one-ninth of the British government's annual budget for its National Health Service. But more tellingly, the figure is 36 times less than the US$246 billion 'developing countries' spent on debt repayments to the West in the same year (this figure was compiled from statistics cited in UNDP, 1998).

13. In relation to land, for example, the 1976 Habitat recommendations state: 'Private land ownership is . . . a principal instrument of accumulation and concentration of wealth and therefore contributes to social injustice; if unchecked it may become a major obstacle in the planning and implementation of development schemes . . . [its] management should be subject to public surveillance or control in the interest of the nation' (Habitat, in Hardoy and Satterthwaite, 1981, p. 227). Levels of inequality in distribution of property have worsened significantly since the 1970s. Despite this fact, this kind of public control over land ownership is rarely recommended today.

CHAPTER 11

1. Pulgar picks up on this theme when he asks: 'Imagine what may be achieved if some of those funds could be diverted to promoting business practices and new technologies that are environmentally friendly? TVE and its partner ITDG did more than imagine, they put the idea into practice.'

2. A full list of programmes and back-up information is accessible on the TVE website: visit www.tve.org.uk and click on 'Hands On'.

3. 'Playpumps' profiles a roundabout which also pumps water; 'Inner Tubes' sees how rubber tyres can be turned into handbags; while 'Cashing In' looks at reverse vending machines where consumers can get their money back if they bring in their old bottles and cans.

4. 'Waste Busters' follows a neighbourhood rubbish collection scheme; 'Vacutug' sees how a new device might be the answer to emptying overflowing city sewers.

CHAPTER 12

1. Paul Jenkins developed and promoted the idea of the North–South Research Network from his position as Director of the Centre for Environment and Human Settlements in Edinburgh. During his doctoral studies, Harry Smith worked on the development and management of the North–South Research Network and collaborated with various activities undertaken by INVESTIGA in Costa Rica, including the 'State of the Art' research project.

2. For a discussion of Nonaka and Takeuchi's (1995) approach to knowledge management in the context of best practices transfer, see Gandelsonas and Lloyd Jones (2001).

3. After working for some 20 years in human settlements in developing countries, and trying to keep in touch with new developments in theory and practice via the professional journals, in late 1996 one of the authors (P.J.) returned to the UK to work in an academic environment. He was surprised to find that the difficulties he had experienced in trying to keep in touch with relevant up-to-date research while overseas were not so dissimilar to the difficulties experienced in the UK, even within academia. This was compounded when a group

of postgraduate students at CEHS asked if there was a source of information in the UK on research into human settlements issues in the developing world. As far as could be ascertained, there was not one physical or documentary source and, after some initial investigation on the Internet, it appeared there was no Internet-based source either, other than the more general development-oriented ID21.

4. This has not yet been successful. The main reason given is that, despite DFID's interest in supporting research dissemination and the North–South Network, it is not viable to support small projects such as this. CEHS is thus currently (mid-2001) suggesting that the Network be associated with wider research dissemination initiatives in a larger package.

5. Specific requests to date have come from Central America, Southern Africa and South Asia.

6. A request for funding to develop and provide this assistance was included in the proposal presented to DFID.

7. Given the level of funding required, it is not surprising that similar experiences are hard to come by. The CDP set up only two other resource facilities – the East African Resource Facility (Kenya, Tanzania and Uganda) and CDP/Asia (Cambodia, Laos, Myanmar, Thailand and Vietnam) – neither of which was developed as much as CERCA.

CHAPTER 13

1. GARNET is an initiative designed to facilitate information exchange between researchers, practitioners and funders of research operating in the water supply and sanitation sector. It aims to achieve this goal through the coordination of low-cost, decentralized subject-based and geographically based networks. GARNET falls under the auspices of the Water Supply and Sanitation Collaborative Council and receives financial support from the UK's Department for International Development

2. Mailbase is a service that runs electronic discussion lists for the UK higher education and research community, based at the University Computing Service, University of Newcastle, UK (www.mailbase.ac.uk).

3. A major activity of WASTE Advisers is the Urban Waste Expertise Programme, a six-year programme that started in 1995. The programme has two stated aims: to improve the living conditions of the urban poor in Southern countries; and to create employment among the urban poor and improve working conditions.

CHAPTER 14

1. The authors are grateful to the industrialists and officials who gave their time in interviews, and to Irfan and Kashif, who assisted with the interviews.

CONCLUSIONS

1. Nothing can express communication problems more clearly than Andrew Buncombe's article 'The world at war' (Buncombe, 2001) in which he describes the infinite care with which wartime propaganda messages are prepared, and their success and failures. The article explains how war propaganda leaflets

were meticulously prepared by teams of linguistic experts as 'not only must they [the messages] be written perfectly in the language of the enemy, they must also take into account various cultural nuances and the mindset of those they are designed to influence . . . The vernacular used in the leaflet is just as important as the message itself. You have to communicate in a language they accept . . . Cultural mistakes will destroy the effectiveness of a leaflet . . .'. His article concludes that although, over the years, the preparation of such leaflets has become more scientific, mistakes are still made. One leaflet had to be withdrawn after a single, simple spelling mistake completely altered the meaning of a message.

References

Abbot, J. (1996) *Sharing the City*, Earthscan, London.

Abrams, C. (1964) *Man's Struggle for Shelter in an Urbanizing World*, MIT Press, Cambridge, MA, USA.

ACHR (2000) *Face to Face: Notes from the Network on Community Exchange*, Asian Coalition for Housing Rights, Bangkok.

Adams, W.M. (1995) Green development theory?, in: Crush, J. (ed.), *Power of Development*, Routledge, London/New York.

Agevi, E. (1998) Networks and Coalitions in Human Settlements – Do they make a Difference? Internal Communication, ITDG, Bourton-on-Dunsmore, Rugby, UK.

Agreda, E. and Contreras, B. (2001) KIS Phase II – Peru Tarapoto Final Report, April 2001, unpublished report, ITDG, Bourton-on-Dunsmore, Rugby, UK.

Ahmed, I. (1998) Crisis of natural building materials and institutionalised self-help housing: the case of Grameen bank in Bangladesh, *Habitat International*, 22(4): 355–374.

Ahmed, I. (2000) Post-flood investigations 1998 and an action agenda for rural housing in Bangladesh, in: Hodgson, R. *et al.* (eds), *Affordable Village Building Technologies: From Research to Realisation*, University of Exeter and BUET, Dhaka, pp. 135–153.

Ahmed, I. and Hodgson, R. (1997) The Tiverton–Sundarban Link: a case of partnership at the grassroots, in: *Proceedings of the 14th Inter-Schools Conference on Development*, Heriot-Watt University, Edinburgh, pp. 90–97.

Ahmed, P., Kok, L. and Lol, A. (2002) *Learning through Knowledge Management*, Butterworth-Heinemann, Oxford.

Albrecht, T., Burleson, B. and Goldsmith, D. (1994) Supportive communication, in: Knapp, M. and Miller, G. (eds), *Handbook of Interpersonal Communication*, Sage Publications, California.

Alcorn, J. (1995) Comments, *Current Anthropology*, 36(5): 802–804.

Ali, M. and Saywell, D. (1999) Experience with electronic conferencing: a case study of electronic discussions on gender and waste management, *Information Development*, 15(1): 47–50.

Allen, D. *et al.* (1993) *Refurbishment Contracts*, HMSO, London.

Allesbrook, C. *et al.* (1988) *Tenant Participation in Housing Design – A Guide for Action*, RIBA Publications, London.

Alvard, M. (1995) Intraspecific prey choice by Amazonian hunter, *Current Anthropology*, 36(5): 789–818.

Anderson, S. (1996) A city called heaven: black enchantment and despair in Los Angeles, in: Scott, A. and Soja, E. (eds), *The City: Los Angeles and Urban Theory at the End of the Century*, University of California Press, London.

Anon. (1950) Royal Charter for Nairobi: from swamp to city within the span of a lifetime, *The Times*, 30 March, p. 7.

Anon. (2000a) Leader, How democratic should we be?, *Building*, 17 March, p. 3.

Anon. (2000b) New Best Value indicators set to stress community role, *Urban Environment Today*, Issue 104, 7 September 2000, p. 1.

Ayittey, G.B.N. (1998) *Africa in Chaos*, extract, *New York Times on the Web* (online archive), www.nytimes.com (accessed 13/10/98).

Azarya, V. (1985) in: Kupper, A. and Kupper, J. (eds), *The Social Science Encyclopaedia*, Routledge & Kegan Paul, London, p. 135.

Barbero, J.M. (1994) Mediaciones urbanas y nuevos escenarios de comunicación, *Sociedad*, 5: 35–47.

Barbrook, R. and Cameron, A. (1996) The Californian ideology, *Science as Culture*, 6(26): 44–72 (www.hrc.wmin.ac.uk/hrc/theory/californianIdeo/main.xml?id= theory.4.2.1).

Barnes, T.J. and Duncan, J.S., eds (1992) *Writing Worlds: Discourse, Text and Metaphor in the Representation of Landscape*, Routledge, London.

Barnett, T. (1988) *Sociology of Development*, Routledge, London.

BBS (1996) *Statistical Bulletin Bangladesh: May 1996*, Bangladesh Bureau of Statistics, Dhaka.

Beall, J. (1997a) *A City for All: Valuing Difference and Working with Diversity*, Zed Books, London.

Beall, J. (1997b) Social capital in waste – a solid investment?, *Journal of International Development*, 9(7): 951–961.

Beall, J. (2000) *Valuing Social Resources or Capitalising on Them? Social Action and the Limits to Pro-poor Urban Governance*, Urban Governance, Partnership and Poverty Working Paper 19, Draft for Submission to International Planning Studies by University of Birmingham, UK/London School of Economics.

Beall, J. and Kanji, N. (1999) *Urban Governance, Partnership and Poverty: Theme Paper Three: Households, Livelihoods and Urban Poverty*, International Development Department, University of Birmingham, UK.

Beder, S. (1997) *Global Spin: The Corporate Assault on Environmentalism*, Books Ltd, Dartington Green, UK.

Berners-Lee, T. (1996) *The World Wide Web: Past, Present and Future*, www.w3.org/People/Berners-Lee/1996/ppf.html.

Berners-Lee, T. (1998) *Realising the Full Potential of the Web*, www.w3.org/1998/02/Potential.html.

de Berry, J. (1999) *Exploring the Concept of Community: Implications for NGO Management*, International Working Paper No. 8, Centre for Voluntary Organisation, London School of Economics.

Brass, E. and Poklewski Koziell, S. with Searle, D. (1997) *Gathering Force: DIY Culture – Radical Action for Those Tired of Waiting*, Big Issue, London.

Broadbent, G. (1984) A last word, in: Hatch, C.R. (ed.), *The Scope of Social Architecture*, Van Nostrand Reinhold, New York, pp. 164–165.

Brooking, A. (1999) *Corporate Memory: Strategies for Knowledge Management*, International Business Press, London.

Brosius, J. (1999) Analyses and intervention: anthropological engagement with environmentalism, *Current Anthropology*, 40(3): 277–309.

Brown, R. (1998) Design games: community participation in urban design, *Urban Design Quarterly*, Issue 65, January, pp. 39–41.

BS (1998) *Directory of Registered Factories*, Bureau of Statistics, Government of Punjab, Lahore.

BSHF (2001) *Harnessing Information Communication Technologies for a more Sustainable Future*, Consultation, St George's House, Windsor Castle, 24–26 April 2001, Building and Social Housing Foundation, Coalville, UK.

Buber, M. (1958) *I and Thou*, T. & T. Clark, Edinburgh.

Buchanan, D. and Cernada, G., eds (1998) *Progress in Prevention of AIDS? Dogma, Dissent and Innovation: Global Perspectives*, Baywood Publishing Company Inc., New York.

Buncombe, A. (2001) The world at war, *The Independent*, 26 October.

Burleson, B., Albrecht, T. and Sarason, I. (eds) (1994) *Communication of Social Support: Messages, Interactions, Relationships, and Community*, Sage Publications, California.

Carley, M. and Christie, I. (2000) *Managing Sustainable Development*, 2nd edn, Earthscan Publications, London.

Carter, M. (1997) *Rural Housing and Affordable Innovation*, Earth Resources Centre, University of Exeter, UK.

Castells, M. (1991) *The Informational City: Information Technology, Economic Restructuring and the Urban-Regional Process*, Basil Blackwell, Oxford, UK.

Castells, M. (1996) *The Rise of the Network Society*, Blackwell, Oxford, UK.

Castells, M. (1997) *The Power of Identity*, Blackwell, Oxford, UK.

CERCA (1997) *Estado del arte de la investigación relacionada con la gestión participativa de los asentamientos humanos. Informe de investigación*, CERCA, San José de Costa Rica.

CERCA (1998a) *Issue Paper SISCOM* (Factsheet), CERCA, San José de Costa Rica.

CERCA (1998b) *Project Profile: Community Development Programme – UNCHS (Habitat): Resource Facility for the Sustainable Development of Human Settlements – Central America*, CERCA, San José de Costa Rica.

CERCA (1998c) *Programa de Investigación, Investiga*, CERCA, San José de Costa Rica.

Chambers, R. (1995) Poverty and livelihoods: whose reality counts?, *Environment and Urbanization*, 7(1).

CHEC (1998) Community learning and information centres as a tool for sustainable development, in: Max Lock Centre, Commonwealth Human Ecology Council, Development Planning Unit, *Communicating for Development, Vol. 2* (2000), University College London and GhK Research and Training (University of Westminster), London.

Chernela, J. (1995) Sustainability in resource rights and conservation: the case of an Awa Biosphere in Colombia, in: Sponsel, L. (ed.), *Indigenous Peoples and the Future of Amazonia: An Ecological Anthropology of an Endangered World*, University of Arizona Press, Tucson, AZ/London.

Chesterman, D. and Stone, C. (1987) New approaches to public housing: an inner-city case study, *Architecture Australia*, 76(4): 37–43.

Chisholm, M. (1979) A study of the provision of rural housing with particular reference to relief and development agencies, BArch thesis, University of Newcastle upon Tyne, UK.

Chitonga, F. (2001) Modelling KIS in two locations, unpublished report, ITDG, Bourton-on-Dunsmore, Rugby, UK.

Chr. Michelsen Institute (2001) From Global Village to Urban Globe, unpublished report, Chr. Michelsen Institute, Bergen, Norway.

Cleary, D. (2000) *Small-Scale Gold Mining in Brazilian Amazonia*.

Colchester, M. (2000) *Salvaging Nature: Indigenous Peoples, Protected Areas and Biodiversity Conservation*, World Rainforest Movement, Uruguay.

Coleman, J.S. (1988) Social capital in the creation of human capital, *American Journal of Sociology*, 94: S95–S120.

Conan, M. (1987) Dwellers' involvement in housing design: a developmental perspective, *Journal of Architectural and Planning Research*, 4(4): 301–309.

Conklin, B.A. (1997) Body painting, feathers, VCRs: aesthetics and authenticity in Amazonian activism, *American Ethnologist* 214(4): 711–737.

Coomes, O.T. (1995) A century of rain forest use in western Amazonia: lessons for extraction-based conservation in tropical forest resources, *Forest and Conservation History*, 39, July: 108–20.

Cox, R.W. (1993) Gramsci, hegemony and international relations: an essay in method, in: Gill, S. (ed.), *Gramsci and Historical Materialism and International Relations*, Cambridge University Press, Cambridge, UK.

Crush, J., ed. (1995) *Power of Development*, Routledge, London.
Cuff, D. (1998) *Architecture: The Story of Practice*, 6th edn, MIT Press, Cambridge, MA, USA.
Cummings, B.J. (1990) *Dam the Rivers, Damn the People: Development and Resistance in Amazonian Brazil*, London.
Dagron, A.G. (2001) *Making Waves: Stories of Participatory Communication for Social Change*, report to the Rockerfeller Foundation, New York.
DARPG (1997) *Statement of the Conference of Chief Ministers on Effective and Responsive Administration*, Department of Administrative Reforms and Public Grievances, New Delhi.
Dasgupta, P. and Serageldin, I. (eds) (2000) *Social Capital: A Multifaceted Perspective*, International Bank for Reconstruction and Development/World Bank, Washington, DC.
Davenport, T. and Prusak, L. (1998) *Working Knowledge*, Harvard Business School Press, Boston, MA, USA.
Davis, J.E. (1991) *Contested Ground: Collective Action and the Urban Neighborhood*, Cornell University Press, Ithaca, NY, USA.
Davis, M. (1992) Fortress Los Angeles: the militarization of urban space, in: Sorkin, M. (ed.), *Variations on a Theme Park: The New American City and the End of Public Space*, Noonday Press, New York.
Debord, G. (1981) Report on the construction of situations and the international Situationist tendency's conditions of organisation and action, in: Knabb, K. (ed.), *Situationist International Anthology*, Bureau of Public Secrets, Berkeley, CA, USA.
DETR (1998) *New Deal for Communities – Phase 1 Proposals – Guidance for Pathfinder Proposals*, Department for the Environment, Transport and the Regions, www.regeneration.detr.gov.uk/newdeal/index.htm.
Devas, N. and Rakodi, C. (1993) The urban challenge, in: Devas, N. and Rakodi, C. (eds), *Managing Fast Growing Cities: New Approaches to Urban Planning and Management in the Developing World*, Longman, Harlow, UK.
Development Alternatives, www.tarahaat.com.
Devlin, K. (1990) An examination of architectural interpretation: architects versus non-architects, *Journal of Architectural and Planning Research*, 7(3); 235–244.
Devlin, K. and Nasar, J.L. (1989) The beauty and the beast: some preliminary comparisons of 'high' versus 'popular' residential architecture and public versus architectural judgements of the same, *Journal of Environmental Psychology*, 9: 333–344.
DFID (1999) *Sustainable Livelihoods Guidance Sheets*, Department for International Development, London (www.livelihoods.org).
DFID (2000a) *India: Country Strategy Paper*, Department for International Development, London.
DFID (2000b) *Sustainable Livelihoods Guidance Sheets*, Department for International Development, London (www.livelihoods.org).
DFID (2001a) *Meeting the Challenge of Poverty in Urban Areas: Strategies for achieving the international development targets*, Department for International Development, London.
DFID (2001b) *Sustainable Livelihoods Project Summary: Information and Communications Technologies (ICTs) for Sustainable Livelihoods, R7371*, Department for International Development, London (www.livelihoods.org).
DFID (2001c) *Bridging the Digital Divide*, www.globalisation.gov.uk/textonly/text three/BridgingTheDigitalDivide.html (accessed 05/06/01).
Downing, J. (1984) *Radical Media: The Political Experience of Alternative Communication*, South End Press, Boston, MA, USA.
Dudley, E. (1993) *The Critical Villager*, Routledge, London.

Dudley, E. and Haaland, A. (1993) *Communicating Building for Safety: Guidelines for Communicating Technical Information to Local Builders and Householders,* IT Publications, London.

Earl, M. (1998) Knowledge as strategy: reflections on Skandia International and Shorko Films, in: Prusak, L. (ed.), *Knowledge in Organizations,* Butterworth–Heinemann, Boston, MA, USA.

Edwards, M. (1996) The getting of wisdom: educating the reflective practitioner, in: Hamdi, N. (ed.), *Educating for Real,* IT Publications, London.

Engel, P.G.H. (1993) Alders, C., Haverkort, B. and van Veldhuizen, L. (eds), 'Daring to share – networking among non-government organizations', in: *Networking for low-external-input and sustainable agriculture,* IT Publications, London. *Linking with Farmers.*

Entwistle, N., Thompson, S. and Tait, H. (1992) *Guidelines for Promoting Effective Learning in Higher Education,* Centre for Research on Learning and Instruction, University of Edinburgh, Edinburgh.

Escobar, A. (1995) Imagining a post-development era, in: Crush, J. (ed.), *Power of Development,* Routledge, London/New York.

Estrella, M. (ed.) (2000) *Learning from Change, Issues and Experiences in Participatory Monitoring and Evaluation,* ITDG Publishing, London.

ETPI (Environmental Technology Programme for Industry) (2000) ETPI impact assessment, in: *ETPI Bi-Annual Update,* Karachi.

Evans, A. (1992) Statistics, in: Ostergaard, L. (ed.), *Gender and Development: A Practical Guide,* Routledge, London.

Featherstone, M. (1995) *Undoing Culture: Globalization, Postmodernism and Identity,* Sage Publications, London.

Fernando, P. (2001) Sustainable Development and Positive Representations of the Third World. MA dissertation. Available from TVE or from Leicester University, cmcr@leicester. ac.uk

Ferretti, S. (1999) Communicating for development with the internet, in: Gandelsonas, C. (ed.), *Communicating for Development: Proceedings of the 16th Inter-Schools Conference, University of Westminster 12–13 April,* University of Westminster, London.

Fischer, C.S. (1982) *To Dwell among Friends: Personal Networks in Town and City,* University of Chicago Press, Chicago/London.

Fisher, W.F. (1997) Doing good? The politics and antipolitics of NGO practices, *Annual Review of Anthropology,* 26:439–464.

Ford Foundation (1999) *Statement of Current Interests,* Ford Foundation, New Delhi.

Foster, M. (2001) *Women and Information and Communications Technologies, Development Studies Association Conference, September 2001.*

FPCCI (Federation of Pakistani Chambers of Commerce and Industry)/Government of the Netherlands (undated) *ETPI: Programme of the Industry for the Industry* (brochure), Karachi.

Frances, J., Levacic, R., Mitchell, J. and Thompson, G. (1991) Introduction, in: Thompson, G., Frances, J., Levacic, R. and Mitchell, J. (eds), *Markets, Hierarchies and Networks: The Coordination of Social Life,* Sage, London.

Freimuth, V.S. (1992) Theoretical foundations of AIDS: media campaigns, in: Edgar, T., Fithpatrick, M.A. and Freimuth, V.S. (eds), *AIDS: A Communication Perspective,* L. Erlbaum Associates, Hillsdale, NJ, USA.

Freire, P. (1967) *Education: The Practice of Freedom,* Paz de Terra, Rio de Janeiro.

Friedmann, J. (1965) *Regional Development Policy: A Case Study of Venezuela,* MIT Press, Cambridge, MA, USA.

Friend, A. (1980) The post-war squatters, in: Anning, N. *et al.* (eds), *Squatting: The Real Story,* Bayleaf Books, London.

Frow, J. (1996) Information as gift and commodity, *New Left Review,* 219: 89–108.

FSF (1996) What is free software?, Free Software Foundation, www.fsf.org/philosophy /free-sw.html.

Fukuyama, F. (1992) *The End of History and the Last Man*, Penguin, London.
Gandelsonas, C. and Lloyd Jones, T. (2001) Communicating good or best practices in different cultural contexts, paper presented at the *World Forum on Urbanizing World and UN Human Habitat II*, Columbia University, New York, June 4–6, 2001, IRFD.
Garcia, K.M. (1997) *Centre for the Development of Indigenous Amazon Peoples, Lima, Peru*, www.latinamericanalliance.
Geise, M. (1996) From ARPAnet to the Internet: a cultural clash and its implications in framing the debate on the information superhighway, in: Strate, L., Jacobson, R. and Gibson, S. (eds), *Communications and Cyberspace: Social Interaction in an Electronic Environment*, Hampton Press, NJ, USA, pp. 123–141.
Ghosh, R.A. (1998) Cooking pot markets: an economic model for the trade in free goods and services on the Internet, *First Monday*, 3(3), www.firstmonday.org/issue/issues3_3/ghosh/index.html
Gibson, T. (1987) Integrating us and them on site, *Architects' Journal*, 11 February, p. 18.
Gibson, T. *et al.* (1986) *Us Plus Them*, Town and Country Planning Association, London.
Giddens, A. (1998) *The Third Way: The Renewal of Social Democracy*, Polity Press, Cambridge, UK.
Gilbert, A. and Gugler, J. (1992) *Cities, Poverty and Development: Urbanization in the Third World*, Oxford University Press, Oxford, UK.
Gill, S. (1992) Economic globalization and the internationalization of authority: limits and contradictions, *Geoforum*, 23(3): 269–283.
Gill, S. (1993) Gramsci and global politics: towards a post-hegemonic research agenda, in: Gill, S. (ed.), *Gramsci and Historical Materialism and International Relations*, Cambridge University Press, Cambridge, UK.
Goetz, A.M. and Jenkins, R. (1999) *Accounts and Accountability: Theoretical Implications of the Right to Information Movement in India*, Institute of Development Studies, Sussex, UK.
Goldberg, D.T. (1993) *Racist Culture: Philosophy and the Politics of Meaning*, Blackwell, Oxford, UK.
Gombin, R. (1971) *Les Origins du Gauchisme*, Editions du Seuil, Paris.
Goodlad, R. (1990) *The Future of the Housing Service*.
Goulet, D. (1995) *Development Ethics: A Guide to Theory and Practice*, Zed Books, London.
GoP/JRC/IUCN (1992) *The Pakistan National Conservation Strategy*, Government of Pakistan/Joint Research Committee/International Union for the Conservation of Nature and Natural Resources, Karachi.
Greenpeace (2001) *Forest Peoples*, Greenpeace Briefing, London.
Groat, L. (1982) Meaning in post-modern architecture: an examination using the multiple sorting task, *Environmental Psychology*, 2: 3–22.
Guijt, I. and Shah, M.K. (eds) (1998) *The Myth of Community: Gender Issues in Participatory Development*, IT Publications, London.
Habitat (1994) On the road to Istanbul, *Signpost*, 1.
Hagstrom, W. (1982) Gift giving as an organisational principle in science, in: Barnes, B. and Edge, D. (eds), *Science in Context: Readings in the Sociology of Science*, The Open University, Milton Keynes, UK, pp. 21–34.
Hall, B.J. (1992) Theories of culture and communication, *Communication Theory*, 2(1): 50–70.
Hall, S. (1994) The West and the rest: discourse and power, in: Hall, S. and Gieben, B. (eds), *Formations of Modernity*, Polity Press, Cambridge, UK.
Halpern, S. (1992) *The United Nations Conference on Environment and Development: Process and Documentation*, Academic Council for the United Nations System (ACUNS), Providence, RI, USA.

Hameed, R. and Raemaekers, J. (1999) The environmental regulation of industry in Lahore, Pakistan, *Third World Planning Review*, 21(4): 429–453.

Hameed, R. and Raemaekers, J. (2001) The state, business and the community: abating industrial nuisance in Lahore, Pakistan, in: Carley, M., Jenkins, P. and Smith, H. (eds), *Urban Development and Civil Society: The Role of Communities in Sustainable Cities*, Earthscan, London, pp. 51–67.

Hammarskjold, D. (1975) *What Now: Another Development?*, Dag Hammarskjold Foundation, Uppsala, Sweden.

Hanna, L. (1991) Sweet charity swings low, *The Guardian*, 18 December, p. 23.

Hardie, G.J. (1988) Community participation based on three-dimensional simulation models, *Design Studies*, 9(1): 56–61.

Hardoy, J.E. and Satterthwaite, D. (1981) *Shelter, Need and Response, Housing, Land and Settlement Policies in Seventeen Third World Nations*, John Wiley and Sons, Chichester, UK.

Hardoy, J.E. and Satterthwaite, D. (1989) *Squatter Citizen: Life in the Urban Third World*, Earthscan, London.

Harris, N., ed. (1986) *The End of the Third World: Newly Industrializing Countries and the End of an Ideology*, Penguin Books, London.

Harris, N., ed. (1992) *Cities in the 1990s: The Challenge for Developing Countries*, UCL Press, London.

Hart, R. (1996) Introduction and overview, in: Hall, N., Hart, R. and Mitlin, D. (eds), *The Urban Opportunity: The Work of NGOs in Cities of the South*, Intermediate Technology Publications, London.

Harvey, D. (1990) *The Condition of Postmodernity: An Enquiry into the Origins of Cultural Change*, Blackwell, Oxford, UK.

Headland, T.N. (1997) CA Forum on Theory in Anthropology: revisionism in ecological anthropology, *Current Anthropology*, 38(4): 605–630.

Henrich, J. (1997) Market incorporation, agricultural change, and sustainability among the Machiguenga Indians of the Peruvian Amazon, *Human Ecology*, 25(2): 319–351.

Hershberger, R. (1988) *A Study of Meaning and Architecture, Environmental Aesthetics*, Cambridge University Press, Cambridge, UK.

Hesse, B. (1997) White governmentality: urbanism, nationalism, racism, in: Westwood, S. and Williams, J. (eds), *Imagining Cities*, Routledge, London.

Hester, R.T. Jr. (1987) Community design: making the grassroots whole, *Built Environment*, 12(1): 45–60.

Hidallage, V. (2001) *Sri Lanka Reports: Analysis of KIS in Two Locations, Country Report - DFID KIS Phase II, August 2001*, Department for International Development, London.

Hill, J. (1998) Introduction, in: Hill, J. (ed.), *Occupying Architecture*, 2nd printing, Routledge, New York, pp. 2–12.

Hill, K. (1995) Comments, in: *Current Anthropology*, 36(5): 805–807.

Holland, J. with Blackburn, J. (eds) (1998) *Whose Voice: Participatory Research and Policy Change*, IT Publications, London.

Homeless International (2001) Zimbabwe: People's Survey in Victoria Falls, in: *Housing by People in Asia*, 12, April 1999, Asian Coalition for Housing Rights, Bangkok.

Hoselitz, A.F. (1953) The role of cities in developing countries, *Journal of Political Economy*, 61: 195–208.

Hugill, B. (2001) Preaching for renewal through participation?, *Regeneration and Renewal*, 23 March, p. 13.

Hulme, D. and Turner, M. (1990) *Sociology and Development: Theories Policies and Practices*, Harvester Wheatsheaf, London.

IACHR (1997) *Annual Report 1996*, Inter-American Commission on Human Rights, Washington, DC.

IDS (1999) *Strengthening Participation in Local Governance*, Institute of Development Studies, Sussex, UK.

Ikara, G. (1996) *The European Union–ACP Relationship: The Case of Eastern Africa* (online archive), Euroforic, www.oneworld.org/ euforic/fes/4gb_iki.htm (accessed 8/3/99).

Ikara, G. and Ndung'u, N. (1999) Kenya, in: van der Geest, W. and ven der Hoeven, R. (eds), *Adjustment, Employment and Missing Institutions in Africa: The Experience in Eastern and Southern Africa*, International Labor Organization, Geneva.

ISS (1996) *Report of International Conference on Kerala's Development Experience*, Institute of Social Sciences, New Delhi.

Janoski, T. and Wilson, J. (1995) Pathways to voluntarism: family socialization and status transmission models, *Social Forces*, 74(1): 271–292.

Johnson, A. (1982) Reductionism in Cultural Ecology: the Amazon case, *Current Anthropology*, 23(4): 413–428.

Johnson, S. Boswell *Life* vol. 2, p. 365, 18 April 1775.

Johnston, R.J., Gregory, D. and Smith, E. (eds) (1986) *The Dictionary of Human Geography*, 2nd edn, Blackwell Reference, London.

Judge, E. (2001a) *Hands On – Energy, Infrastructure and Recycling*, ITDG Publishing, London (www.itdgpublishing.org.uk).

Judge, E. (2001b) *Food Chain: The International Journal of Small Scale Food Processing*, Impact Assessment, unpublished report, ITDG, Bourton-on-Dunsmore, Rugby, UK.

Judge, E. (2001c) *Hands On – Food, Water and Finance*, ITDG Publishing, London (www.itdgpublishing.org.uk).

Katsiaficas, G. (1987) *The Imagination of the New Left: A Global Analysis of 1968*, South End Press, Boston, MA, USA.

Keith, M. and Pile, S. (1993) The place of politics, in: Keith, M. and Pile, S. (eds), *Place and the Politics of Identity*, Routledge, London.

Khan, A.U. (undated) *Industrial Operations and Interaction with Ecology: The Case of Pakistan*, www.etpi.org.pk.

Kleinman, N. (1996) Don't fence me in: copyright, property and technology' in: Strate, L., Jacobson, R. and Gibson, S. (eds), *Communications and Cyberspace: Social Interaction in an Electronic Environment*, Hampton Press, NJ, USA, pp. 59–82.

Kripa, A. and Prasad, G.S. (2000) *Governance and Media: Use of Radio in Disseminating Information on Participatory Governance in Mysore District*, Ford Foundation, New Delhi.

Kumar, K. (1994) *Communication Approaches to Participation and Development*, in: White, S. with Nair, S. and Ascroft, J. (eds), *Participatory Communication: Working for Change and Development*, Sage, New Delhi.

Lang, B. (1998) Free software for all: freeware and the issue of intellectual property, *Le Monde Diplomatique*, January, www.monde-diplomatique.fr/md/en/1998/01/12freesoft.html.

Lerner, D. (1958) *The Passing of Traditional Society*, Free Press, Glencoe, Illinois.

Lewando-Hundt, G. and Al Zaroo, S. (1999) Evaluating the dissemination of health promotion research and information, in: Thorogood, M. and Coombes, Y. (eds), *Evaluating Health Promotion*, Oxford University Press, Oxford, UK.

Leys, C. (1975) *Underdevelopment in Kenya: The Political Economy of Neo-colonialism, 1964–1971*, Heinemann, London.

Lillington, K. (1998) No! It's not OK, computer, *The Guardian*, 6 April, Online Section, pp. 2–3.

Lipietz, A. (1992) *Towards a New Economic Order: Postfordism, Ecology and Democracy*, Blackwell, Oxford, UK.

Local Government Act (2000) Chapter 22, Stationery Office, Norwich, UK, p. 3.

Lowe, L. (1998), unpublished report presented at *Engineering Knowledge and Research Knowledge Transfer Project Workshop*, Charney Manor 1–3 July 1998.

MacDonald, J. (1999) *Understanding Knowledge Management*, Cox and Wyman, London.

Magne, S. (1999) *The H&H Rural Workshops – Realising Potential*, Earth Resources Centre, University of Exeter, UK.

Malo, G. (1999) ENVIRONMENT–ECUADOR: indigenous communities seek more reserves, *World News*, www.worldnews.com.

Mangin, W. (1967) Latin American squatter settlements: a problem and a solution, *Latin American Research Review*, 2: 65–98.

Marx, K. (1973) *Grundrisse*, Penguin, London.

Maslow, A. (1987) *Motivation and Personality*, 3rd edn. Revised by Frager, R., Fadiman, J., Reynolds, C. and Cox, R., Harper & Row, New York.

Mauss, M. (1990) *The Gift: The Form and Reason for Exchange in Archaic Societies*, Routledge, London.

Max Lock Centre (2001a) *Communication for Development, Vols 1–3*, University of Westminster, London.

Max Lock Centre (2001b) *Improving Knowledge Transfer in Urban Development: Guides 1–8*, Max Lock Centre School of the Built Environment, University of Westminster, London, www.wmin.ac.uk/builtenv/maxlock.

Max Lock Centre (2002) *Localising Habitat Agenda: Inception Report*, University of Westminster, London.

Maxwell, K (1991) The tragedy of the Amazon, *New York Review*, 7 March.

McAdam, S. (2000) Base neighbourhood strategies on residents' visions, *Urban Environment*, 4 May, p. 10.

McClintock, A. (1994) *Imperial Leather: Race, Gender and Sexuality in the Colonial Contest*, Routledge, London.

McLuhan, M. (1994) *Understanding Media: The Extensions of Man*, MIT Press, Cambridge, MA/London.

Meggers, B.J. (1971) *Amazonia: Man and Culture in a Counterfeit Paradise*, Chicago.

Mezirow, J. (1990) How critical reflection triggers transformative learning, in: Mezirow, J., *Fostering Critical Reflection in Adulthood*, Jossey-Bass Publishers, San Francisco, CA, USA.

Mhonda, E. (1997) Development through radio with rural communities, *Appropriate Technology*, 24(3): 12–14.

Michell, P. (2001) Event – public conversation, Diploma-level Professional Studies paper, University of East London, p. 5.

Michiels, S.I. and van Crowder, L. (2001) Discovering the 'magic box': local appropriation of information and communication technologies (ICTs), Communication for Development Group Extension, Education and Communication Service (SDRE) Research, Extension and Training Division, June 2001, www.fao.org/sd/2001/kn0602a_en.htm

Midgley, J., Hall, A., Hardiman, M. and Narine, D. (1986) *Community Participation, Social Development and the State*, Methuen, London.

Monge, P. (1985) in: Kupper, A. and Kupper, J. (eds) *The Social Science Encyclopaedia*, Routledge & Kegan Paul, London, p. 130.

Moser, C. (1989) Community participation in urban projects in the Third World, *Progress in Planning*, 32: 71–133.

Moser, C. (1996) *Confronting Crisis: A Comparative Study of Household Responses to Poverty and Vulnerability in Four Urban Communities*, ESD Series 8, World Bank/UNCHS, Washington, DC.

Narayan, D. (1996) The contributions of people's participation: evidence from 121 rural water supply projects, in: Rietbergen-McCracken, J. (ed.) *Participation in Practice: The Experience of the World Bank and Other Stakeholders*, World Bank Discussion Paper No. 333, World Bank, Washington, DC.

National Environmental Consulting (Pvt) Ltd and Haskoning Consulting Engineers and Architects (1996) *Environmental Technology Programme for Industry (ETPI), Progress Report, September–November 1996*, FPCCI/Government of the Netherlands, Karachi.

Netwizards (2000) *Internet Domain Survey 2000*, www.isc.org/dsWWW-2000/report.htm.

New Economics Foundation (2000) *Research on Community Sustainable Development Indicators*, draft report, Environ, Leicester.

Newton, K. (1997) Social capital and democracy, *American Behavioral Scientist*, 40(5): 575–586.

Nicol, D.J. (1997) *Research on Learning and Higher Education Teaching*, UCoSDA Briefing Paper 45, University of Sheffield, Sheffield.

Nonaka, I. and Takeuchi, H. (1995) *The Knowledge-Creating Company*, Oxford University Press, New York.

Norton, A. (2001) *A Rough Guide to Participatory Poverty Assessments: An Introduction to Theory and Practice*, Overseas Development Institute, London.

Nugent, S. (1981) Amazonia: Ecosystem and Social System, in *Man*, New Series, 16(1): 62–74.

O'Dell, C. and Grayson, C.J. Jr (1998) *If Only We Knew What We Know*, Free Press, New York.

O'Farrell, C. (2001) *Information Flows in Rural and Urban Communities: Access, Processes and People*, Paper for Development Studies Association Conference, 10 September 2001.

O'Farrell, C., Norrish, P. and Scott, A. (2000) *Information and Communication Technologies (ICTs) for Sustainable Livelihoods: Briefing Document*, Final Technical Report DFID/ESCOR 7173, Department for International Development, London, www.rdg.ac.uk/AcaDepts/ea/AERDD/ICTs.home.htm.

ODA (1995) *Guidance Note on how to do Stakeholder Analysis of Aid Projects and Programmes*, Overseas Department Agency (now DFID), London.

OECD (1996) *Shaping the 21st Century: The Contribution of Development Co-operation*, Development Assistance Committee, Organisation of Economic Co-operation and Development. (www.oecd.org/pdf/M00003000/M00003334.pdf)

Owens, R. (1988) Parker Morris in the pub, *Architects' Journal*, 29 June, pp. 52–61.

Partners in Charge (2000) *Taking The Lead*, from a training programme developed by Levitt Bernstein in association with Rod Laird Associates on behalf of Wherry Housing Association, Housing Corporation, London.

Phillips, S. (2002) Social capital, local networks and community development, in: Rakodi, C. with Lloyd-Jones, T. (eds) *Urban Livelihoods: A People-Centred Approach to Poverty Reduction*, Earthscan, London.

Planning Commission (1997) *Ninth Five-Year Plan (1997–2002)*, Planning Commission, New Delhi.

Polanyi, M. (1966) *The Tacit Dimension*, Anchor Day Books, New York.

Porter, R. and Samovar, L. (1988) Approaching intercultural communication, in: Samovar, L. and Porter, R. (eds), *Intercultural Communication: A Reader*, 5th edn, Wadsworth, Belmont, CA, pp. 15–31.

Porterfield, K. (1998) *Information Wants to be Valuable*, report from the first O'Reilly Perl conference, www.netaction.org/articles/freesoft.html.

Portney, K. and Berry, J. (1997) Mobilizing minority communities: social capital and participation in urban neighborhoods, *American Behavioral Scientist*, 40(5): 632–644.

Posey, D.A (2000) Biodiversity, genetic resources and indigenous peoples in Amazonia: (re)discovering the wealth of traditional resources of native Amazonias, in: Hall, A. (ed.) *Amazonia at the Crossroads. The Challenge of Sustainable Development*, Institute for Latin American Studies, London.

Communicating for Development*

Powell, W. (1991) Neither market nor hierarchy: network forms of organization, in: Thompson, G., Frances, J., Levacic, R. and Mitchell, J. (eds), *Markets, Hierarchies and Networks: The Coordination of Social Life*, Sage, London.

Power, A. (1993) *From Hovels to High Rise: State Housing in Europe since 1850*, Routledge, London.

Pretty, J.N., Guijt, I., Thompson, J. and Scoones, I. (1995) *Participatory Learning in Action*, Participatory Methodology Series, International Institute for Environment and Development, London.

Public Affairs Centre (1995) *Public Services for the Urban Poor: A Report Card on Three Indian Cities*, Public Affairs Centre, Bangalore, India.

Pulgar, D. (2001) *Hands On: It Works*, Final Evaluation, unpublished report, TVE.

Puri, R. (1995) Comments, in: *Current Anthropology*, 36(5): 805–807.

Putnam, R. with Leonardi, R. and Nanetti, R. (1993) *Making Democracy Work: Civic Traditions in Modern Italy*, Princeton University Press, Princeton, NJ, USA.

Rabben, L. (1998) *Unnatural Selection. The Yanomami, the Kayapo and the Onslaught of Civilisation*, Pluto Press, London.

Rabrenovic, G. (1994) Women and collective action in urban neighborhoods, *Urban Affairs Annual Review*, 42: 77–96.

Rahman, M.A. (1995) Participatory development: toward liberation or co-option?, in: Craig, G. and Mayo, M. (eds), *Community Empowerment: A Reader in Participation and Development*, Zed Books, London.

Rakodi, C. (1999) A capital assets framework for analysing household livelihood strategies, *Development Policy Review* 17(3).

Ramos, A.R. (1994) The hyperreal Indian, *Critique of Anthropology: A Journal for the Critical Reconstruction of Anthropology*, 14(2): 153–171.

Ramos, A. (1998) *Indigenism: Ethnic Politics in Brazil*, University of Wisconsin Press, Wisconsin.

Rapoport, A. (1977) *Human Aspects of Urban Form*, Pergamon Press, Oxford, UK.

Rapoport, A. (1982a) *The Meaning of the Built Environment: A Nonverbal Communication Approach*, Sage Publications, Beverly Hills, CA, USA.

Rapoport, A. (1982b) Design, development and man–environment studies, *Environments*, University of Waterloo, Faculty of Environment Studies, 14(2).

Raven, B.H. and Rubin, J.Z. (1983) *Social Psychology*, 2nd edn, Wiley, New York.

Raymond, E. (1998) The Cathedral and the Bazaar, *First Monday*, 3(3), www.first monday.org/issues/issue3_3/raymond/index.html

Redford, K. and Stearman, A.M. (1993) Forest-dwelling native Amazonians and the conservation of biodiversity: interests in common or in collision?, *Conservation Biology*, 7(2), June: 248–255.

Rheingold, H. (1994) *The Virtual Community: Finding Connection in a Computerised World*, Secker and Warburg, London.

Rietbergen-McCracken, J. (ed.) (1996) *Participation in Practice: The Experience of the World Bank and Other Stakeholders*, World Bank Discussion Paper No. 333, World Bank, Washington, DC.

Rocha, J. (1999) *Murder in the Rainforest. The Yanomami, the Gold Miners and the Amazon*, Latin American Bureau, London.

Roche, C. and Bush, A. (1997) Assessing the impact of advocacy work, *Appropriate Technology*, 24(2): 9–15.

Ruskulis, O. (1998) Informing the urban poor? An assessment of information and dissemination media for informing urban development, presented at *Engineering Knowledge and Research Knowledge Transfer Project Workshop*, Charney Manor 1–3 July 1998.

Ruskulis, O. (2000) Literature Survey: Strengthening Poor People's Knowledge and Information Systems, unpublished paper prepared for DFID Infrastructure and Urban Development Division, Department for International Development, London.

Samovar, L., Porter, R. and Jain, N. (1981) *Understanding Intercultural Communication*, Wadsworth, Belmont, CA, USA.

Sandel, M.J. (1984) The procedural republic and the unencumbered self, *Political Theory*, 12: 81–96.

Sarap, M. (1993) *An Introductory Guide to Post-Structuralism and Postmodernism*, 2nd edn, Harvester Wheatsheaf, New York.

Saravia, M. (2001) *Strengthening Knowledge and Information Systems of the Urban Poor: Final Country Report, Peru*, ITDG, Lima.

Scarbrough, H. and Swan, J. (1999) *Case Studies in Knowledge Management*, Institute of Personnel and Development, London.

Schilderman, T. (2001) Strengthening Poor People's Knowledge and Information Systems, A Summary of Research Findings – January to April 2000, unpublished, ITDG, Bourton-on-Dunsmore, Rugby, UK.

Schmidt, M. (1996) Popular participation and The World Bank: lessons from forty-eight case studies, in: Rietbergen-McCracken, J. (ed.), *Participation in Practice: The Experience of the World Bank and Other Stakeholders*, World Bank Discussion Paper No. 333, The World Bank, Washington, DC.

Schneider, S.C. and Barsourx, J. (1997) *Managing Across Cultures*, Prentice Hall, London/New York.

Schon, D.A. (1983) *The Reflective Practitioner: How Professionals Think in School*, Basic Books, New York.

Schroeder, D., Penner, L., Dovidio, J. and Piliavin, J. (1995) *The Psychology of Helping and Altruism: Problems and Puzzles*, McGraw-Hill, New York.

Schuman, T. (1991) Forms of resistance: politics, culture and architecture, in: Dutton, T.A. (ed.), *Voices in Architectural Education*, Bergin and Garvey, New York, pp. 3–28.

SEARCH (1999) *Strengthening Participation in Local Governance: Use of Participatory Methods*, SEARCH Training Centre, Bangalore, India.

Sennett, R. (1996) *The Uses of Disorder*, Faber and Faber, London.

Shadrack, B. (2001) Conference Moderator, e-conference on the KIS of the Urban Poor, unpublished report, ITDG, Bourton-on-Dunsmore, Rugby, UK.

Shelter (2001) Regional Statistics Briefing: London, unpublished, Shelter, London.

Soja, E.W. (1996) Los Angeles, 1965–1992: from crisis-generated restructuring to restructuring-generated crisis, in: Scott, A. and Soja, E. (eds), *The City: Los Angeles and Urban Theory at the End of the Century*, University of California Press, London.

Staeheli, M.A. (2001) Information Providers; Strategies to Provide Information to Poor People: Qualitative Study with Institutional Information Providers, unpublished report, ITDG, London.

Starkey, P. (1998) *Networking for Development*, International Forum for Rural Transport and Development, London.

Stiefel, M. and Wolfe, M. (1994) *A Voice for the Excluded: Popular Participation in Development: Utopia or Necessity?*, UNRISD and Zed Books, London.

Theis, J. and Grady, H. (1991) *Participatory Rapid Appraisal for Community Development: A Training Manual Based on Experiences in the Middle East and North Africa*, IIED/Save the Children Federation, London.

Till, J. (1998) Architecture of the impure community, in: Hill, J. (ed.), *Occupying Architecture*, 2nd printing, Routledge, New York, pp. 62–75.

Turner, J.F.C. (1987) The enabling practitioner and the recovery of creative work, *Journal of Architecture and Planning Research*, 4(4): 273–280.

Turner, T. (2000) Indigenous rights, environmental protection and the struggle over forest resources in the Amazon: the case of the Brazilian Kayapo, in: Conway, J., *et al.* (eds), *Earth, Air, Fire and Water: The Humanities and the Environment*, University of Massachusetts Press, Amherst.

UN (1993) United Nations Draft Declaration on the Rights of Indigenous Peoples, *Spiritual Ties to Land,* Part 6, Article 25 of the UN Draft Declaration of the Rights of Indigenous Peoples, United Nations, New York.

UN (1995) *World Urbanisation Prospects: 1994 Revision,* United Nations, New York.

UN (2001) *Road Map Towards Implementation of the UN Millennium Declaration,* United Nations (www.un.org/law/counsel/info.htm).

UN/WHO (2000) *AIDS Epidemic Update: December 2000,* Joint United Nations Programme on HIV/AIDS/World Health Organization, UNAIDS, Geneva.

UNCHS (1998) *The Istanbul Declaration and the Habitat Agenda,* United Nations Centre for Human Settlements, Nairobi.

UNCHS (2001) *Cities in a Globalizing World,* Global Report on Human Settlements 2001, UN Centre for Human Settlements/Earthscan Publications, London.

UNDP (1997) *Human Development Report 1997,* United Nations Development Programme/Oxford University Press, Oxford, UK.

UNDP (1998) *Human Development Report 1998,* United Nations Development Programme/Oxford University Press, Oxford, UK.

Vaneigem, R. (1972) *The Revolution of Everyday Life,* Practical Paradise, London.

Ventriss, C. (1987) Critical issues of participatory decision making in the planning process: a re-examination, *Journal of Architecture and Planning Research,* 4(4): 281–288.

Villas Boas, O. and Villas Boas, C. (1973) *Xingu, The Indians, Their Myths,* Condor Book Souvenir Press, London.

Visscher, J.T. (1998) *Information, Key for Sector Improvement, With Resource Centres Matching the Demand and Supply,* IRC, The Hague, The Netherlands.

Wall, K. (1993) Personal insights: involving urban communities in decision-making, *Planning,* no. 128, July, pp. 22–25.

Wallace, J. (1997) *Overdrive: Bill Gates and the Race to Control Cyberspace,* John Wiley, New York.

Ware, A. (ed.) (1989) *Charities and Government,* Manchester University Press, Manchester, UK.

Warren, D., Michael, L., Slikkerveer, J. and Brokensha, D. (1995) *The Cultural Dimension of Development: Indigenous Knowledge Systems,* Intermediate Technology Publications, London.

Watson, J. and Hill, A. (2000) *Dictionary of Communication and Media Studies,* 5th edn, Arnold/Hodder Headline Group, London.

Webster, A. (1990) *Introduction to the Sociology of Development,* Macmillan, London.

Werlin, H.H. (1974) *Governing an African City: A Study of Nairobi,* Africana Publishing Co., London.

Wheeler, D. (2000) *Racing To The Bottom? Foreign Investment and Air Quality in Developing Countries,* Development Research Group, World Bank, www.worldbank.org/nipr/work_paper/RaceWP1.pdf.

White, S. (ed.) with Nair, S. and Ascroft, J. (1994) *Participatory Communication: Working for Change and Development,* Sage, New Delhi.

WHO (2000) *WHO Report on Global Surveillance of Epidemic-prone Infectious Diseases,* World Health Organization, London.

Widner, J. with Mundt, A. (1998) Researching social capital in Africa, *Africa,* 68(1): 1–24.

Wilsing, M. and Wilsing, N.A. (2001) *Idea-Arch-Practice Concept in Architecture Education,* 19th European Association of Architectural Education International Conference, Ankara, Turkey (from Bruce Nyland, from material by Edgar Dale, from Dr Richard Felder's Teaching Effective workbook).

Wilson, J. and Musick, M. (1997) Who cares? Toward an integrated theory of volunteer work, *American Sociological Review,* 62: 694–713.

Wishart, G. (1996) *BASIN Evaluation – Building Partnerships,* unpublished document, SKAT/Ashton Court, St Gallen, Switzerland.

Wolch, J. (1996) From global to local: the rise of homelessness in Los Angeles in the 1980s, in: Scott, A. and Soja, E. (eds), *The City: Los Angeles and Urban Theory at the End of the Century*, University of California Press, London.

Woolcock, M. (2000) *Friends in High Places? An Overview of Social Capital*, World Bank Development Research Group, World Bank, Washington, DC.

World Bank (1997) *World Development Report*, World Bank, Washington, DC.

World Bank (1998) *World Development Report*, World Bank, Washington, DC.

World Bank (2000a) *World Development Indicators 2000*, World Bank, Washington, DC.

World Bank (2000b) *Greening Industry: New Roles for Communities, Markets and Governments*, Oxford University Press, New York.

World Bank (2001) *World Development Report, Attacking Poverty*, Oxford University Press, Oxford, UK.

Wratten, E. (1995) Conceptualizing urban poverty, *Environment and Urbanization*, 7(1): 11–36.

Index

academic networks   5
actions, communication process
   113
AIDS (acquired immunodeficiency
   syndrome)   211–19
alliances   65
Altimira conference   125
Amazonia   123–34
anarcho-communism   46–51
architectural perceptions   101,
   110–11
Asian Coalition for Housing Rights
   71

Bangladesh
   building safety   198–210
   Hands On response   158
BASIN *see* Building Advisory
   Service and Information
   Network
BBC World TV   28, 149, 152
Beira Lake Restoration Project   35
best practice model of knowledge
   transfer   21–4
Bolivia, *Hands On* response   159
Brazil
   indigenous population   124–33
   Mutirao 50 Network   71
Building Advisory Service and
   Information Network (BASIN)
   72
building safety, Bangladesh
   background   198–9
   evaluation   207–8
   fieldwork   202
   new agenda   199–201

participatory workshops
   203–6
replication project   208–10
supporting activities   206–7
Building and Social Housing
   Foundation   72

Cambodia   84
case studies
   building safety in Bangladesh
      198–210
   electronic conferencing   179–86
   Hands On   149–61
   HIV/AIDS prevention in Vietnam
      211–19
   Internet-based research
      networks   162–78
   knowledge transfer in India
      220–34
   lessons learnt   238–9
   pollution abatement in Pakistan
      187–97
   SDI   120–1
CBOs *see* community-based
   organizations
Central America, INVESTIGA
   171–7
Centre for the Development of
   Indigenous Amazon Peoples
   127
CERCA *see* Resource Facility for the
   Sustainable Development of
   Human Settlements in Central
   America
city growth   61
coalitions   65

Zimbabwe
  information priorities   75
  key informants   32, 74
  KIS research   41
  malaria   41

midwives   38–9
modelling information flows
  30–2, 38–9
Zone One Tondo Organization
  Network (ZOTO)   71–2